From Mann To Mysore

The Indian Careers of Col. Mark Wilks FRS and Lt. General Sir Mark Cubbon

L. B. Thrower

CENTRE FOR MANX STUDIES MONOGRAPHS 4

From Mann to Mysore: The Indian Careers of Col. Mark Wilks FRS and Lt. General Sir Mark Cubbon

First published 2006 by Centre for Manx Studies

CENTRE FOR MANX STUDIES MONOGRAPHS 4

Produced with financial assistance from the Manx Heritage Foundation.

Published by: Centre for Manx Studies
6 Kingswood Grove
Douglas
Isle of Man
IM1 3LX

http://www.liv.ac.uk/ManxStudies/

General Editor: Dr P J Davey
Technical Editor: Philippa Tomlinson

Cover photographs: (upper) Tynwald Hill, St. Johns, Isle of Man. Site of the annual open-air Tynwald Ceremony (lower) Gateway and part of the wall around grounds within which the Maharajah's palace is situated (SLT, 1992).

Cover design: Ruth Sutherland

Printed by SHORT RUN PRESS LIMITED

© Centre for Manx Studies, 2006

ISBN: 1899338-12-8

For Stella, as a token of my affection and esteem,

and in gratitude for her unfailing support

Detail of Equestrian Statue of Sir Mark Cubbon, Cubbon Park, Bangalore (Baron Carlo Marochetti: SLT, 1992).

Contents

List of illustrations ii
List of colour plates iii
Acknowledgements iv
Abbreviations v

CHAPTERS
   Introduction.. 2
1. The Isle of Man 7
2. Two Manx Families 16
3. South India to 1780 23
4. Mark Wilks's First Tour 1782 –1795 37
5. Mark Cubbon's Youth 1785 – 1801 52
6. Interlude 1795 – 1799 59
7. Together under Mornington's Regime 1799 – 1805 67
8. Together with a Government Adrift 1805 – 1808 84
9. Mark Cubbon Alone 1808 – 1834 99
10. Prelude to the Commission : Mysore & Coorg 1799 – 1834 113
11. Commissioner for Mysore 1834 – 1843 121
12. Commissioner for Mysore & Coorg 1843 – 1860 132
13. Cubbon's Administration 1834 – 1861 151
14. Charles Trevelyan and the Transfer of Mysore 1860 163
15. The Journey Home 1861 178
    Epilogue 183

Appendix 1 : Biographical Names.. 189
Appendix 2 : Geographical Names... 195
Appendix 3 : Glossary... 197

Maps 201

Index 205

i

Illustrations

Frontispiece

Detail of Equestrian Statue of Sir Mark Cubbon, Cubbon Park, Bangalore.

Figures

Some family relationships	vi
Pater familias, the Rev. James Wilks	19
Mark Wilks as a Lieutenant in 6 Madras Native Infantry	43
Barry Close when Adjutant-General of the Madras Army	45
Harriot Wilks (née Macleane), probably painted 1795-99	50
Fort Hill, Bellary	95
Maharajah Krishnaraja Wadiyar III in 1827	115
Commissioner's residence, Bangalore as Cubbon knew it	131
Sir Mark Cubbon about 1855	147
Sir Mark Cubbon, aged about 73 years	179
Cubbon remembered: Mysore Cottages, Ramsey	187

Maps

1: The Isle of Man with main places and the road system of 1789	201
2: Indian Sub-continent	202
3: South India showing main places mentioned in the text	203
4: Mysore and Coorg as in Cubbon's time.	204

Colour Plates - between pages 103 and 106

1: St. Mary's Chapel, later the Grammar School, at Castletown, seen from the south-west. The arches are part of an arcade between the 13th century nave and an aisle (now demolished). The wing with chimney was added in early 18th century, mainly to provide for the new Academic School. (SLT, 1995)

2: Maughold Church, where the Rev Thomas Cubbon was Vicar. The pillar-cross stands on the left of the gate-way. (A Heaton Cooper, 1909: Courtesy of the Director, Manx National Heritage)

3: Landing over the surf on to the open beach at Madras, as experienced by both Wilks and Cubbon. (Lt. R. Thompson ca 1850, Courtesy of the Director, National Army Museum, London)

4: The former Residency in Mysore City, from south. Built by Mark Wilks and completed in 1805, it was later known as Government House. (SLT, 1992)

5: Within the fort at Mercara, Coorg: statues of Vira Raja's elephants. (SLT, 1992)

6: Nandidrug from Nandi village, about 48 km north of Bangalore. In the 18th century Hyder and Tipu constructed extensive fortifications around its summit; and within these Mark Cubbon built his house. (SLT, 1992)

7: Gateway in the outer wall of fortifications on Nandidrug. In Cubbon's time the hill was ascended by means of 1,175 steps. (SLT, 1992)

8: Front of Mark Cubbons's house near the summit of Nandidrug. (SLT, 1992)

Acknowledgements

Material has been collected from the British Library's Manuscripts Collection and its Oriental and India Office Collections, Centre for Kentish Studies at Maidstone, Manx National Heritage Library, National Library of Wales, and the Robinson Library of the University of Newcastle-upon-Tyne. I am grateful to the Librarians and their staff in all these institutions. I am particularly indebted to Mr. Roger Sims, Librarian and Archivist in the Manx National Heritage Library, and his staff, for much help and friendship.

I am grateful to Lady Errington and Cambridge University Press for approval to quote from letters of Lord Macaulay in the possession of Lady Errington, which have been printed in volumes edited by Professor T. Pinney and published by Cambridge University Press; to The Trustees of the Trevelyan Family Papers held in the Robinson Library of the University of Newcastle-upon-Tyne for allowing me to quote from some letters of Sir Charles Wood; to the family of the late Brigadier H.R. Norman for approval to quote from the Norman papers deposited in the Centre for Kentish Studies, and to Mr. Stuart Bligh for his assistance; finally and particularly to the Director of Manx National Heritage, Mr. Stephen Harrison, for permission to quote extensively from the correspondence of the Wilks and Cubbon families.

For permission to reproduce illustrations I am indebted to Messrs Christies; the Director of the National Army Museum, London; the National Portrait Gallery, London; the Oriental and Indian Office Collections of the British Library; and to Manx National Heritage. All other photographs were taken in India and the Isle of Man by Dr Stella Thrower (SLT).

Among the individuals have helped in a variety of ways, I am particularly grateful to the Hon. Donald J.Gelling CBE MLC, Chief Minister of the Isle of Man; to Professor C. A. Bayly FBA of St Catharine's College, Cambridge for encouragement at the beginning of the project; to Mr. P. V. Chandrashekar both for enabling me to secure the photograph of Cubbon's statue in Bangalore that has been used as the frontispiece, and for his continuing help; to the late Professor G.H. Choa CBE, MD, FRCP, formerly Director of Medical & Health Services in Hong Kong and latterly founding Dean of the Faculty of Medicine in The Chinese University of Hong Kong, for his diagnosis of the probable immediate cause of Cubbon's death; to Dr N.H.M. Chancellor for sharing some of his insights into Mysorean politics as they were in the years preceding Cubbon's Commissionership; to the late Mrs M.I. Quirk for giving me insights into Manx life in earlier times, and for encouragement that continued until her death; to Mr. G. E. Radcliffe of Ballakissack for lending books that were not available elsewhere in the Isle of Man.

Several members of the Centre for Manx Studies have given invaluable help. Dr. Peter Davey (Director), Dr. Fenella Bazin and Dr. Philippa Tomlinson have seen the book through to publication. Dr. Rosaline Stott kindly read Chapter 1 and gave advice that enabled me to avoid some errors.

My wife, Dr. Stella Thrower, has helped, as so often in the past, with the collection of data, suggestions, constructive comment and encouragement.

Abbreviations

BL	British Library, London
BL (OIOC)	British Library (Oriental and India Office Collections)
CKS	Centre for Kentish Studies (Kent Archives Office), Maidstone
MNH	Manx National Heritage, Manx Museum, Douglas
MNHL	Manx National Heritage Library, Douglas
NLW	National Library of Wales, Aberystwyth
PP (H of C)	Parliamentary Papers, House of Commons
UNL	University of Newcastle-upon-Tyne, Robinson Library

SOME FAMILY RELATIONSHIPS

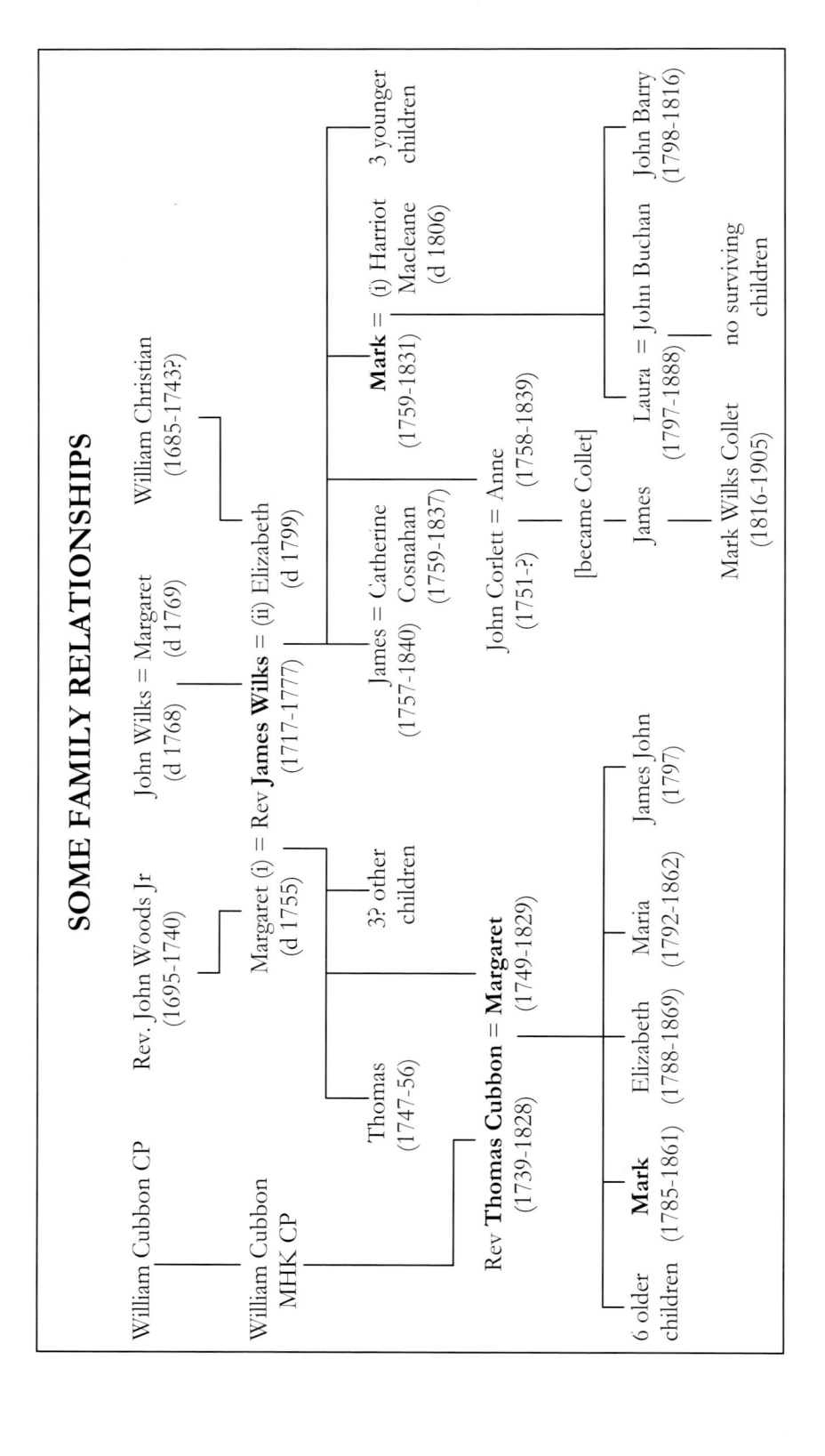

```
William Cubbon CP      Rev. John Woods Jr         John Wilks = Margaret       William Christian
                         (1695-1740)                (d 1768)    (d 1769)       (1685-1743?)
         |                    |                         |_____|                |
William Cubbon                |                                 |                    |
   MHK CP                     |                                 |                    |
         |       Margaret (i) = Rev James Wilks = (ii) Elizabeth                     |
         |         (d 1755)      (1717-1777)          (d 1799)                       |
         |              |                  |                                         |
   Thomas         3? other            James = Catherine         Mark  =  (i) Harriot        3 younger
  (1747-56)       children           (1757-1840) Cosnahan     (1759-1831)   Macleane        children
                                                (1759-1837)                 (d 1806)
                                     John Corlett = Anne
                                      (1751-?)     (1758-1839)
                                                |
                                          [became Collet]
Rev Thomas Cubbon = Margaret                    |
   (1739-1828)      (1749-1829)          James      Laura = John Buchan       John Barry
         |_____|                         (1797-1888)                (1798-1816)
                 |                                       |
                 |                              Mark Wilks Collet       no surviving
                 |                                (1816-1905)              children
  6 older    Mark      Elizabeth    Maria      James John
  children (1785-1861) (1788-1869) (1792-1862)  (1797)
```

Introduction

> Looking back over this period, it almost seems that the British succeeded in dominating India by a succession of fortuitous circumstances and lucky flukes. With remarkably little effort, considering the glittering prize, they won a great empire and enormous wealth, which helped to make them the leading power in the world.[1]
>
> > Jawaharlal Nehru
> > (Prime Minister of India 1947-64)

Another opinion, and one more complimentary to Indians, was given by Lord Macaulay a century before the future Prime Minister of India recorded his judgement. Having referred to the triumph of Cortes over the Aztecs in one of his most flamboyant passages, Macaulay went on

> The people of India, when we subdued them, were ten times as numerous as the Americans whom the Spanish vanquished, and were at the same time quite as highly civilized as the victorious Spaniards. They had reared cities larger and fairer than Saragossa or Toledo, and buildings more beautiful and costly than the cathedral at Seville. They could show bankers richer than the richest firms of Barcelona or Cadiz, viceroys whose splendour far surpassed that of Ferdinand the Catholic, myriads of cavalry and long trains of artillery that would have astonished the Great Captain.[2]

In any event, the period that both Nehru and Macaulay had in mind – when British authority was being established in India – was the very time that Mark Wilks and Mark Cubbon were there. Altogether, the Indian careers of uncle and nephew spanned nearly eighty years, including some eight years when they were together. Wilks had gone there when Warren Hastings still had three years before him as Governor-General of Fort William in Bengal; and Cubbon left the country four years after the Sepoy Rebellion, when Canning's Viceroyalty was nearing its end and the Crown had already assumed direct responsibility for governing the sub-continent.

My interest in these two Manxmen came about through, in Nehru's words, a lucky fluke. Soon after settling in the Isle of Man I re-read Lord Trevelyan's 'The India We Left' and came across a reference to 'Sir Mark Cubbon …a wily old man.'[3] Cubbon is a Manx name, so how did a Manxman come to govern Mysore? A little research brought me into contact with two remarkable men. Sir Mark Cubbon was the most famous Manxman of the mid-19th century, as shown by the 'international' pages of Manx newspapers. His uncle, Colonel Mark Wilks had a distinguished career in India and wrote extensively about the

---

[1] Jahawarlal Nehru, *The Discovery of India* (Calcutta 1946) 276
[2] T. B. Macaulay, 'Lord Clive' *Edinburgh Review*, Jan 1840, reprinted G. M. Young (ed) *Macaulay: poetry and prose* (London 1967) 306-73
[3] Humphrey Trevelyan, *The India we Left* (London 1972) 73-4

history of South India; later he was Governor of St. Helena and Speaker of the House of Keys in his native Island.

Inevitably, my reading about, and travels in, India led me to form opinions about the milieu within which Wilks and Cubbon worked. Two of those opinions may be stated; neither is original through both may be unfashionable. First, I subscribe to Nehru's assessment of 'fortuitous circumstances and lucky flukes' which, often enough, meant the right men being in place when most needed. On the other hand, the magnitude of the achievement, as outlined by Macaulay, must not be diminished. Now that the British Empire has run its course, attempts are being made to explain why and how it came about in the first place. Some see an 'imperialist design' underlying everything. Such notions may be useful in respect of the African Colonies, which were acquired long after the Empire in the East had been established, but I believe Nehru's view to be a more accurate assessment of what happened in the Sub-continent, Sri Lanka and Malaysia. There, the East India Company acquired some territories as trading posts, others as by-products of European wars, some others by deliberate conquest, and some by annexation. Moreover, as the Company moved into a position of ascendancy it attracted a significant number of Indians to itself by the order and military virtue it afforded. Once the Company had established itself in India there followed a need for it, and the Home Government, to secure lines of communication between Great Britain and the Sub-continent, and with the predominantly European settlements in New Zealand and Australia. Suitable stations along the way were acquired for victualling and coaling ships, thus giving rise to the 'all-red route' which was seen by my own and earlier generations of Australians as a wholly desirable arrangement.

The second opinion concerns relationships between Indians and British as Wilks and Cubbon experienced them – before the cataclysm of 1857. For those relationships I prefer to rely on sources of the time rather than later interpretations. For example, a contemporary of Mark Cubbon's, General John Briggs, set out his ideas for proper intercourse between British and Indians in a series of letters to a fictitious pair of brothers: George who was nineteen when he joined the civil service in India, and Charles who was only sixteen when he left Great Britain for the Madras Army. The main thrusts of his advice to them were to:

— become well-versed in Indian languages, beginning with Hindustani, and familiar with the customs of Indians so as to avoid giving offence through ignorance;
— behave decently toward all Indians, but especially to those in inferior situations such as servants.

Briggs also warned against a feeling of prejudice because of dark colour, such as may arise from ideas about African slaves; and of aversion toward comparative 'nakedness' which was entirely sensible in the Indian climate but unknown in Europe. Indeed he almost went so far as to suggest that Europeans were over-dressed for Indian conditions.[4]

It is only reasonable to judge individuals according to the standards of their own place and time rather than our own. I have tried to observe that principle in writing an account of people and events of 1780-1860 and have, therefore, quoted verbatim from letters and other documents of the time.

Both Wilks and Cubbon were the sons of clergymen, which poses a question whether sons of the Manx Vicarage favoured careers in the East India Company's armies. Heathcote has recorded the social origins of officers in the Bengal Army during 1820-34, whose fathers had not served in India. Of 1403 officers, 331 (23.6 per cent) had fathers who were army officers, 307 (21.9 per cent) had fathers in clerical orders, 96 (6.8 per cent) in the legal profession, 68 (4.8 per cent) were tradesmen, and fathers of the remainder pursued a wide variety of callings. There is no reason to believe that origins of officers in the Madras Army were much different. Of the four Manxmen mentioned in this book two (Wilks and Cubbon) had fathers in clerical orders, and the fathers of two (James Mark Cosnahan and Thomas Moss McHutchin) were in the legal profession – both, in fact, were Deemsters. Heathcote has pointed out that officers in the Company's Armies were drawn predominantly from the middle classes. Reasons included the large families of the times, lack of prospects for younger sons, and a wish to leave a social environment that hampered their personal advancement.[5]

Two matters are mentioned repeatedly in accounts of army life in India during the 18th and 19th centuries. One is ill-health, which twice drove Wilks from the country, partially incapacitated Cubbon, and prematurely struck down many contemporaries. Indeed the death-rate among officers (let alone other ranks) in India was much higher than among men of all social levels in England. Thus, over the period 1800-47 the annual death-rate per thousand officers in India was 24 at age 20 years and 30 at age 40 years; corresponding figures for men in England were 9 and 14. To his great credit Sir Charles Trevelyan (whom we shall meet in Chapter 14) brought his formidable energy to bear on improving health and hygiene among military personnel in India.[6]

The second matter that concerned officers in the Company's Armies was the slow rate of promotion, particularly in comparison with the King's (British) Army. For example, in 1855 the average European officer in Madras Infantry Regiments was promoted to major after 27 years service, whereas in King's Regiments the period was 11 years. Consequently, the average age of serving

---

[4] John Briggs, *Letters Addressed to a Young Person in India* (London 1828) 49-57
for ability in languages; 14-16, 24-5, 27-8 for attitudes to colour and nakedness.
[5] T. A. Heathcote, *The Indian Army: the garrison of British Imperial India 1822- 1922.* (London 1974) 122-3
[6] PP (H. of C) 1863. Vol 19 Part 1. Paper C3184 Sanitary State of the Army in India: report of the Commissioners with a précis of evidence.

majors was 49 years in the Madras Infantry but only 32 years in the British Army.[7] Given this unpromising prospect many capable and ambitious officers with five to ten years service sought appointments on the Staff (like the Commissariat) or in civilian employment (such as the Mysore Commission) where allowances were better and duties more varied and interesting. This draining away of its more capable officers diminished both the efficiency and morale of the Madras Army. As we shall see, both uncle and nephew quitted regimental duty in favour of more rewarding work as representatives at a Princely Court.

Consequently, the careers of Wilks and Cubbon reveal something of the origins and development of the Foreign and Political Department of the Government of India. A historical perspective has been given by Coen

> The British went to India to trade, not to conquer; and again and again expansionist policies in India were severely criticized or even forbidden by the home authorities …. The Company was, at first, purely a trading organization not, indeed, confined to India….When, very gradually, some of its officials began to look up from their ledgers to the land around them and the problems of its rule, it was not as civil servants administering British 'districts'….All around them were the 'country powers' as they were called (and) it was as diplomatic representatives to these powers, not as direct administrators, that the Company's non-commercial officers served.[8]

Macaulay described the position as it was about 1773

> The English functionaries at Fort William had as yet paid little or no attention to the internal government of Bengal. The only branch of politics (namely, diplomacy) about which they had much busied themselves was negotiations with the native princes.[9]

From early times army officers became diplomats, and we shall see how Cornwallis considered their abilities superior to those of Madras civil servants. Eventually, they made up some 70% of the Foreign and Political Department, which had two principal functions. One was to represent the Government of India in independent territories, either through permanent legations, or on special missions such as those of John Malcolm to Persia. The second was to represent the Government of India at the Courts of Indian Princes, either as a Resident like Wilks in Mysore, or as a Commissioner (having much greater authority) like Cubbon in the same State.

Having lived beside Wilks and Cubbon for several years, one is tempted to assess their relative merits and the places they occupy in the history of Anglo-

---

[7] T. A. Heathcote, *The Indian Army* 132-3
[8] T. C. Coen, The Indian Political Service: a study in indirect rule (London 1971) 8
[9] T.B. Macaulay, 'Warren Hastings' Edinburgh Review Oct 1841 reprinted G. M. Young (ed) Macaulay: poetry and prose. 373-469

India. Wilks, I believe, possessed the greater heart and the nobler character. He was able to make smooth many rough places for his nephew. He had enjoyed no such benefit at the start of his own career, but had to make his way by his own efforts alone. In many ways, Mark Cubbon was his creation, formed by his precepts and example. Both men attracted highly favourable opinions from some of the most notable figures of their day, and Wilks secured the abiding friendship of Arthur Wellesley – a singularly cool judge of mankind.

Professionally, the younger man went further. He may be placed, I believe, in the second rank of the British who served India during the early years; below the greatest such as Charles Theophilus Metcalfe, Barry Close, John Malcolm, Thomas Munro and Mountstuart Elphinstone, but nevertheless a man of formidable attainment. He stands, perhaps, with William Sleeman and others who achieved much in a single endeavour. He spent sixty years in India and was Commissioner in Mysore for twenty-seven. By contrast, Wilks was in India for only nineteen years, in two periods separated by four years on sick-leave, so that at the beginning of his second tour he had almost to start afresh. He was dogged by such persistent ill-health as to prevent him from achieving all that was within the scope of his abilities. Yet he carried away with him an almost unique knowledge of the region which was later distilled into publications – notably his 'Historical Sketches of the South of India' – that have placed us in his debt and have led a prominent scholar-administrator of modern Karnataka State to call him 'the Mysore historian'.[10] Had his Indian career extended to thirty years he might well have come close to equalling the greatest men of Anglo-India.

Inevitably, accounts differ about some events, such as the precise relationship between the restored Maharajah of Mysore (1799) and that predecessor who was set aside by Hyder Ali. Where Wilks deals with an event in his 'Historical Sketches' I have followed his version – both from deference to one of the subjects of this book and out of respect for his scholarship. On matters where his guidance is lacking I have made a judgement between conflicting versions. Similarly, so far as possible I have used the participants' own words, in the hope of conveying a flavour of the times.

In general, names of places in India have been spelt as they appeared in atlases and guide-books about the time of Independence. However, when a direct quotation is given the writer's own spelling is used; for example, Mark Wilks always wrote 'Mysoor' for the more usual 'Mysore'. Some personal and geographical names, therefore, may appear in two or more forms.

Three Appendices provide additional information. Biographical Names describes some of the people; Geographical Names does the same for places, especially those not mentioned in general atlases. The third Appendix is a Glossary of Indian and Anglo-Indian words – to which a few Manx terms have been added for the benefit of those unfamiliar with the Island.

---

[10] T. P. Issar, *The Royal City*. (Bangalore, 1991) 55

Wilks and Cubbon employed Imperial and Indian units of measurement. However, since the former will soon disappear, metric units have been used here, except in quotations from letters and the like.

CHAPTER ONE

The Isle of Man

Mark Wilks was born at a time that saw some of the most far-reaching changes in the history of the Isle of Man; changes that continued to have an effect throughout the youth of Mark Cubbon and beyond his sailing for India in 1801. The Island's constitutional position was being transformed, as was its social and economic structure. A rehearsal of the state of the Isle of Man as it was when Wilks and Cubbon were growing to manhood may be helpful to those without Manx connections, and remind Manx readers of how different was their Island then.

The Isle of Man is a small place, only 572 sq km in area; but within it there is a surprising variety of landscape. Two large blocks of mountains (to 620m), separated by a valley running from west to east, have determined the patterns of communication and land-use. It has never been a part of the United Kingdom nor was it, for that matter, within the Roman Empire. At various times it had been attached to the kingdoms of Norway, Scotland or England. Then, in 1333, Edward III of England took back the Island from Scotland and appointed William de Montacute as tributary King of Man. Thereafter it passed through several hands before being given by Henry IV to Sir John Stanley with the condition that he render two falcons to Henry as an act of homage, and that the same be done at the coronation of future monarchs of England – a practice that was continued until George IV was crowned in 1821. In 1460 the ruling Stanley became 1st Earl of Derby. The family continued as Lords of Man until 1594 when Elizabeth I took control of the Island, which duly passed to her successor James VI and I. Both monarchs appointed Governors. There was a restoration of the Stanley's in 1610, but in 1651 the Island came under the Lordship of Thomas Fairfax until 1660 when the Stanleys were again confirmed as Lords.

Following the death of the 10th Earl without issue in 1736, James Murray 2nd Duke of Atholl, a descendant from a daughter of the 7th Earl, succeeded as Lord of Man after a period of contention with other claimants. Though generally sympathetic to his new dominion, the Duke spent little time in the Isle of Man, which is not surprising given the extent of his interests elsewhere. The Atholl family has their seat at Blair Castle near the village of Blair Atholl, and Defoe wrote this about them more than a decade before they became Lords of Man

> The Duke of Atholl is lord, I was almost going to say king of this country, … and has the greatest share of vassalage of any nobleman in this part of Scotland. I have been told that he can bring a body of above 6000 men together in arms at

very little warning. The pomp and state in which this noble person lives is not to be imitated in Great Britain; for he is served like a prince, and maintains a greater equipage and revenue than five times his estate would support in another country.[11]

Within three decades the Island's constitutional position was changed yet again, but for an economic reason. At that time the 'running trade' – smuggling – had grown in importance so that, by the mid-18th century, it was by far the most profitable activity in the Island and, indeed, acted to the detriment of other enterprises. In this instance the 'trade' consisted of importing commodities such as tea, tobacco, wines and spirits into the Island from continental Europe, paying a (legally) low customs duty at Manx ports, and then moving them to secluded harbours in Great Britain or Ireland so as to avoid paying the much higher duties prevailing in those countries. On the one hand, this trade was highly profitable to those who had invested in it, whether they lived on or off the Island; and on the other hand it deprived the British Government of revenue it should have received in duties. The solution perceived by that Government was for the King of Great Britain, George III, to resume sovereignty over the Island.

In 1764 the 2nd Duke of Atholl died and was succeeded by his son-in-law and nephew as 3rd Duke. He was immediately faced with a proposal from the British Government to buy out the Lordship. After some argument a sum of £70,000 was agreed and the Isle of Man Revesting Act (1765) was passed by the British Parliament.

The 'running trade' brought wealth to those engaged in it and, indeed, some measure of prosperity to the wider community. Unfortunately, it was accompanied by neglect of other elements of the economy. Farming and fishing were comparatively inefficient, being intended to provide mainly for the small domestic market, and little thought was given to opportunities for exporting the produce. Fishing competed with farming for labour during the summer, which depressed the efficiency of agriculture even further.[12] In fact, not for the last time the Island had put all its economic eggs into one basket and, when the bottom fell out of it, the economy lay almost in ruins. During the next sixty years the Island struggled to rebuild its economy. For a time, conditions were very hard, but later they improved gradually. This general economic malaise is one reason for Mark Cubbon's often-expressed wish to provide his parents with financial assistance. On the other hand, the day-to-day running of the Island probably showed little change with revestment. For example, John

---

[11] Daniel Defoe, *A Tour through the Whole Island of Great Britain, 1724-6*, Pat Rogers (ed) (London 1971) 673-4

[12] Basil Quayle, *General View of Agriculture in the Isle of Man* (London 1794) 14 (Reprinted in one volume with report having the same title by Thomas Quayle (1812) and an introduction by F. Quayle (Douglas 1992))

Wood, who had been appointed Governor and Commander-in-Chief in 1761, continued in that post until 1777, some twelve years after Revestment.

When the 3rd Duke died in 1774, his successor began to press for an additional payment for the Lordship of Man that had passed from his family. The House of Keys opposed this, and the British Parliament refused it; but a face-saving measure was found for the Duke. Since 1285 the Lords of Man had been represented in the Island by a deputy who carried one of a variety of titles: accordingly, the Duke was appointed Governor-in-Chief and Captain General in 1793.[13] Unfortunately he showed a strong tendency toward nepotism, and filled many public posts with his own relatives. His kinsman, Lord Henry Murray, was Lieutenant-Governor during 1804-5 and would have enjoyed a longer tenure had not death deprived him of it. His nephew, George Murray, was appointed to the great office of Lord Bishop in 1814. When this man is remembered, it is for trying to impose a tithe of twelve shillings per acre on the potato crop and thus provoking riots.[14] The Duke remained Governor-in-Chief until 1808 when he was replaced, as Lieutenant-Governor, by Colonel Cornelius Smelt who was much more in sympathy with the Island's needs.

Civil Government

Throughout this period the affairs of the Island were carried on through institutions and public offices that had existed for centuries. Among the secular offices, that of Governor has already been noted. He was supreme within the Island subject, of course, to instructions from the Lord or, after Revestment, from the British Government. Castletown was the capital and here, within the medieval Castle Rushen, the Governor resided.

There were two Judges of the High Court of Justice, who bore the title 'Deemster' (of Scandinavian origin) and had extensive authority. Their appointment reflected the ancient division of the Island into 'north' and 'south' for there was a Northern and a Southern Deemster. In addition there was a third senior Judge, the Clerk of the Rolls, and a stipendiary magistrate, the High Bailiff. The Lord's Treasurer was the Receiver-General, who collected revenues and customs duties from all sources and arranged for the maintenance of Castle Rushen, but after Revestment these duties were transferred to other hands so that the post faded away. More enduring was the office of Attorney-General, principal legal adviser to the Governor. In exercising his authority the Governor was assisted by the Lord's Council, a body of variable composition which usually included the Bishop, Deemsters, Attorney-General and Receiver-General.

In so far as the community – or its more wealthy and influential members – had any representation, it was through the House of Keys, a body of twenty-

---

[13] R. H. Kinvig, *The Isle of Man: a social, cultural and political history* (3rd ed, Liverpool, 1975) 117
[14] R.H. Kinvig, *The Isle of Man.* 118

four members led by its Speaker. At this time the House of Keys had its home in a stone building in Parliament Square Castletown, under the shadow of Castle Rushen. Until 1866 the Keys were essentially self-electing in that when a place became vacant the remaining members proposed two names to the Governor from which he chose one; thereafter the member could serve for life. Moreover, the House met in camera until the Revesting Act required it to meet in public. These imperfections notwithstanding, the House of Keys exerted itself to achieve a measure of prosperity for the Island.

Of all the Island's institutions the open-air Tynwald ceremony was, and remains, the most moving manifestation of the identity of Man. Of Scandinavian origin, and possibly dating from 979 AD, the ceremony had long been held on mid-Summer's Day (24 June), but even this had been changed a few years before Mark Wilks was born, with introduction of the Gregorian adjustment to the calendar in 1752. Consequently, 11 days had to be omitted from that year so that the old calendar 24 June became Gregorian calendar 5 July and the Tynwald ceremony has since been held on that date – but it was still an innovation when Mark Wilks first attended.

As today, the ceremony took place at St. John's, on and around a stepped hill that was tented for the occasion. The hill itself is not an insignificant structure, for its base now covers about 480 sq m and the uppermost of its four tiers has an area of 26.5 sq m.[15] During the ceremony, this tier was occupied by the Governor, Bishop, Deemsters, and other members of the Council; and on the next level were the members of the House of Keys. These two groups together comprised the Tynwald Court. Lesser dignitaries and officials were on the tiers below them. The citizens gathered around the hill and listened intently as laws that had been passed during the preceding year were announced in English and Manx – for those laws became effective only after they had been proclaimed in this way. At the same time the citizens were able to sum up the men who had made those laws.

Such a large gathering of people was reason enough for a fair. If a painting of 1795 is a true representation both the fair and the ceremony itself were less restrained, more frolicsome, affairs than today. Doubtless, young Mark Cubbon, as son of a prominent clergyman and grandson of a member of the House of Keys, was present at that Tynwald ceremony and took a ten-year-old's interest in the happenings.

For civil purposes the country was divided into six sheadings: in the north were Glenfaba, Michael and Ayre; and in the south Garff, Middle and Rushen. Every sheading had a Coroner who carried out a variety of tasks intended to keep the peace and uphold the law – essentially those of a sheriff. The sheadings were sub-divided into seventeen parishes: five sheadings with three parishes but one with only two. The parishes had their origins in military

---

[15] E. H. Stenning, *Portrait of the Isle of Man* (4th ed. London 1978) 61 (Dimensions of Tynwald Hill converted into metric units)

organization, in recognition of which each had a Captain. He was appointed by the Lord and was responsible for selecting and organizing a small force to maintain security and discipline within his parish; and he served as a means of conveying official orders and information. As might be expected the parishes also had an ecclesiastical purpose, and the names of several was derived from that of the Saint to whom the Parish Church is dedicated.

The Church

The Manx Church is a part of the Anglican Communion and, since the Reformation at least, its organization has reflected the situation in England. Methodism was brought to the Island in a meaningful way about 1776, and John Wesley himself made visits in 1777 and 1781. This new presentation of Christianity achieved considerable popularity with the community; indeed, in many Manx people there may be an element of austerity, coupled with 'fellowship', that finds Methodism peculiarly attractive. However, the incoming preachers received a mixed reception from the established clergy: some were welcoming but others were distinctly antagonistic.

At the head of the Manx Church was (and remains) the Lord Bishop of Sodor and Man, whose title harks back to Norse times when Man was united with the Sudreys or Southern Isles, the Hebrides in fact. For centuries it had been the practice for the Bishop to be appointed by the Lord of Man, and the Archdeacon of Man was appointed in the same way. Unique to the Manx Church, since the Reformation, was the office of Vicar-General. Indeed, during the 18th century there were two such: one usually holding his court in the north and the other in the south but, when necessary, holding a combined court. Within their jurisdiction came all cases touching upon Church discipline including the behaviour of parishioners, as well as wills and probate.

Some of the Island's bishops impinged directly upon the Wilkses and Cubbons in a variety of ways, though perhaps most forcibly over the matter of tithes. To Bishop Simon of Argyll (1229-48) belongs the unenviable distinction, in his first synod, of introducing tithes to the Island: on grain, livestock and woven cloth. Later in that century Bishop Mark of Galloway (1275-1305) imposed a tithe on fish caught at sea. Some 500 years later Mark Wilks's father was to be charged with the pursuit of tithes on behalf of the Manx clergy. Bishop Isaac Barrow (1663-71) was a formidable character who acted as Governor or 'Sword Bishop' for a time from 1664. Much concerned by the low level of education possessed by the Island's clergy he set about improving the situation – and with that in mind sequestered two farms in order to establish a fund, later named 'Bishop Barrow's Trust', intended to provide education for those who aspired to the cloth. A third Bishop of concern to this story is Thomas Wilson (in office 1698-1755), a prelate who was at once highly supportive of his clergy, much concerned with popular education and personally frugal, but so obsessed with ecclesiastical authority as to jeopardise the position of his Church. Indeed, his position vis-à-vis civil authority was similar to that of the nonjuring Bishops who had been influential in England when he was a young man.[16]

During the years following their introduction by Bishop Simon in the 13th century tithes were extended to a greater range of produce. In 1712 Bishop Wilson imposed a tithe on potatoes, which had recently been brought to the Island, arguing that the area planted with tithe-free potatoes and turnips had increased greatly at the expense of other crops on which tithes were payable, so that the income of the clergy was reduced. Traditionally tithes were collected 'in kind' and sometimes under circumstances demeaning to the donor.[17]

Popular opposition brought about the withdrawal or lapse of liability to tithes: Bishop Wilson's potato tithe lapsed after 1750, and fish tithes were not collected after 1770. By about 1812 the position had become: no tithe was levied on milk, but there was a four penny tithe on a cow that had calved within the year; a tithe was payable on crops secured by cutting; no tithe was payable on crops dug up or pulled.[18] The situation was made worse by a system of 'tithe farming' under which a clergyman let the tithes to another person, from whom it might pass to three or four other people with each taking a profit.[19] This served neither the farmer nor the clergyman.

No wonder that as early as 1794 the point had been well made that 'a greater blessing could not fall on this country than universal payment of the tythes in a settled sum of money'.[20] This did not come about until 1839 when Tynwald passed the Tithe Commutation Act as a consequence of indirect pressure from the British Government.

The Way of Life

In 1757, two years before Mark Wilks was born, the Island's population was estimated at 19,144 people. The largest town, and already the chief place of trade, was Douglas (pop.1814). The other towns were the capital Castletown (915), Ramsey (882) and Peel (805); the five largest villages accounted for perhaps 1000 people between them. Consequently, almost 72 percent of the population was rural, living on farms, in small villages or coastal crofting communities. By 1792 the population had grown to 27,913.[21]

As a small insular community the Manx were disadvantaged by what would now be called their 'transportation infrastructure'. External transportation links seem to have been forged in response to existing demand. The first service was provided by cutters which were ready to sail at short notice between the Island and its neighbours, with Whitehaven as a favoured port in Great Britain. In

---

[16] G. M. Trevelyan, *England under Queen Anne* vol 1 Blenheim (London 1965) 76
[17] B. Quayle, *General View of Agriculture* 11
[18] Thomas Quayle, *General View of Agriculture in the Isle of Man* (London 1812) 29-30
[19] B. Quayle, *General View of Agriculture* 40
[20] B. Quayle, *General View of Agriculture* 11
[21] Pigot and Co's *National Directory of Scotland and of the Isle of Man* (London 1837) 824

1750 Tynwald established a packet-boat service, which sailed at regular intervals, to carry letters and goods between Douglas and Whitehaven. This arrangement was refined in 1767 when the Government chartered a packet to carry mail, once per week, between the same pair of ports. At the same time a postal service was established for the Island, and postage on a single letter cost two (old) pence.[22] By 1798 there were thirty-two vessels on the Liverpool run: twenty-five serving Douglas and seven sailing from Ramsey, but only two of these ships carried passengers and mail. Douglas Bay is wide, faces eastward, and was not ideal for landing passengers. The position was improved when the Red Pier in Douglas was opened during 1793, but even then arriving passengers transferred to small boats and had to scramble over slippery rocks to reach the Pier.[23] About 1812, Ramsey was described as 'an indifferent harbour but has a good roadstead' and it seems that passengers arrived on to the open beach.[24]

Internal means of transportation were unsatisfactory until at least 1713. The so-called roads were so bad as to be impassable by wheeled vehicles. Travellers on foot or horseback preferred to use paths, which often ran over private land, with the consent of owners. Farmers used the same paths when driving their animals or conveying goods on sleds. The Highways Act of 1713 made demands on ordinary folk for money or labour to maintain the roads. Matters may not have improved much because the Act of 1776 imposed a further obligation in order to ensure that adequate roads were built, eight yards (7.3 m) wide from ditch to ditch. By 1794, one-horse gigs and carts drawn by two or three horses were replacing sleds for the transport of corn, lime and manure.[25] A further impediment to inland travel was a lack of bridges. For example, until the late 18th century travellers between Maughold and Ramsey had to pass the Ballure river either by going along the shore at low tide or by using the ancient ford. In 1787 thirty-three prominent residents of Ramsey and Maughold petitioned Tynwald to build a bridge over the river upstream of the ford, and divert the Ramsey to Douglas highway so as to pass over it; among the petitioners were John Frissell, High Bailiff, and the Rev Thos Cubbon of Maughold.[26] Their petition was granted but pedestrians continued to use the ford for years afterwards. In 1821 regular stage-coach services began operation in the Island, largely in consequence of steam-ship services to the Island with which they connected; but until 1835 the coach between Ramsey and Douglas travelled via Bishop's Court[27] – which was little help to the people of Maughold.

---

[22] A. W. Moore, *History of the Isle of Man* 2 vols with pages numbered consecutively throughout. (London 1900) 426, 614
[23] Vaughan Robinson and Danny McCarroll (eds), *The Isle of Man: celebrating a sense of place* (Liverpool 1990) 177
[24] B. Quayle, *General View of Agriculture* 9
[25] B. Quayle, *General View of Agriculture* 18-19, 21
[26] J. W. and C. K. Radcliffe, *A History of Kirk Maughold* (Douglas 1979) 205
[27] J. W. and C. K. Radcliffe, *A History of Kirk Maughold* 206

Country folk brought poultry and other produce to Saturday markets that were held in the towns. Fairs were held somewhere in the Island on most days of the week, and these served as a place for dealing in horses and cattle, and for selling clothing and other goods made on the Island.[28]

In their overall standard of living ordinary Manx people probably differed little from their counterparts in Great Britain: probably no better and possibly no worse. Both breakfast and supper usually consisted of meal pottage and milk, but dinner was made up of potatoes with either fresh or salt fish.[29] Indeed, existing folk memory recalls a staple diet of potatoes and herrings helped down with buttermilk, reasonably nutritious though monotonous. The small professional and landed elements of society enjoyed standards similar to those of equivalent groups in Britain, and secured many commodities at a lower cost. Moreover, the few very wealthy families were decidedly cosmopolitan in their mode of living.

So far as their cultural environment was concerned, Wilks and Cubbon grew up within a community that used the Manx language as a matter of course. It had been entirely a spoken medium without significant literature until about 1756 when the Manx Prayer Book was published. In 1764 the greater part of the population spoke no English. By 1812 'the yeomanry and inferior ranks of the people' still spoke Manx, but English was coming in quickly especially among the young.[30] For the educated Manx person English provided an essential medium for receiving information and opinions from the world beyond Man. The intellectual climate of the time was stimulating, for many previous accepted practices and beliefs were being subject to critical reappraisal in the spirit of the European Enlightenment by scholars such as Montesquieu, Voltaire, Hartley, Buffon and Hume. This constituted a remarkably congenial and challenging intellectual environment for a lively mind such as that of Mark Wilks.

As a Preparation for Mysore, 1783

In some ways their youthful experience of the Isle of Man gave Wilks and Cubbon a good preparation for what they would meet in South India. For example, their departure from Douglas or Ramsey would have been over the rocks or beach to boats that carried them out to their ships. Similarly, at Madras they disembarked into massula boats and were landed upon the open beach, though the massula boats were comparatively large vessels able to carry 40 to 60 tonnes.

Both communities were essentially rural, with many small villages but few towns. In the Island, villages provided services for farms and crofts in their vicinity, such as a blacksmith, a carpenter, a store and so on, which was not far

---

[28] B. Quayle, *General View of Agriculture* 24
[29] B. Quayle, *General View of Agriculture* 15
[30] T. Quayle, *General View of Agriculture* 164-5

removed from the situation in Indian villages described by Pandian (Chapter 7). In both countries, communication between villages was indifferent and, indeed, may have been inferior in the Island to that in South India. Animals were the only source of locomotive power, and South India had an advantage in the shape of its trotting bullocks, about which more will be said later. When the first regular postal service to Ramsey was established about 1779, a man was employed to meet the packet in Douglas and carry any letters to Ramsey, stay there for a day, and return to Douglas with mail for the next sailing.[31] This arrangement was little different from the tappal or dak that carried letters for Mark Wilks in South India.

Local government in the Island was largely carried on by Coroners of Sheadings and Captains of Parishes, but higher authority was either at some distance in Castletown or far away in London. Similarly, local government in South India depended on village headmen and Amildars, but highest authority lay with the Princely Courts at Seringapatam or Hyderabad, or with the Presidency Government in Madras.

Mention has been made of the 'tithe farming' that existed in the Island as late as 1812. An analogous system of 'tax farming' grew up in Mysore, which eventually led to serious revolts by the peasants and thus to Mark Cubbon's appointment as Commissioner there.[32]

---

[31] Constance Radcliffe, *Ramsey 1600-1800* (Douglas 1986) 83
[32] N.H.M. Chancellor, pers. com.

CHAPTER TWO

Two Manx Families

Origins

The names of the two men, who are the concern of this book, reflect the origins of the families from which they sprang: the Cubbons were wholly Manx but the Wilkses were incomers. The two families were united by the marriage of the Rev Thomas Cubbon with Miss Margaret Wilks, who was half sister to Mark Wilks. Thomas and Margaret became the parents of Mark Cubbon.

Paradoxically, the story of the Cubbons is less well documented than that of the later arrivals. The probable reason is that Thomas's immediate ancestors were well-to-do farmers and thus self-employed; prominent in their community, they were answerable to no man so that written records are sparse. The Wilkses, however, were dependent upon others, and this dependence entailed written applications, records and reports that spell out the family's story.

An earlier version of Cubbon – M'Cubbon – is recorded in the Island from 1430. Thomas's family was from Ballacallin, Kirk Marown and had long enjoyed considerable standing in the community. Both his father and grandfather were named William and both were Captain of their Parish; in addition, Thomas's father was a Member of the House of Keys from 1748 to 1797. Thomas attended school for about eleven years at the charge of his maternal grandfather, the Rev G. McLean, and for a time was tutor to the Governor's children.[33]

By contrast, the name 'Wilks' first appeared in Manx records only in 1717. While sources agree that the family were comparatively recent arrivals in the Isle of Man, there are two accounts of how they came here. One suggests that the family may have originated in Somerset, whence it moved to Leighton Buzzard in Bedfordshire, and from there to the Island. A second account asserts that the family came originally from Yorkshire, and that the first Wilks to reach the Isle of Man moved first to Dublin as a young man. Later he and his own son moved to the Island. The accounts agree that the family settled in Ballasalla.[34]

Certainly one George Wilks was a smith in Ballasalla about 1723, and apparently engaged in minting coin during 1733-34. He was assisted by one of his sons, named John, who had married a girl called Margaret and the baptism of their first son (also named John) on 30 June 1717 at Kirk Malew is that first written record of 'Wilks' in the Island. The couple had a least five children, and

---

[33] Centenary of the Popularly Elected House of Keys. (MNHL D1511/41)
[34] MNHL MD 436 10/3

the baptism of their second son is entered in the Register of Santon as 'James Wilks, son of John and Margaret of Newton in Asholt July 26, 1719.'[35] It seems that Asholt (or Holt's Hill) was a large intack, part of which is known now as Mount Murray. A property named Newton was built there just before 1717, and this fact has been invoked as evidence that the Wilks were recent arrivals in Santon. Later, Newton passed into the ownership of Lord Henry Murray, a kinsman of the Duke of Atholl, who was Lieutenant Governor for a short period.

The Rev James Wilks

Little is known of James Wilks's early life. In 1742 he was ordained by Bishop Wilson, and then served as Curate of St German's. Three years later he became Vicar of St John's. About that time, he was sent by Bishop Wilson to Dublin to obtain arrears of interest on money left to the Academic Fund under Bishop Barrow's will and invested there; his mission was completed successfully, as was his commission from the Bishop to secure plate for Marown church.[36] In 1750 Wilks was made Episcopal Registrar, and in 1752 was moved to Kirk Michael so that he would be close to Bishop's Court, residence of the ageing Thomas Wilson who had become much dependent upon him: indeed by the modern road the Old Vicarage (as it is now known) is little more than a kilometre from Bishop's Court. The Vicarage had been built only nine years previously and stood beside a substantial glebe farm. The house itself is placed well back from the road, and its exterior has a pleasant, simple dignity.

The Rev Wilks married twice. His first wife was Margaret, daughter of the Rev John Woods Jr (former Vicar-General who had died in 1740), whom he married at St German in 1745. Their oldest child was Thomas, born in June 1747. In July 1749 he was followed by Margaret, known as Peggy within the family, who would become Mrs Cubbon. Next came Deborah and Elizabeth at intervals of two years; the former was named for Mrs Wilks's sister then living in Ireland for who she felt a warm affection.[37]

Margaret Wilks suffered from ill-health for much of her short life: for example, in her will of 30 August 1750, made when she was only twenty-six, she recorded herself as being 'in a moderate state of health and of sound mind and memory.'[38]

Bishop Wilson died in 1755. Later that year Wilks was sent to London 'on account and at the request of the Clergy of this Isle', about a chancery suit against the Earl of Derby for the recovery of tithes which, it was claimed, had been annexed by the Earl's family. In London he dined with James, 2nd Duke of Atholl and Lord of Man. Soon afterwards the Duke introduced him to the Rev

---

[35] Manx Genealogies (mss, n.d.) (MNHL MD 10036)
[36] MNHL MD 10036
[37] MNHL MD 10036
[38] Episcopal Wills, 1750: Kirk German, Margaret Wilks. (MNHL, MF/ GL719).

Dr Mark Hildesley, whom he had appointed to succeed Bishop Thomas Wilson. Clearly the two men got on well together, and Hildesley was favourably impressed by Wilks.

At the time of James's journey Margaret was expecting their fifth child, but matters went badly wrong. The child was baptized James on 9 June but died next day, and Mrs Wilks herself died on 13 June aged thirty-one years.[39] Perhaps fortuitously, Wilks was staying at 'Mr Wood's a surgeon in Brook Street' but it may be he was consulting the surgeon about his wife's state of health. In any event, without having been able to return home for the funeral, Wilks had the onerous task of seeing Bishop-designate Hildesley and his family to the diocese. Bishop's Court was undergoing repairs – doubtless necessary after being for fifty-six years the residence of one man. He went on ahead, being 'gently wafted over the Pond' from Liverpool to Douglas: the weather in mid-July was very good but nevertheless his small sloop took nineteen hours in the crossing. Having seen his children, Wilks inspected Bishop's Court and reported that it was not quite ready; but reassured the Hildesleys about the crossing, that the beds would be thoroughly aired, and advising Mrs Hildesley about which provisions she might bring with her and which would be cheaper on the Island.[40]

Next year James Wilks suffered another blow when his son, Thomas, died tragically on 1 May (old style). In a house at Ramsey gunpowder was being prepared for use in celebrations to be held later that day. There was an explosion, the house collapsed, and Thomas was killed.[41] The Bishop, to give him due credit, rallied round generously. During all this time James's mother did much to care for his young children. For example, in 1756 he was again in London in pursuit of tithes, and he obviously treasured 'my Mother's letter of July 21 1756. Rec^d 1 August' in which she reported that the Bishop himself was carrying out James's duties on holy days, and assured him Peggy goes to school to a mistress living in the white house so doth Debbie.

> The children are very well and I have got their new cloathes made...the good woman at the white house whom my Lord Bishop encourages to teach ten girls of the Parish...his Lordship will give her £5 per annum and also a green gown for each girl to distinguish them, and whom he intends to educate after his own way.[42]

Mrs Wilks's reference to the 'white house' indicates what was then a well-known property in Michael village that had been built some time before 1688 but no longer exists.[43] Hildesley's establishment was perhaps the earliest

---

[39] Burials, 1755: Kirk Michael, Margaret Wilks. (MNHL MF/ PR24)
[40] MNHL MD 436 3/16
[41] Burials, 1756: Kirk Michael, Thomas Wilks. (MNHL M/F PR24).
[42] MNHL 436 6/24.
[43] John Grimson, *Kirk Michael* (Douglas 1991) 23

Pater familias: the Rev. James Wilks. (Courtesy of Director MNH)

school for girls in the Island, for it pre-dated Halsall's School in Castletown which had been founded with a bequest from Catherine of that name as a free school for teaching girls to read, sew, knit and spin.

In June 1756 James Wilks married, as his second wife, Elizabeth Christian, daughter of William Christian, the Vicar-General, of Ballamooar, Jurby. Their first child, James, was born in June 1757, and he was followed by Anne (1758), Mark (1759) and two more.[44] Mark was named for Bishop Hildesley, who stood Godfather to the lad, and so his Christian name became established in the family. Anne, or Nancy in the family, was a prolific letter-writer who sought to keep every brother informed of what the others were doing, especially after they had gone their several ways. In 1782 she married John Corlett – which was changed to Collet when they emigrated to North America. A grandson of that name appears near the end of this story.

James's career continued to prosper. He was sent, yet again, to London in May 1768 in order to manage, in conjunction with Counsel Mr Hamersley, the clergy's litigation with the fishermen over tithes, and remained away until August.[45] Next year he was made a Vicar-General, and felt compelled to consult the clergy for their opinion on whether he should continue to press

---

[44] MNHL MD 10036.
[45] MNHL MD 436 3/53.

claims for those tithes which, as we have seen, would not be collected after 1770. In 1771 he became Rector of St Mary de Ballaugh, a post that Philip Moore had held eleven years before. Moreover, he had influential friends: Bishop Hildesley and, through him, the Duke of Atholl, Lord of Man.

Mark Wilks was particularly fond of his half-sister Margaret or Peggy, who was older by ten years and sometimes may have seemed more like an aunt. Perhaps, therefore, he had mixed feelings when, in August 1769, at the age of twenty, she married the Rev Thomas Cubbon – ten years her senior and recently appointed Vicar of Maughold in succession to her great uncle, the Rev Thomas Woods. As we have seen, the Cubbons came from Marown, and Thomas had already served for four years as Vicar of the neighbouring parish of Santon. The vicarage at Maughold (now the 'Old Vicarage') was in need of repairs when the Cubbons moved in, but an expenditure of £19 Manx seems to have been sufficient to put the house into satisfactory order for the next fifty years! In the fashion of the time, children arrived regularly; there were ten in all, including Mark who was born in 1785 as the seventh among them.[46]

The Rev Wilks died in June 1777, but seemingly had possessed the foresight to make provision for his son's future. On 7 November 1776 James Wilks, Samuel Wattleworth of Kirk Malew (the Archdeacon) and Mark Wilks of Castletown entered into a bond by which they acknowledged that they were

> Indebted to HE John Wood Esq[r] Governor and Commander of this Isle, the Right Reverend Richard, Lord Bishop of Sodor and Man, and other [named] Trustees or Feoffees in trust nominated and appointed by the late Right Reverend Bishop Barrow one hundred pounds lawful money of Great Britain, [and] Mark Wilks has been allowed of and admitted to be one of the Academic scholars and thereby intitled [sic] to a certain Annual Sum or benefaction while he continues upon said Benefaction or Foundation, or he be provided for in the Ministry and service of the Church in this Isle. Mark Wilks...shall carefully apply himself to the study of Academic Learning ... and at all times be ready when required to enter into Holy Orders.[47]

The Scholars were selected from among pupils at the Grammar School. Since Mark was already in Castletown and appointed an Academic Scholar he must have been a pupil at the Free Grammar school there. This occupied the mediaeval Chapel of St Mary's which had long served the town as both church and school. A new St Mary's had been built between 1698 and 1701 so that the Chapel could be given over exclusively to education, and an annex had been added to fit it better for that purpose.[48] Under the educational reforms of

---

[46] MNHL MD 436 10/3

[47] Miscellaneous documents relating to Colonel Wilks. Bond of 7 Nov 1776 (CKS U1287 96/2)

[48] A. M. Cubbon, 'The Mediaeval Chapel of St Mary's Castletown – later the Castletown Grammar School' reprinted from Proceedings of the Isle of Man Natural History and Antiquarian Society VII No. 3 (1971).

Bishop Barrow an Academic School was established and shared the premises with the Grammar School. The Schoolmaster taught in the Grammar School and also read logic and philosophy to the Academic Scholars – who were usually four in number. A contemporary account states 'they are habited in black, wide-sleeved gowns and square caps and have lodgings in the castle and a salary of £10 a year a piece.'[49]

Mark was fortunate in his teacher for the Master was the Rev Thomas Castley, Fellow of Jesus College Cambridge, Senior Wrangler, Second Medallist. Precisely what had induced the man who had taken top place in the Mathematics Tripos at Cambridge to make his career in Castletown remains a mystery. He was, however, a successful teacher as well as a distinguished scholar. By 1776 he had been in post for nearly twenty years but had not yet gained the reputation for harshness that was to come his way near the end of the fifty years he spent at the school. In any event, there can be no doubt that Mark's scholarly development owed much to his influence.[50]

Mark Wilks's Lucky Chance

So there was Mark, a Scholar at the Academic School and seemingly destined to follow his father into the Manx clergy. By a long chance, however, another career open to him. During the middle of the 18th century Fencible Corps were raised in several parts of Great Britain, though not at that time in the Isle of Man. Their purpose was essentially to replace the regular army in its duties at home when a substantial part of it was abroad. Their members were volunteers who received a bounty (usually three guineas) together with the same pay and allowances as the regulars. In July 1779 measures to raise a Manx Fencible Corps were put in train, and in November these were approved: its headquarters were to be in Castletown, there would be three Companies, and it would serve only in the Island. The Lieutenant-Governor, Richard Dawson, a former Lieutenant Colonel in the Engineers, was appointed Major-Commandant. Two other officers commissioned at the same time were Captain John Taubman, aged 33 years, who had resigned from the 6th Dragoon Guards in 1774 after ten years service, and Lieutenant Mark Wilks, aged 21 years.[51]

Thus was Mark at once given experience of the profession of arms and brought into company with a member of one of the most influential families in the Island. The outcome, as reported in a letter of 23 August 1782 by sister Anne was that

> Mark was to have sailed from Spithead on 20th of this month in the capacity of Cadet in India service as will be recommended as any young man could be through the interest of our truly worthy friend Captain Taubman he has the

---

[49] MNHL 5132 Castletown Grammar School (Misc. notes)
[50] MNHL BH 4432C Academic Scholars (1761)
[51] B. E. Sargeaunt, *The Royal Manx Fencibles.* (Aldershot 1947) 14, 20

interest of Sir Henry Fletcher, Deputy Chairman of the Court of Directors, Sir Thomas Rumbolt one of the Company whose wealth make him of consequence to them, Lady Rumbolt and several others of less consequence …
He sails in the Montague…[52]

Sister-like she recorded also that he was 5 ft 11 ½ ins tall!

The 'interest' to which Anne referred was, of course, patronage. The institution was wide-spread over much of western Europe at the time, and was not without merit. Among others, it gave Joseph Haydn the opportunity to realize his musical potential under the aegis of the Esterhazy family (1761-90) and thus lays a debt upon all of us. In those days it offered virtually the only route to employment in the East India Company's service. Not to labour the point, the function of patronage as exercised by the Company's Directors was to place a young man's feet upon the first rung of the career-ladder; how high he climbed thereafter was a matter for himself. Mark Wilks's cadet papers have not come to light, but the way in which he secured patronage is reasonably clear. He was fortunate in having the interest of three highly influential men in the Island: Sir George Moore who had recently resigned as Speaker of the House of Keys, John Taubman Sr the current Speaker, and his son, Captain John Taubman, who had been a Member of the Keys since 1777. Sir George procured letters to introduce Mark into the right circles in Madras, but Captain John Taubman was the key figure. The Taubmans had been a prominent Manx family for several generations, giving at least one Deemster to the Island. John Taubman Sr (1720-99) was a merchant who had accumulated the wealth that enabled him, in 1776, to buy the Island's finest private estate, the Nunnery, and to make influential friends in Great Britain: indeed he became known as the 'Great Taubman.' Captain Taubman, Mark's comrade in the Fencibles, had served in a fairly fashionable cavalry regiment before entering the House of Keys. Much of his time was spent in England, where he bought a house in Bath and had his portrait painted in London by Romney.[53] He would have moved in the same circles as men like Sir Henry Fletcher, a Director of the East India Company from 1769, and his warm recommendation would have sufficed to persuade Fletcher to nominate Mark for a cadetship. The part played by Thomas Rumbolt is more problematical: although Governor of Madras 1780-82, he was already under the suspicion of corruption that led to his dismissal by the Court of Directors.

In this way was Mark launched on his career in South India.

---

[52] Letters of Anne Corlet (néeWilks) and others (CKS U1287 94/2) letter of 23 Aug 1782

[53] A. M. Cubbon, 'The Romney Portraits of the Taubman Family' *Journal of the Manx Museum* VII, No. 88 (1976) 232-3

CHAPTER THREE

South India to 1780

What are the geographical limits of South India, and what kind of country is it? Its northern limit is marked by two rivers: the Narmada which flows from east to west for 1200 km, and the Mahanadi which runs to the east coast; at one point they are only about 160 km apart (Map 2). These two rivers are also the northern boundary of the Deccan, a high plateau occupying much of the Indian peninsula and ranging from 400 to 900 m above sea level. The Deccan is bounded on east and west by ranges of mountains called Ghats. The Western Ghats are the higher, reaching almost 3000 m and producing a rain shadow on their inland side; the Eastern Ghats are less substantial. Eventually the two ranges meet to form the delightful Nilgiris, which constitutes the southern limit of the Deccan, but the Western Ghats extend further south, almost to Kanya Kumari – the southern limit of the sub-continent. On the plateau to the north of the Nilgiris lies the region formerly known as Mysore. To the south-east of the Deccan is a great quadrant of lower country.

The Deccan itself is rather dry, and is given a distinctive appearance by outcrops of granite and sandstone. It is traversed by two major rivers: the Godavari (1500 km) and the Kistna (or Krishna, 1300 km), both of which rise on the inland slopes of the Western Ghats and reach the sea through fertile deltas on the east coast. Between the Ghats and the sea are coastal plains: in the west carrying the lush vegetation of the wet tropics which reaches its exuberant best in the former States of Travancore and Cochin, but much less luxuriant near the east coast where the effect of low rainfall is exacerbated by light soils as around Rameswaram. The rain-bearing south-west monsoon arrives in the region between late May and early June but is preceded, from March to May, by a dry period with increasing temperatures.

Essentially four political units existed in South India as Wilks encountered it: Mysore, Hyderabad, the Maratha Confederation, and the Madras Presidency (Map 3). These were the contenders for primacy in the South. The first three had been brought into being by a combination of wholly Indian factors, comprising diverse southern institutions, northern influences upon them, and southern reactions. By contrast, Madras was a British trading settlement in the process of becoming a military power.

Having to begin somewhere, one could say that in the 12th century the South comprised a diversity of peoples possessing different languages and cultural norms, but united within the broad tolerance of Hinduism; indeed some similarities to pre-Reformation Europe come to mind, albeit without a papacy. Later came Muslim invasions from the north, which either destabilized or stimulated indigenous Hindu communities and introduced new populations, new ruling groups, and a new religion – Islam. For example, in 1310-11 a Muslim army advanced almost to Kanya Kumari and returned with loot comprising 312 elephants, 20,000 horses, 1250 kg of gold and chests of jewels. In due course, the Muslim governor who had been left in Madurai set up an independent sultanate.

Contact between the south and north of India varied in intimacy from time to time, and for considerable periods events taking place in the north had little relevance to the south.

In 1526 a new Muslim dynasty, the Mughals, came to North India in the person of Zahir-ud-din Muhammad commonly known as Babur. The fifth Emperor of his line, Aurangzeb, seized power in 1658 and embarked on a series of campaigns that were mainly directed southward. The Marathas, the independent Muslim kingdoms of the Deccan, and the Sikhs of the Punjab all felt the weight of his arms. At his death in 1707 the Mughal Empire extended almost to Madurai in the extreme south – little wonder, therefore, that he took the title of Alamgir or 'Universe Grasper'. His activities, however, led to the decay of the Mughal dynasty. Indian and Western commentators agree that the greatest campaign to bring the Deccan under control of Delhi failed after an expenditure of men, treasure and effort unequalled in the history of India. Indeed, in the opinion of a Western historian 'By the time of Aurangzeb's death, imperial finances were already in disarray, strained to breaking point by the need to maintain constant campaigning throughout the whole subcontinent'[54] After his death, dissolution of authority gained pace, exacerbated by invasions from the north-west. There were to be thirteen more Mughal Emperors before the accession, in 1760, of Shah Alam II who was still in place when Mark Wilks arrived in the subcontinent.

When Europeans arrived in India they encountered the cultural milieu and administrative structures created by the Mughals. Almost until its end in 1858 the Emperor's court at Delhi held a special place in the cultural life of the sub-continent. Indeed, a comparison has been drawn between the influence of the Mughal court on Indian conventions and that of the court at Versailles upon other courts of Western Europe. Its cultural writ ran from Punjab to Madurai and, within this vast region behaviour and forms of address reflected standards of the capital. Persian, for example, was the language of diplomacy, of polite society and, in large measure, of administration. Consequently, Europeans had compelling practical reasons for coming to grips with the language. In the process some, like Wilks, were captivated by its poetry. Moreover, the British adapted Mughal administrative structures and methods to their own purposes.

Against this background, we may consider the four political entities that dominated South India when Wilks arrived there.

---

[54] C. A. Bayly, *New Cambridge History of India Vol II / I. Indian Society in the Making of the British Empire.* (Cambridge 1988) 7

Mysore

The Hindu Hoysala dynasty had long ruled in the South with its capital at Halebid. A raid by Mohammed bin Tughlaq in 1328 severely weakened it, but his withdrawal allowed two states, one Muslim and the other Hindu, to establish themselves. In the northern part of the region the Governor of the Deccan revolted against Mohammed bin Tughlaq in 1347 and set up the Muslim Bahmani kingdom of the Deccan with its capital first at Gulbarga, but later at Bidar. Then, in 1489, the Bahmani kingdom broke into five separate states, which are often referred to as the Deccani Sultanates. Eventually, the five states disappeared piecemeal with the last falling to Aurangzeb in 1687.

This fragmentation of Muslim power in the south allowed the remnant of the Hoysala dynasty to combine with two other Hindu kingdoms and found the kingdom of Vijayanagara in 1336. In 1378 Madurai, with the Muslims remaining from Tughlaq's colonization, was added. Vijayanagara was the largest state in the entire history of South India, and probably the most splendid. Its capital city bore the same name; and the main part of that city was situated on the south bank of the Tungabhadra river where it ran through a gorge surrounded by massive granite boulders. Its religious centre was close to the river, near the present-day small town of Hampi. To its south was an irrigated valley that received water from the river by way of channels. Further south of this was the so-called urban core, an oval site measuring 4 km in the longer axis, and surrounded by well-built granite walls more than 6 m high.[55]

The kingdom reached the zenith of its power under the rule of Krishnadevaraya (reigned 1509-29), who introduced an innovation that was to have far-reaching consequences. In order to counteract the minor chieftaincies that existed within his realm he created local war-chiefs or poligars, men who held one or two villages from which they derived an income on condition of giving him military service. They were intended to be vassals of the kings of Vijayanagara but matters sometimes turned out differently. Maintenance of the royal authority was also aided by the construction of fortresses at strategic points within the empire such as those on the hills between Bellary and Anantapur, north of Bangalore.

Vijayanagara issued extensive series of gold and copper coins, called pagodas, which bore the image of one or more Hindu deities on the obverse. They formed the pattern for later coinages of Indian states and of various European powers in South India, and gave rise to the notion of 'shaking the pagoda tree' as a euphemism among European traders for making one's fortune more or less illegally.

The Tungabhadra river is a tributary of the Kistna, and in the triangular no man's land between them, at least twenty-eight battles were fought between Vijayanagara and one or more of the Sultanates. The last, recorded in history as

---

[55] George Michell, *Penguin Guide to the Monuments of India vol 1 Buddhist, Jain, Hindu.* (London 1989) 397-401.

the Battle of Talikota, brought complete ruin to the great Hindu State. Four of the Deccani Sultanates settled their differences sufficiently to combine against their larger neighbour. In mid-January 1565 the Muslim forces came together at Talikota and moved southward, to meet their enemy near the village of Tandihal. Estimates vary for the number of soldiers involved, with one account suggesting that the Hindus put 82,000 cavalry, 900,000 infantry and 2000 elephants into the field, and the Muslims perhaps half that number of men with 600 guns.[56] What European power of the time could have raised such forces?

The army of Vijayanagara was completely routed. The chief minister, was slain and there is a story that his head was displayed annually in the city of Ahmadnagar for 200 years.[57]

So great was its dismay that the defeated army made no attempt to defend the capital city, which was sacked. Despite this calamity, something of the kingdom survived, for the king and much of the royal treasure were carried to Penukonda where a new capital was established. Some provinces asserted their independence but at least three, including Mysore, remained under control of the truncated Vijayanagara. However, the kingdom did not prosper and, about 1600, its capital was moved to Chandragiri. This was a place having good natural defences and a fort set upon a granite hill 180 m above the surrounding country; and within the fort an imposing palace was built. However, the move did not bring good fortune because more of the poligars declared their independence. The most important of these was in Mysore where the poligar seized the nearby fortified island of Seringapatam (Srirangapatna) and established the Wadiyar dynasty. He and his descendants extended and consolidated their state. His fourth successor, Chikka Devaraja (reigned 1672-1704), made the kingdom one of the most powerful in South India, acquired Bangalore from the Marathas, and formed a friendship with Aurangzeb who is said to have presented him with the famous throne of Mysore. For its part, Chandragiri became a prize for any who could take it, and was eventually ceded to the East India Company in 1792.

During the time of Chikka Krishnaraja Wadiyar in Mysore (reigned 1734-66) Hyder Ali made himself master of the State. His father had been a Muslim soldier in the service of the Wadiyars, who had risen to command the fort at Bangalore. By 1760 Hyder himself was already a leading general, and had gone some way toward supporting the French against the British but whose better judgement made him avoid this kind of `problematical entanglement. His next step on the way to power was to imprison the Diwan of Mysore in an iron cage and assume that post himself. In 1762 he set aside the Rajah and thus became de facto Head of State, but the Rajah was kept under palace arrest and shown

---

[56] Wolseley Haig (ed), *The Cambridge History of India vol 3 Turks and Afghans* (Cambridge, 1928) 448-50.
[57] V. A. Smith, *The Oxford History of India*. Percival Spear (ed) (3rd ed Oxford, 1958) 298-9.

to the people once a year with Hyder himself standing in the background.[58] It was left to Hyder Ali's son, Tipu, to secure for himself the title of Sultan.

In reviewing the history of Mysore State the most important places are the cities of Mysore and Bangalore, and the island of Seringapatam. By the tenth century Mysore was already the main town of a district containing seventy villages. It grew steadily, but suffered a setback in 1610 when the first Wadiyar Rajah established his capital at Seringapatam. This island in the Cauvery river was more easily defended than Mysore, so that both Hyder Ali and Tipu retained it as the site of their capital. They greatly strengthened the island's defences and gave particular attention to the fort at its western end, which came to enclose the Ranganathaswami Hindu temple together with the Jami Masjid that Hyder constructed nearby. Hyder and his son also built a fine palace of two storeys, the Lal Mahal, within the fort while outside it Tipu had his summer palace, the Daria Daulat. As a further defensive measure Tipu demolished the Delhi Bridge across the northern arm of the Cauvery.

According to tradition Bangalore was founded in 1537 by Kempe Gowdar I, a local chieftain who had to make his own way in the world. With astonishing confidence he set up four towers to mark what he foresaw as the eventual boundaries of his city and, as its nucleus, he built a mud-walled fort and laid out a bazaar. He named the place Bangaluru or 'village of half-baked beans' because, so legend says, he wished to commemorate an encounter with a generous peasant woman who had given him a meal of pulses when he became hungry while hunting.[59] Eventually the city passed into the hands of the Wadiyar family, and then of Hyder Ali when he took over the State. In 1761 he rebuilt the fort in stone as a considerable structure, some 735 m from north to south by 550 m from east to west, which contained both an arsenal and the main palace. The bazaar had grown into a small town surrounded with a ditch and a thorn hedge, so that it became known as the Pettah. Less than a kilometre south of the fort Tipu built his summer palace – a pleasant, airy structure.

Hyderabad

This name belonged to both the former princely state and its capital. Hyderabad city was founded in 1591 by the Sultan of Golconda under the name of Bhagnagar or 'City of Gardens'. In February 1687 Aurangzeb captured the place and in October of the same year overthrew the crumpling kingdom of Golconda. Thereupon, he created a post of subadar of the whole Deccan, the Nizam-al-Mulk or 'Regulator of the Realm', whose capital was at Aurangabad and under whom was a governor of each of its six provinces including

---

[58] H. H. Dodwell (ed), *The Cambridge History of India. vol 5 British India.* (Cambridge 1929) 275

[59] M. H. Mari Gowda, 'History of Lal Bagh' in T. B. Issar, *The City Beautiful.* (Bangalore, 1988) 256.

Hyderabad. In 1713 a distinguished Turkoman soldier, Chin Qilich Khan, was appointed Nizam-al-Mulk. There is no doubt that from the first he aspired to establish an independent state, and that the condition of the Mughal dynasty would permit him to do so, there having been nine Emperors since the death of Aurangzeb in 1707. Suffice it to record that, in a convoluted series of moves, he achieved de facto independence by 1724 and established his capital in Hyderabad city. He possessed ample financial resources, amounting to nearly fifty percent of the revenue of the Mughal Empire, for his six provinces of the Deccan had a standard revenue of some Rs160 million whereas the remaining twelve provinces of the Empire commanded about Rs170 million between them.[60] Those six provinces now enjoyed a period of peace for the first time since Aurangzeb's invasion forty years before. From then on, Hyderabad represented the cultural legacy of the Mughal Empire in South India and, like that Empire, comprised a Muslim aristocracy ruling over a Hindu majority.

The first action of the independent Nizam was to try to reach a settlement with the Marathas. His efforts were complicated by the fact that both chauth and sardeshmuki of the Deccan provinces had been granted to the Marathas by the Emperor in 1718 'for services rendered' provided these taxes could be collected peaceably. The Nizam accepted this situation but still saw himself as heir to Aurangzeb's territories, subject to the grant of 1718. Somehow this gave the Marathas an impression he was trying to exclude them from Hyderabad – which they saw as part of their natural home range. The situation has been well described as leading to an inevitable clash between an established authority (in the shape of the Nizam) and a new dynamic power seeking its place in the sun.

The Marathas

Broadly speaking, the Marathas are a Hindu people of the western part of Maharastra: a roughly triangular block of country measuring some 610 km along the coast from Goa to the Gulf of Cambay, eastward along the Satmala range for 640 km, and thence 880 km south-west to the coast near Goa. Most of it stands on the Deccan plateau. The Marathas have their own language and an indigenous literature. Moreover, they seem to possess a strong sense of place which confers a peculiar unity upon them. The rise of these people is linked to the Hindu hero Sivaji, one of the most romantic and dashing figures in all Indian history.

In the seventeenth century the land of the Marathas had the Mughal Empire to its north and the independent Sultanates of Bijapur and Golconda to the south. Within this region Shahji Bhonsle held a small jagir near Poona. He was later granted a more substantial holding near Daulatabad, but this grant was soon reversed. Enraged by this treatment, Shahji offered his services to the Sultan of Bijapur and so practically exiled himself from his homeland. However

---

[60] Wolseley Haig and Richard Burn (ed),. *The Cambridge History of India vol 4 Mughul India* (Cambridge 1937) 378

he showed marked ability as a soldier and eventually became Governor of the Bijapur Carnatic. His son Sivaji had been born in 1627, and to him was given the small jagir near Poona; and indeed it seems that Sivaji and his mother were virtually abandoned by Shahji. In any event, from the age of twenty Sivaji had to make his own way and, like many youngsters of character in the same position, he prospered; in less than ten years he had more than doubled the area and revenue of his possessions, chiefly by taking lands on the boundary of Bijapur.

Sivaji still occupies a special place in Maharastra, in western India, and among Hindus generally. Tales of his exploits are recited by itinerant story-tellers and have been used time and again by film-makers. An episode from his career will show why this should be so, and gives an insight into acceptable behaviour of his day. In 1659, when Bijapur sent an army against him, Sivaji and its leader, Afzal Khan, agreed to meet in private parley at a point between their armies, unarmed and each attended by only one armed follower. Tradition has it that both men were dressed in white muslin, but Sivaji wore light chain mail beneath robe and puggari, carried a dagger and wore, on his left hand, a waghnagh or 'tiger's claws' which consisted of four razor-sharp curved steel claws fastened by rings to his fingers. One version says that when the men embraced, Afzal Khan tried to stab Sivaji with a hidden dagger but the thrust was turned by the chain mail. In retaliation Sivaji disembowelled the Khan with his waghnagh and stabbed him. The Maratha army then fell upon the unprepared Bijapuris and dispersed them.[61]

Sivaji died in 1680. His principal achievements, perhaps, were three. In the first place he welded a number of scattered clans into a working unit – almost a nation. Indeed, his reputation was sufficient to maintain a measure of unity among his peoples, thus giving rise to a Maratha Confederation. Secondly, he withstood the power and authority of the Mughals under their most aggressive Emperor. Finally, the fact that he and most of his associates were not Brahmins was itself a challenge to the Hindu hierarchy; Sivaji himself was a Vaisya, or cultivator, and firmly rejected all pretentious pedigrees drawn up to suggest otherwise.

Sivaji's grandson, Shahu, appointed a Brahmin (Balaji Vishvanath Bhat) as Peshwa or Chief Minister, and thereafter the office became hereditary within the man's family. Shahu's descendants continued as rulers of the modest principality of Satara, but within Maharashtra as a whole four great families arose: the Gaekwar of Baroda, Holkar of Indore, Sindia of Gwalior, and the Bhonsla of Nagpur. These names, and that of the Peshwa continued in the story of the Marathas.

---

[61] Wolseley Haig and Richard Burn (ed). *The Cambridge History of India.* vol 4 272

Madras

This was the fourth political unit, which eventually became the most important European settlement in all of South India, and capital of a Presidency with the same name.

Three European States established a presence on the coasts of South India, beginning with Portugal when Vasco da Gama arrived at Calicut on the south-west or Malabar coast in 1498. In 1500 Pedro Alvarez Cabrera (Cabral) demonstrated the feasibility of using the counter-clockwise wind system of the south Atlantic by sailing south-westward from Lisbon almost to Brasil before turning eastward to pass the Cape and make his landfall on Cochin Island. Two years later Gama, on his second voyage, established a factory there, the first European settlement in India. The profits to be made from such an enterprise at that time were enormous: for example, pepper purchased in Cochin could be sold in Lisbon for forty times its original cost. In due course the Portuguese established settlements at various other places around the coast of India, notably Goa, and in the coastal region of Ceylon. So began what Sardar K. M. Panikkar has described as 'invasion by the sea nomads', which was quite different from the previous overland invasions of India. Pursuing this theme he remarked that

> pressure from the sea has a relentlessness which the sporadic threats from the side of the land do not possess. Once the coasts of a country become open to pressure from the sea, they remain perpetually under threat, for though the particular power which exercised the pressure might itself be destroyed, the indivisibility of the sea enables any other power, however distant, to step into the vacant place.[62]

Whereas Portuguese navigators and merchants were essentially agents of their royal government, other European States channelled their activities in the East through trading companies. Of these, the most long-lasting and influential were those of England and Holland, and they will be considered in some detail. First, however, the whole assemblage may be reviewed.

The earliest to be established was the London Company which received its Charter on 31 December 1600 from Elizabeth I under the name 'The Governor and Company of Merchants of London trading into the East Indies' and was given a monopoly of English trade for fifteen years within a region from the Cape of Good Hope eastward to the Straits of Magellan.

The Dutch *Vereenigde Oostindische Compagnie* (VOC) was founded in 1602, followed by the Danish East India Company in 1616. The Danes began their operations in 1626 by establishing a settlement at Tranquebar, on the east or Coromandel Coast about 480 km south of modern Madras. However, the enterprise did not prosper despite several 'new beginnings'. Finally, in 1845 Tranquebar and their other territories were sold to the English Company for

---

[62] K. M. Panikkar, *Geographical Factors in Indian History*. (Bombay 1955) 83-4.

Rs12,500; the fort there became a dak bungalow which was described in the mid-1970s as 'not good'.

Attempts to establish a Scottish Company as early as 1617 failed because of English competition and the dissipation of its resources in a disastrous effort to set up a colony at Darien in Central America. Thereafter, Scottish entrepreneurs turned their attention to the London Company within which they secured a disproportionate influence by the 1780s.

The French showed no serious interest until 1664 when the *Compagnie des Indes Orientales* was founded with the encouragement of Louis XIV. Its first trading post was set up in 1668 at Surat. In 1672 Pondicherry, on the Coromandel Coast was purchased from the Nawab of Bijapur, and a two years later a trading settlement was established there. This place became the capital of French possessions in India and remained under French control until 1954. The *Compagnie* itself enjoyed varying fortunes, which reached their zenith under the brilliant Governor-General Joseph Dupleix, but then faded away to disappear during the Revolution.

From the outset the Dutch Company was better organized and more powerful than the English. Its seventeen Directors – the *Heeren XVII* – were among the most influential men in the Dutch Republic and closely connected to the Government. Moreover, its Charter of 1602 enabled the VOC to make war, conclude treaties, hold territory and erect forts, so that it became an instrument of conquest.[63] It exercised its powers with energy. In addition to its activities in Indonesia, the VOC attacked the Portuguese in Ceylon in 1638 and had expelled them from the Island by 1658. Their occupation of Galle, Colombo and Negombo not only forestalled any Portuguese counter-attack but also gave them effective control of cinnamon production. In 1641 Malacca was taken. From there, and from their headquarters at Batavia, they held control of shipping lanes between the Indian Ocean and the China Sea. During the period 1658-63, all Portuguese possessions on the Malabar Coast south of Goa were captured, including Cochin and Cannanore. Since they also held Quilon the VOC had secured a virtual monopoly of the pepper trade in the region.

In 1652 Jan van Riebeeck established a settlement at the Cape of Good Hope on behalf of the VOC. In due time the name *de Indische Zeeherberg* or 'Tavern of the Indian Ocean' was applied to it, and it was seen as such for 200 years by mariners sailing between Europe and the Indies. Both Wilks and Cubbon were to spend time there, recruiting their health.

Meanwhile the London Company had not prospered to the same extent as its Dutch counterpart. From the outset its affairs were managed in a more democratic but commercially less efficient way. Its Governor, Deputy-Governor, Treasurer and twenty-four Directors were elected annually in a general court of all stock-holders. By 1635 these twenty-seven officials held more stock than the other 400 share-holders combined, but their authority was

---

[63] H. H. Dodwell (ed), *The Cambridge History of India.* vol 5 30-3

limited by the fact that every stock-holder had the same number of votes in general court. This meant that the smaller share-holders could exert pressure upon the Directors to distribute all profits, so that the Company was unable to accumulate capital in support of long-term enterprises. Moreover, it was not closely linked to the government, nor did it possess the extensive diplomatic and military powers of the VOC.

In July 1698 the London Company suffered what could have been a mortal blow. Parliament passed an Act that gave a new company exclusive rights of trading to the East Indies, but permitted the existing London Company to continue operating until the end of a three-year period of notice, namely until September 1701. In conformity with the Act, William III granted a Charter to the new Company as 'The English Company trading to the East Indies' on condition that its capital of £2 million was lent to the government at 8 percent interest, a rate which yielded insufficient income for the Company to be able to trade on an adequate scale. The London Company, however, held two good cards. It had subscribed £315,000 to the capital of the new English Company in the name of its treasurer so that it could continue to trade in his name, and it had some well-established bases from which the English Company could not dislodge it.[64] Clearly, English interests were not being well served by this kind of competition. In 1702 the two Companies agreed to amalgamate, with a seven-year transition period. The combined group received a new Charter as 'The United Company of Merchants of England trading to the East Indies' and will be referred to hereafter as 'The East India Company' (EIC).

The merger was completed successfully in March 1709, when the Company's privileges were extended for a further fifteen years. During negotiations to bring about amalgamation two principles were established that would have great future importance. One was the right of Parliament to control concessions to the Company; the other was a requirement for the Company to make a contribution to the nation's finances.

What were the relative positions of Dutch and English interests in the East? Like the VOC, the London Company had been attracted to the Indonesian archipelago, but the Dutch had established themselves before the English arrived in force. In 1619 the energetic and ruthless Dutch Governor-General, Jan Piertersoon Coen, had conquered the Javanese city of Jacatra and founded Batavia (now Jakarta) upon its ruins. The London Company had set up a factory at Bantam on the west coast of Java in 1602, and in 1619 reached an agreement with the VOC for its merchants to be admitted to Dutch settlements including Batavia. For several reasons the arrangement did not work and the English found themselves excluded from Indonesia – especially after the affair at Amboina (Ambon) in 1623 when ten English, ten Japanese and a Portuguese were executed after being charged with attempting to overthrow Dutch authority there.

---

[64] H. H. Dodwell (ed), *The Cambridge History of India*. vol 5 98-100

It has been well said that the main influence of the Dutch on the course of Indian history was that they excluded the British from the Indies and thus directed their attention to India. Moreover, the London Company not only concentrated on India as the sole available place of trade, but also turned away from spices as the main commodity. The early alternatives were indigo, saltpetre, cotton piece-goods and sugar. Although these goods were less valuable than spices the potential market for them was much larger. Indeed, as Spear has pointed out, the English were operating in an inherently difficult market-place, for they had little except silver to attract their Indian clients so that they had to make a close study of markets and potential purchasers. Consequently, they gained a detailed knowledge of the country that provided an invaluable basis for their political activities in the next century.[65]

British authority came to be based upon the Presidencies of Madras, Bombay, and Bengal which had its capital at Fort William, the nucleus of Calcutta. Bengal, the last to be established, eventually became the grandest. All three were developed pragmatically as the products of false starts and revised decisions.

Madras was typical. In 1605 the Dutch had started a factory at Masulipatam, which was about half way along the east coast and was the chief port of the Kingdom of Golconda. The English followed in 1611 with the intention of trading in cotton piece-goods, but they soon found that these materials were available at a lower price in the territory of the Rajah of the Carnatic so that, in 1626, the merchants at Masulipatam set up a subsidiary factory at Armagon. Since this place had a rather shallow anchorage they looked about for something better. In 1639 the Chief Factor, Francis Day, secured permission from the nayak of the Rajah of Chandragiri to construct a fortified factory further south of Armagon, near the small town of Madrasapatam. Quite soon a new Rajah succeeded to the gaddi and the merchants deemed it prudent to seek confirmation of the concession. A delegation was sent to Chandragiri where, in November 1645, the Rajah confirmed the grant of a coastal strip 5.5 km long by 1.75 km wide; and the agreement was recorded on a plate of gold. The Company had acted just in time for next year the Rajah was displaced by Mir Jumla, Sultan of Golconda. Yet again they were able to secure confirmation of the concession, though subject to his receiving a share of customs duties paid by strangers – an arrangement which continued with various amendments for more than a hundred years.

The merchants had moved to their new site in February 1640 and their fortified factory was completed on St George's Day of that year, so that the settlement was named accordingly. In September 1641 Fort St George became the Company's headquarters on the Coromandel Coast. The English had neighbours for, in 1522, the Portuguese had colonized Myalopore, or San Thome, (about 8 km from Fort St George) and built a church there to receive

---

[65] Percival Spear, *India: a Modern History*. (Ann Arbor 1961) 167-8

the relics of St Thomas the Apostle. The place was taken by the Dutch in 1674, and occupied by the British in 1749.

Madras, as it came to be known, developed so steadily that its population reached 40,000 by 1670. In 1676 the ancient village of Triplicane was acquired. Governor Streynsham Master established a Superior Court of Judicature in 1678, and built St Mary's Church inside the fort. Its design and construction were placed in the hands of William Dixon, Master Gunner and bastion designer, who applied familiar techniques to the work. The original building was a simple rectangular structure measuring 27.5 by 18 m, with outer walls of brick and polished chunam almost 1.25 m thick; and the curved roof was 0.6 m thick. The first marriage in the church was that of Catherine Hynmer and Elihu Yale – later to become President of Fort St George and a founder of the American university that bears his name. In 1753 Robert Clive and Margaret Maskelyne were married there.[66] [67]

From its beginning Fort St George had been subordinate to Bantam in Java, but it became independent in 1683 when its first President was appointed. Five years later it was chartered to 'be a Corporation by the name and title of the Mayor, Aldermen and Burgesses of the Town of Fort St George and City of Madrassapataam' – the first such municipality in India. By this time its population was 300,000 souls. In 1717 five additional villages were absorbed, and this process was repeated over the years.

During the 18th century Madras was menaced many times by hostile forces. The threats began in 1702 when Aurangzeb's general, Daud Khan, unsuccessfully attacked the place. The Marathas repeated the operation in 1741, also without success. However, the greatest danger came from the French, who were established at Pondicherry 85 km to the south. There, the ambitious, energetic and able Joseph Dupleix became Governor-General of the French Indies in 1741. Quite apart from their local rivalries, Pondicherry and Madras were caught up in two European wars that involved Great Britain and France: the War of Austrian Succession (1740-48) and the Seven Years War (1756-63) so that Madras was threatened by French forces. These recurring dangers made the President and Council of Fort St George look to their defences so that, in 1767 the fort was strengthened and given its present form. Two years later, however, Hyder Ali appeared before the city with a large force of cavalry and dictated the terms of a treaty which included a defensive alliance between himself and Madras, and so drew the Presidency more deeply into the politics of South India.[68]

---

[66] Philip Davies, *Penguin Guide to the Monuments of India Vol. 2 Islamic, Rajput, European.* (London 1989) 545.
[67] S. Muthiah, *Madras Discovered.* (New Delhi 1987). 26-30.
[68] H.H. Dodwell (ed), *The Cambridge History of India.* vol 5 276

Concern at Home

As they became more confident the Presidencies acquired additional territory, and this was especially true of Bengal. Meanwhile Parliament looked on with interest, and some alarm, as a commercial company became a great power in Hind. When minded to take action, Parliament was not inhibited by any previous agreement with the Company – a favourable position that derived from the well-known indolence of Charles II. His Charter to the London Company gave it inter alia a right to appoint Governors who, with their Councils, were to exercise civil and criminal jurisdiction within the Presidencies, each of which would deal directly with the Directors at home. But although the Company urged the King to have the Charter confirmed by Parliament, he never did so.[69]

Within Parliament, the extreme opinions were for non-intervention on the one hand, and for transferring the Company's territories to the Crown on the other. Edmund Burke expressed the consensus of opinion 'The East India Company did not seem to be merely a company formed for the extension of British commerce, but in reality a delegation of the whole power and sovereignty of this kingdom sent into the East.'[70]

Three critical inter-relationships had to be resolved: (i) between the Company and the British State; (ii) between the administrations of the Company in Britain and in India; and (iii) between the administrations of the three Presidencies. This last had become urgent because Bengal, though a late-comer, had outstripped the other two.

Parliament's opportunity came in 1772 when the EIC experienced a problem of cash-flow and applied for a loan. It was not given as the Company hoped. Instead, in July 1773, Parliament passed two linked Acts: one granted the Company a loan of £1.4 million at four percent per annum; the second was the Regulating Act which came into effect on 1 August 1774 and addressed the three relationships mentioned above.

In pursuit of the first inter-relationship, the Directors were to provide the Treasury all correspondence with India that dealt with the revenues, and to a Secretary of State everything dealing with civil or military matters.

To reform the second inter-relationship, the constitution of the Company was to be remodelled. The qualifying stock-holding for a vote in the Court of Proprietors was raised from £500 to £1000, and stock had to be held for a year before the stock-holder became eligible to vote. The twenty-four Directors were to be elected for four-year terms (instead of only one year at a time) with a quarter to retire each year and remain out of office for at least twelve months.

Finally, there was to be a Governor-General at Fort William in Bengal together with a Council of four members. Simple majority voting was to be used and the Governor-General was to have only a casting vote. Warren

---

[69] H. H. Dodwell (ed), *The Cambridge History of India*. vol 5 95-6
[70] H.H. Dodwell (ed), *The Cambridge History of India*. vol 5 182

Hastings was named as Governor-General, and the four Councillors were also named in the Act. This Supreme Council was to have powers to superintend the two subordinate Presidencies in making war and peace, a provision which Hastings described as 'giving us a mere negative power.' There was to be a Supreme Court of Justice with a Chief Justice and three Puisne Judges. Thus Parliament took a first step toward regulating the affairs of the Company.[71]

Much more was achieved by William Pitt's India Act of August 1784, which had the following main provisions: (i) there were to be six Commissioners of the Affairs of India, known popularly as the 'Board of Control'; they were a Secretary of State (to be President), the Chancellor of the Exchequer, and four Privy Councillors appointed by the King; (ii) urgent or secret orders of the Commissioners were to be transmitted to India through the Secret Committee of the Directors (to be not more than three Directors, and nearly always only the Chairman and Deputy Chairman); (iii) the Court of Proprietors was deprived of any power to annul or suspend a resolution of the Directors that had been approved by the Commissioners; and (iv) the Government of India was made the responsibility of a Governor-General and Council of three members in Bengal, and the other Presidencies were to be clearly subordinate in all matters of revenue, diplomacy and war.

Obviously, these measures linked the Board of Control closely to the Home Government of the day, for at least two members changed with each ministry, and the Board held control over non-commercial activities of the Company. On the other hand, the Directors retained direction of commercial operations, patronage, and the right to dismiss the Company's servants.[72] [73] Immediately on the legislation being passed, Henry Dundas was appointed President of the Board of Control. Thereafter, management of the Board's affairs was virtually in his hands for, in addition to being President until 1801 he was concurrently its Home Secretary (from June 1791) and Secretary for War (from July 1794).[74] For good measure he is said to have been ruler of Scotland for thirty years.

In 1786 three supplementary measures were passed, the most important of which empowered the Governor-General, in special cases, to overrule the majority of his Council but allowed the dissidents to record their arguments in writing. The Governor-General was also enabled to hold the office of Commander-in-Chief in an emergency.[75]

All this may be summarized by saying that the Home Government had progressively developed an administrative structure for dealing with the Company's possessions in India and, indeed, for controlling the Company itself. Moreover, during the 1780s Indian affairs were placed in capable hands, both at Home (Dundas) and in India (Warren Hastings).

---

[71] H.H. Dodwell (ed), *The Cambridge History of India*. vol 5 187-9
[72] H.H. Dodwell (ed), *The Cambridge History of India*. vol 5 200-4
[73] C. H. Philips, *The East India Company 1784-1834*. (Manchester 1940)
[74] C. H. Philips, *The East India Company*. 338
[75] H. H. Dodwell (ed), *The Cambridge History of India*. vol 5 203

CHAPTER FOUR

Mark Wilks's First Tour 1782 – 1795

The Journey
Mark travelled to Portsmouth by way of London, there to go through the obligatory formalities at East India House in Leadenhall Street, and pay his respects to his patrons Sir Henry Fletcher and Sir Thomas Rumbolt. The latter, long in the Company's service and recently retired as Governor of Madras, was in a good position to inform the young man of Hyder Ali's possible actions, and of the long-term prospects for Madras Presidency and the Company as a whole.

Sister Anne's information was proved incorrect for Mark had to wait nearly three weeks in Portsmouth. His enquiring mind would have had much to occupy it as he prepared himself for an active military career. Portsmouth was then beyond comparison the largest fortification in England and offered the navy its best security. Portsea Island, on which Portsmouth had been built, and the adjoining promontory with Gosport at its apex, enclosed a fine harbour. Its narrow entrance was guarded on both sides – the Point and the Gilkicker – by formidable assemblages of cannon. Both consisted of a brick structure that housed two tiers of guns, one above the other, and gave such excellent cover that the gunners could not be driven from their guns and the guns themselves could not be easily overthrown. Even the outer roadstead of Spithead was commanded by cannon from South-Sea-Castle.[76] Formidable indeed, and giving much food for thought to the young officer soon to encounter the fortifications of Hyder Ali and Tipu.

Mark's ship, 'Montagu', sailed from Portsmouth on 11 September 1782. She was a vessel of 755 tons, commanded by Captain Thomas Brettrell, and with six other officers. The standard crew for ships of the East India Company was 12½ men for every 100 tons so that Montagu had about 94 men including a Gunner and his Mate. Their journey to India and back was to be a long one, for Montagu did not return to the Downs until 17 June 1784. In the following year she was blown up! Capt Brettrell, however, went on to greater things, as commander of 'Canton' of 1198 tons on its voyage to Bombay and China during the 1790-91 season.[77]

At first the fleet, of which 'Montagu' was part, retraced the course pioneered by Cabral 280 years before. It picked up the north-east trade wind which carried it to the coast of Brasil; thence it travelled southward along that coast

---

[76] Daniel Defoe, *A Tour through the Whole Island of Great Britain, 1724-6* 150-1
[77] H.C.Hardy, *A Register of Ships Employed in the Service of the Honorable the United East India Company from the Year 1760 to 1812* (London 1812)

with the aid of the Brasilian current; beat south-east to meet the prevailing westerlies, passed the Cape of Good Hope and caught the monsoon for the final run into the Bay of Bengal. How did Mark occupy his time? Among other things he kept a journal, which he began rather later than one would wish.

> At Sea Novr 18th 1782.
> Yesterday our fleet sailed from St Salvador. The evening before I went on shore to deliver my letters for Europe (which I was concerned thro' hurry to have left unfinished) into the charge of the Intendant. About ten at night accompanied by eleven fellow passengers I took a country boat with two Negroes, in order to return on board. Within about half a mile from our own ship & quarter of a mile from the Bristol one of our Gentlemen suddenly alarmed us by declaring the boat was sinking; we found there was some water in the boat, but without suspecting any danger laughed very heartily at his apprehensions. The water gained upon us, every person was glad to make use of his hat to keep her clear, but in spite of every exertion, in less than three minutes the boat was more than half full of water; the matter now became truly serious, the Negroes laid down their oars and began to say their <u>Ave Marias,</u> there was a universal cry for assistance. The Bristol's boat was immediately manned and with an exertion the (sic) does honour to His Majesty's Naval Service, and the discipline of the Bristol in particular, saved us from inevitable destruction at a time when it was impossible to continue above water many seconds longer, & only three persons in the boat could swim. I shall leave you to imagine our reflections on this providential escape, and proceed in my account of Saint Salvador, which I fear you will be sorry to see resumed. There is one way – skip it. …..[78]

Late on 17 November, 'Montagu' and the rest of the fleet sailed from Sao Salvador and laid a course for the Island of Trinidad: not the 'great' island of that name, but a very small one at 20° 30' N. latitude and 28° 50' W longitude. The island was only 6.5 km long by 5 km broad, and Mark saw it as a huge disjointed rock covered with shrubs of Oleander wherever there was an inch of soil. Despite its inhospitable appearance, the Navy had tried to establish a victualling station there at a time when the Cape was closed. The fleet reached Trinidad on 28 December and departed three days later. From Trinidad onward the fleet's route was largely determined by the possible presence of enemy forces. European settlements in the East had been caught up by French entry into the American Revolutionary War (1775-83). Ile de France (Mauritius) was a French possession, and French naval forces had secured dominance in the Bay of Bengal and adjacent parts of the Indian Ocean. The British admiral in command of the region, Sir Edward Hughes, lacked both adequate forces and the spark of genius necessary to combat Suffren de Saint Tropez, one of France's greatest admirals. As Mark Wilks recorded in his journal

---

[78] Wilks Papers vol 1, Correspondence of Lt. Col Mark Wilks concerning India 1782-1826 (BL Mss Coll. Add. Mss 57313) fol 1-5 (Journal of 18 Nov 1782 to 22 Jul 1783).

Madras Ap[l] 18th 1783.
Since our departure from Trinidad nothing very material has occurred we doubled the Cape in the latitude of 42.0 S° a climate of cold and tempest, where within half a mile of another ship her mast heads are often invisible. You will easily perceive by casting your eye on the map that, we went into this horrid climate to keep clear of the Mauritius. To avoid Ceylon which we justly suspected to be in the hands of the Enemy we went nearly as far as the streights (sic) of Malacca, and after escaping the Enemy more by accident than the good management of Admiral Hughes arrived in this road on the 16th instant; seven months and five days since our departure from the Mother bank, having run by our own log the distance of 17,000 miles. And now if you please we will rest till I have an opportunity to say something about Madras.[79]

'Montagu's voyage amounted to 27,200 km, in contrast to the 17,500 km covered by a liner of the 1930s between England and Madras via the Cape. At Madras, protocol required the Fort to hoist a flag in order to show that a safe approach was possible. The ship then exchanged single-cannon salutes with the Fort and dropped anchor. The customary first, unofficial, sign of welcome was the appearance of several catamarans, each constructed of five logs lashed together and carrying one or two almost naked men. Sometimes the rower stood upright so that he seemed to be walking on the water as he plied his paddle, first on one side and then on the other. One catamaran brought messages for the Captain.

At that time Madras lacked a wharf or enclosed anchorage, so that passengers and goods were landed through its notorious three lines of surf on to the open beach. This was done in massula boats. Quite narrow but deep, and pointed both fore and aft, these surf-boats had their planks sewn together so that they were pliant and yielded to the pressure of the breakers.

Several were engaged to carry 'Montagu's passengers ashore. Each boat had about ten oarsmen who chanted in unison, the tempo becoming faster or slower depending on the manoeuvre being attempted. Chanting and rowing were slow when the boat lay in a trough, but both reached almost feverish speed as it prepared to ride an incoming wave, and then diminished again. This happened three times, until the last line of breakers brought the boat to the beach, where it was seized and dragged on to the sand with its passengers almost dry.

South India about 1783

When Mark arrived in Madras the Presidency's prospects remained uncertain. It had powerful neighbours, whose intentions were often unclear: Dutch and French settlements, Hyderabad and, most formidable, Mysore.

The Dutch possessed factories and forts on the Coromandel Coast, notably at Sadras 98 km south of Madras, but their influence on India's east coast was

---

[79] Wilks Papers vol 1 (BL Mss Coll Add Mss 57313) (fol 7- 11)

fading. However, they had a firm grip on the coastal regions of Ceylon and were well established at Cochin on the Malabar Coast. France was still a monarchy, and the headquarters of its Indian possessions seemed secure at Pondicherry, 160 km south of Madras. Moreover, since 1768 they had secured considerable influence in Hyderabad through the initiative of Michel Raymond who had raised and trained 15,000 good soldiers there. Nizam Ali (reigned 1762-1802) had to choose judiciously between the French, who were strong on the ground, the British, and Hyder Ali of Mysore.

Mysore was then about twice the area it was later to become. There, also, was a Muslim ruler and a Hindu population, but the country was given a sense of purpose by the ability, energy and success of Hyder Ali. The Company's first Mysore War had been begun through diplomatic bungling by the Nizam, Mysore and the Company, and had ended in March 1769 when Hyder Ali appeared before Madras with his formidable cavalry. The Madras Council had resolved upon peace, and secured generous terms including, however, a defensive alliance with Mysore that drew it further into the cockpit of South India.

The next stage of the Company's conflict with the Powers of South India began in 1775 and continued until 1784. Two inter-related struggles may be recognised: the First Maratha War (1775-82, which mainly concerned Bombay) and the Second Mysore War (1780-84). Moreover, they occurred at a time when the Home Government was fully occupied with the Revolutionary War in North America and by the prospect of facing a hostile European coalition (1778-83). Inevitably, the North American War spread to India and open conflict was resumed between France and Great Britain. At that time the Madras Presidency was sunk in misrule and corruption, and insubordination toward any who attempted to rectify its condition. Its ineptitude encouraged Mysore and the Nizam to make common cause with the Marathas. Indeed, its Second Mysore War was begun when the Madras Government sent a military force to the French possession of Mahé on the west coast in 1779. Hyder Ali disapproved, attacked the Presidency and defeated Col William Baillie at Pollilur; one of his captives was David Baird, who was to spend nearly four years in the prison at Seringapatam and of whom more will be heard later. Soon afterwards Mysore's cavalry again appeared near Madras City.

However, Warren Hastings saved the day for the Company by a combination of military initiative and diplomatic skill. He transformed the military situation by reinforcing Madras with troops under an outstanding commander. In July 1781 the redoubtable Eyre Coote, with 8000 men and 41 guns, defeated Hyder Ali, who had 40,000 men and 100 guns, near Porto Novo. Next year he repeated the achievement at Arni. By diplomacy Hastings managed to detach the war-weary Marathas from their allies and to make peace with them through the Treaty of Salbai (May, 1782).

In December 1782 Hyder Ali died, leaving for his successor written advice to make peace with the Company which, he believed, would prevail in South

India. Characteristically, Tipu ignored his father's advice and so the struggle between Mysore and the Company continued. Early in 1783 an expedition was mounted from Bombay to relieve pressure on Madras. With surprising ease it captured Mangalore and Bednur, capital of the province of that name. Tipu Sultan reacted quickly by withdrawing most of his forces from the Carnatic, rolling up piecemeal the Company's scattered detachments in Bednur, and besieging Mangalore.

Meanwhile, on the east coast the Company was in danger of suffering a serious reverse at the hands of much more capable French leaders who had established their forces at Cuddalore. In June, Maj. Gen. James Stuart conducted a lethargic campaign to capture the place. It was unsuccessful and, to make matters worse, the British naval squadron had to withdraw its support. Only luck saved Stuart's forces: the American Revolutionary War was to be ended by the Treaty of Paris in September 1783, but a preliminary peace agreement was signed much earlier and word of it reached Madras late in June. The French observed it punctiliously, and thus Tipu was deprived of their active support.

By January 1784 Tipu was with his army before Mangalore. In that city, on 7 March, he and commissioners from Madras agreed the Treaty of Mangalore. Under its term both parties were to give up their conquests and all prisoners were to be released, among them David Baird whose ordeal in the dungeon of Seringapatam engendered bitter resentment toward Tipu. The decision to end hostilities was made by Lord Macartney, who had become Governor of Madras in 1781. While more capable than his recent predecessors he had a predilection for following an independent line which was often at variance with that of Hastings, and this did not advance the Company's cause.

Hastings disapproved strongly of what Macartney had done, calling it 'humiliating pacification'; and the Treaty displeased many of the British. It is true that a major condition of the Treaty of Mangalore required all captured territories to be returned. To that extent the struggle was inconclusive. However, Smith has suggested that the war marked an important turning-point for the Company in South India for, without any significant support from Britain it had withstood a coalition of the principal Indian Powers. From that long struggle the Company had emerged as the strongest power in the South India.[80]

Military Service

Mark had been posted to the 6th Regiment, Madras Native Infantry. In uniform he cut a fine figure that would have delighted sister Anne. Red coat with lapels, collar and cuffs of the facing colour – blue at the time but changed to green in 1785 – worn open and with only one epaulette. Waistcoat and trousers were of

---

[80] V. A. Smith, *The Oxford History of India*. 513

white linen in hot weather and ordinary white cloth at other times. Boots were black, as was the tricorne hat that had a white cover in hot weather.[81]

The journal of his voyage describes his early experiences in Madras

Madras July 22d 1783.
Believe me my dear friend 'tis all a take in: an Officer here exists on his pay with greater difficulty than in England. The Die is cast and I must make the best of it. But let me give you an account of my proceedings hitherto. And first of letters. On my enquiring for the persons to whom they were addressed, I found one half of them either dead or gone home & the major part of the remainder in the field. Sir Jn. Burgoyne received me as a person particularly recommended to his protection, & at my request did everything in his power to get me permission to go with the Army to the Siege of Cuddalore but Gen[l] Stuart positively refused me and many others saying the young men do not know what they ask, it would be certain death to take the field before they are a little seasoned to the Climate. I find he was perfectly right, I have had a little seasoning which in camp must have done my business, for here I was within a squeak, or two…He (Sir John Burgoyne) has not seen a shot fired since he came into the Country and probably will not – his being cut for the liver, the disease of this infernal Country, has hitherto kept him inactive, and he has lately had an accident of a broken arm which will probably prevent him ever being able to manage a horse again, – indeed were his health and strength re-established the Government here do not wish to send a man into the field who does not know his own mind for two minutes; I had an instance of his steadiness – the second time I called on him he hardly knew me. My letter from Lady Rumbold was received in the true Madras stile, a formal dinner…..R has irrevocably ruined this country, the history of his villainy is too long and complicated for a letter. Captain Smart, General Stuart's Aid de Camp, is as honest a fellow as his correspondent Christie, to him I am principally indebted for getting me ranked above every Cadet in our or Bickerton's fleet, even above one who had been in the Regulars whose Commission was dated subsequent to mine, 'tis a step of one hundred and twelve, but still the prospect is poor – very poor. The letter from George Moore's friend, though merely introductory, procured me a genteel reception, & a general welcome to the House of a hospitable pleasant man, he is a Senior Merchant & should he ever get into the Council I am clear I shall not be without interest. I beg you will return my thanks to Geo: Moore, Major D'Arcey and Captain Christie. On my letter from D'Arcey to Lord McCartney's Secretary I at present place my greatest Dependence. He has given proof of his inclination to serve me, by getting me without any solicitation appointed, 'pro tempore', an assistant Aid de Camp to attend the Committee sent with a flag of truce to Cuddalore, unfortunately I was extremely ill and could not go. I have now got stout again and think I shall be able to fight the Climate and a long fight it must be, for in less than 15 years I cannot possibly expect a Batalion of Seapoys, and until then it is almost impossible to save

---

[81] Boris Mollo, *The Indian Army*. (Poole 1986) 30-1

Mark Wilks as a Lieutenant in 6 Madras Native Infantry probably painted 1795-99 (Courtesy of Director MNH).

anything of consequence. Formerly when Subalterns got 500 and 1000 Pagodas prize money at a siege it was pretty pickings, but these days are over, and in retaking every place we have lost, we shall get nothing but hard knocks.[82]

Although Mark had seen no action during 1783-84 reports of events had thrown Anne, now in Philadelphia, into a flutter about him as shown by her letter of 14 December 1784 to 'Tomas' Wilks

> Poor Mark is in the 5th batt[n] sepoys which were not with him but heaven knows where he is or what his suffering may be. How dreadful it is to have such an uncivilized enemy. Death in the field is paradise to the tortures they inflict and I am really divided whether to pray for his life or death if he is a prisoner which God forbid. I have not acquired so much outward philosophy as Mother, for

---

[82] Wilks Papers vol 1 (BL Mss Coll Add Mss 57313) (fol 1-5)

my heart really bleeds for a Brother who would not have disgraced a crown and I doubt not will wear an immortal one.[83]

About this time Mark had a pleasant experience that he recorded later

> I became accidentally known to [an old Nevayet gentleman] at an early period of my residence in India, from having lost my way in a dark night, and wandered into a village about a mile from his habitation, whence I received an immediate invitation, conveyed by two of his sons, and a reception that might have graced a castle of romance...the dignified manners, the graceful, almost affectionate politeness of the old gentleman ...left an indelible impression.[84]

Also about this time Mark met Lt Barry Close, also of 6 MNI, who was only a year older but nine years senior in the service and who had already earned a reputation for dashing leadership. Physically the two men were quite different: Wilks was tall and spare with a fresh complexion whereas Close was rather swarthy and short with a tendency to put on weight despite the very active life he led.[85] The initial attraction between the two was undoubtedly their shared interest in the languages and culture of India.

In 1786 Mark was appointed Deputy Secretary to the Military Board of the Madras Army. Next year, when Capt Close led a mission to negotiate boundary alignments with Tipu Sultan, Mark was its secretary and so able to study the leader of Mysore and his senior advisers at close quarters. They included Poorniah, a Brahmin who was described in 1800 'Poorniah appears clever with a good-natured countenance; he is quite a short man.'[86] Certainly this appointment says much about Mark's competence in Indian languages, especially Hindustani and Persian. Close himself excelled in these languages and was described as 'a most capital Persian scholar, and the best Hindustanee student in the peninsula.' It indicated also that Mark's prospects were improving: by August 1787 his income was £350, but his health was not very good for he was experiencing severe stomach cramps.

Warren Hastings had left Calcutta in February 1785, and Sir John Macpherson acted as head of Government. An old-style servant of the Company, his term in office was described by his successor as 'a system of the dirtiest jobbing.' Also early in 1785 Tipu Sultan took the first step along the path toward fulfilling his ambitions by attacking a hill-top post belonging to an ally of the Marathas. Invoking the Treaty of Salbai, the Marathas requested the Company's aid against Tipu. Macpherson returned only prevarication – though

---

[83] CKS U1287 C 94/3

[84] Mark Wilks, *Historical Sketches of the South of India*. (2nd ed, 2 vols Madras, 1869) 1 151 footnote.

[85] Lord Sidmouth, 'Sir Barry Close Baronet 1756-1813.' *Journal of the Society for Army Historical Research* 6 (1968) 246-7.

[86] Powis, Henrietta Antonia Clive, *Journal of a Voyage to the East Indies*. Publ 1857 80 (BL (OIOC) WD 4235)

Barry Close when Adjutant-General of the Madras Army (Miniature by John Smart, 1794: Courtesy of Christies).

he was sufficiently disturbed to appoint a Resident to Poona, the Marathas' capital. Thrown back upon their own resources, the Marathas and the Nizam formed an alliance that checked Tipu and brought about another drawn contest.

After considerable hesitation the Earl Cornwallis accepted the Governor-Generalship on condition that the post of Commander-in-Chief should be combined with it, and that he would be able to over-rule his Council if he thought it necessary. He was the first Governor-General to be nominated by the Cabinet, and from outwith the ranks of the Company's establishment. His brief was non-military, covering such matters as behaviour of the Company's servants, maintaining the rights of zamindars and land-owners, and ensuring equality and justice for Indians and Europeans alike. Cornwallis arrived in Calcutta in September 1786, aged forty-eight years, lacking personal knowledge of India and therefore dependent upon his subordinates for local advice. As a soldier he had survived the surrender of Yorktown in 1781; as a man he has been described as

...incorruptible without being sour and clear headed without being brilliant. His rule of bluff common sense and genial simplicity was neither faultless nor always wise, but it imported a new spirit into British Indian affairs which was never again wholly lost.[87]

Important as were Cornwallis's civil contributions to British India, they are not a part of this story. Germane to it, however, is the next stage in the conflict between Tipu Sultan and the Company – which had been foreseen by both Tipu and Cornwallis. The Governor-General's room for manoeuvre was restricted by a clause in the India Act of 1784, which stated 'to pursue schemes of conquest and extension of dominion in India are measures repugnant to the wish, honour and policy of this nation.'[88] On the other hand, Cornwallis believed that, in the event of war with Tipu, 'a vigorous coöperation with the Marathas would certainly be of the utmost importance to our interests in this country.'[89] His response at the beginning of the conflict was to ignore the Act and be guided by military realities but, when making peace, to pay some attention to the restriction it imposed upon conquest and the acquisition of territory.

As early as 1785 Tipu had let the French know of his plans: to defeat the Nizam and the Marathas and then, building upon that success, to crush the Company in Madras. Equally, by 1788 Cornwallis foresaw a rupture with Tipu as inescapable and set about securing the Marathas and the Nizam as allies. In this endeavour he was aided by their fearing Tipu more than the Company; though the Nizam's position was complicated by his having engaged Michel Raymond and other French officers to train a corps of 15,000 soldiers in the European manner. Nevertheless, treaties were signed with the Marathas in June 1790, and next month with the Nizam.

In December 1789 Tipu reasserted an historic claim to two districts on the west coast, and attacked Travancore when it was contested by the Rajah. War began between Tipu and the Nizam in May 1790. Mark served throughout as Brigade-Major and ADC to Col James Stuart.

At first, the Madras Army was directed by its new Commander-in-Chief, Gen Sir William Medows, an energetic officer who lacked an adequate appreciation of logistics and the importance of securing his lines of communication. Moving up from the south through Coimbatore he extended his supply lines until he was 95 km from his nearest base, whereupon Tipu's mobile forces attacked his more isolated detachments and came close to destroying them. Cornwallis himself then took command and moved against Mysore from the east, by way of Vellore and Ambur, to take Bangalore fort by storm on 21 March 1791 – and this despite the presence in the vicinity of Tipu with a large army. By mid-May he was only 15 km from Tipu's capital,

---

[87] V. A. Smith, *Oxford History of India* 530
[88] Percival Spear, *India: a Modern History* 211
[89] H. H. Dodwell (ed), *The Cambridge History of India*. vol 5 334

Seringapatam. Then the monsoon broke and the sluggish Madras Government showed itself incapable of maintaining its forces in the field. Cornwallis was therefore forced to destroy his battering train and withdraw.

Mark had met his future wife, Miss Harriot Macleane, a year or two before. His wooing was certainly that of a soldier who expects his fiancée to understand military matters, as his correspondence reveals. In October 1790 he was among a force of 9500 men under Col Maxwell which entered the Baramahal district, some 225 km south-west of Madras. They approached Khistnagherry, the capital and strongest fortification of the district: a tremendous rock with defences that had recently been improved.

> Camp at Caveripatam
> 3 November 1790
>
> My dearest Harriot,
> I received yours of the 25th Octr last night. I had just before sent off one which had been two days waiting for a Tappal – Since I wrote it I have had a very severe attack of Bile, some Fever and much Headache occasioned by riding all day in the Sun looking at Kistanagherry the day after I wrote to you. I tell you this because I have completely got the better of it, and am now in very perfect health. So much for myself. We marched the 1st instant to within three miles of the much famed Kistnaghirry, where we encamped, & different parties went completely round it to reconnoitre it thoroughly. It is horribly strong by nature, and art has been well employed in adding to its force. The Works are all very well built, and well situated. But yet, I think it might be taken soon – but alas we have no heavy guns; without a few it would be madness to attempt it; even with them many men must fall in ascending the Rock, which alone would be a business of some hours. I do not know anything more provoking than to be two days in sight of an Enemy Garrison, which as this did, does you the honor to fire at you whenever you approach it, and to know it is not in your power to take it from them. The worst of it is that while it is theirs' we want Provisions – all the Grain of the Country being within its walls.[90]

Seemingly the rest of the letter has been lost, but attached to the foregoing fragment was Mark's annotated sketch of Khistnagherry in silhouette. It stood about 700 feet (213 m) high, and a battery of six guns had been placed at its summit. At its foot was the pettah with, beyond it,

> a slope to the Rock [Khistnagherry itself]; large low rocks with stones and trenches. Steep rock above the slope – smooth and extremely steep for about 60 feet to the foot of the wall. This is the place we want, it may be taken by storming it. Tho' it would be difficult, as the wall is about 500 feet from the mountain, the ascent steep and rugged, and exposed to the rolling down of large stones when near the summit.[91]

---

[90] Wilks Papers vol 1 (BL Mss Coll Add Mss 57313) (fol 12, letter of 3 Nov 1790)
[91] *ibid*

Fortunately, Maxwell decided not to take a chance by attacking the place, but Harriot must have been apprehensive when she read the letter.

With the onset of the next dry season (1791-92) campaigning was resumed. Tipu led off by recapturing Coimbatore, but Cornwallis refused to be diverted from his deliberate northerly advance toward Seringapatam. On the way he captured the reputedly impregnable fort of Nundidroog after a bombardment of twenty-one days: it fell on 19 October 1791 with the loss of only thirty casualties, most of which were caused by rocks rolled down from the heights. In December 1791 Mark was in Bangalore where he had just recovered from a complaint in his bowels brought on by a severe cold; but his general health was good, and a few days later he went on to join the battering train before Seringapatam.

Cornwallis's army comprised 19,000 European and 29,000 Indian troops with 400 guns, supported by large contingents of Maratha and Hyderabad cavalry. By February 1792 it was assembled at Hirode (or French Rocks) to the north-west of Seringapatam. On the north side of the river, opposite the fort, was a 'bound hedge' of thorn that extended 5 km along the river and enclosed a space up to 2.5 km wide which was defended by six redoubts. Its purpose was to provide a place into which cattle could be moved when hostile cavalry approached, and as an outer line of defence. On the night of 6 February the army carried these defences and secured a foothold on the Seringapatam island itself – a considerable feat given the width of the river and lack of cover. In the attack Cornwallis commanded the central column, which suffered by far the most casualties, and after issuing his orders he is said to have 'fought like a common soldier.'[92] Mark had a share in the business and his horse was shot under him, but he escaped unhurt and remained on the island. On 21 February he wrote an account of the affair to 'My dearest Sister' – presumably Anne. Like his letter to Harriot this one included an annotated sketch of the place in contention, and he gave the Company's casualties by 7th February as: Killed – Indians 28, Europeans 67; Wounded – 162 and 211; Missing – 13 and 21.[93]

Cornwallis's guiding principle was to destroy Tipu's power rather than make a grand gesture by capturing the Sultan's capital; in short, to leave him with some 'face' among the other Indian rulers. The signing of a preliminary treaty was followed by protracted negotiations during which malaria and other diseases increased seriously among the Company's forces, much to Tipu's advantage. Capt Close therefore urged Cornwallis to set a deadline for peace or a resumption of war. This put an end to Tipu's procrastination, and final terms were settled on 23 April.

In the event, those terms were hard enough. A half of Tipu's territories were to be forfeit: large parts went to the Nizam and the Marathas, while the Company secured his possessions on the west coast between Travancore and

---

[92] Mark Wilks, *Historical Sketches of the South of India*. (3 vols London 1810-17) vol 3 217, 223

[93] Wilks Papers vol 1 (BL Mss Coll Add Mss 57313) (fol 13, letter of 21 Feb 1792)

the Kaway river, together with the Baramahal and Dindigul districts in the east. The state of Coorg was restored to its Rajah. Thus Mysore came to be encircled by the victorious Powers. An indemnity of Rs330 lakhs (£3 million) was exacted, all prisoners were released, and two of the Sultan's sons were given up to ensure he kept faith, as was customary in the 18th century. Transfer of the hostages was done in considerable style. The two boys, Abdul Khaliq aged about ten, and Muiz-ud-din some two years younger, were carried to the site on elephants together with Tipu's authorized representative, the lame Vakil Ghulam Ali Khan. At the Company's camp a special tent had been erected and a splendid carpet laid outside it. There Cornwallis received the boys in a humane manner. He was supported by Sir John Kennaway, Resident at the Nizam's Court; Mir Alam represented the Nizam, and Buchaji Pandit the Peshwar. According to a contemporary account

> the princes appeared in long white muslin gowns, and red turbans. Each had several rows of large pearls around his neck, from which hung an ornament consisting of a ruby or an emerald, of considerable size, surrounded by large brilliants, and in his turban a sprig of valuable pearls. The correctness and propriety of their conduct evinced that they had been bred up with infinite care, and taught in their youth to imitate the reserve and politeness of age.[94]

They were to remain with the Company for more than two years.

As we have seen, the settlement brought a large accession of territory to the Madras Presidency. This placed Cornwallis in a perplexing position because of the unreliability of that administration. For more than thirty years the Madras Government had been responsible for the districts immediately surrounding it and, further afield, for the North Circars. In neither case had the responsibility been discharged properly.

Indeed, Cornwallis and others believed there were three great and inter-related defects within these districts: continuing insubordination among the poligars, an uncertain system of land revenue, and lack of established laws and law courts. These defects could not be allowed to spread into the newly acquired territories; but the Madras civil servants as a body, sluggish and intent upon corrupt gains, were clearly unfit for the task ahead. On the other hand, he had been much impressed with the quality of officers of the Madras Army: men like Barry Close, who had been Deputy Adjutant-General throughout the war. Cornwallis therefore made the position clear: administration of the Company's territories in the South – not trade – would in future be the chief duty of its servants, and there would be rewarding careers for those who equipped themselves for that work by acquiring a knowledge of local languages and customs. Moreover, for the immediate future the Army would be called upon to shoulder the task. Therefore, in the Baramahal, a triangle of land cut from

---

[94] T. P. Issar, *The Royal City* (Bangalore 1991) 166

Harriot Wilks (née Macleane), probably painted 1795-99
(Courtesy of Director MNH).

the eastern part of Mysore and having uncertain boundaries, he showed what was intended by appointing Capt Alexander Reid, with three other soldiers as assistants, to settle the country. Read himself was an outstanding man, and one of his assistants, Thomas Munro, was to become the finest administrator in the history of Madras Presidency.

This arrangement would have suited Mark Wilks perfectly, for he was already fluent in some of the languages and knowledgeable about the ways of the people. For the present, however, civil employment was not for him; in 1793 he was appointed Assistant Adjutant-General.

He had other things also to occupy his mind. On the twenty-first day of September 1793 Lt Mark Wilks married Miss Harriot Macleane, aged twenty years, in St Mary's Church, Fort St George. She was the daughter of John Macleane, who had been Assistant to the Chief Engineer in charge of the defences of Madras. Her mother was dead, so she went to the church from the house of a Mrs Hume. The Rev A. Bell, Chaplain, officiated and the witnesses were Mr A. Evant and Capt P. A. Agnew, who was already a close friend of Mark.[95] The old church was shaded by fine trees and its interior was dim and cool. Now more than a century old, it had accumulated some notable treasures including a painting behind the altar of 'The Last Supper' in the style of Raphael, who had himself painted the chalice – so legend said.[96] The young couple probably held their reception in the Officers' Mess nearby. On the first storey was a long ballroom with a cool stone floor, overlooked at one end by a minstrels' gallery, and thus an ideal place for such an occasion. Next year Mark was made Military Secretary to Maj-Gen James Stuart, so that his career seemed to be set fair. But then persistent stomach trouble and recurrent fever overcame him, and he was sent home on furlough beginning 31 March 1795. And so he met his nephew and namesake for the first time.

---

[95] Brig H. R. Norman to Mr Megaw, 23 June 1952 covering copy of Mark Wilks's marriage certificate (MNHL Mss, Individual 5371)
[96] Philip Davies, *Monuments of India* vol 2 545-6

CHAPTER FIVE

Mark Cubbon's Youth 1785 – 1801

Mark Cubbon was born in Maughold. His father, Thomas Cubbon, was Vicar of Kirk Maughold and Mark's first cries were heard in what is now known as the Old Vicarage. He was not the first, nor yet the last, for the Cubbons had ten children of whom Mark was the seventh. His two younger sisters, Elizabeth and Maria, remained closest to him throughout his life. The youngest child of the family died in infancy.

In summer at least, Maughold must have been an idyllic place for a boy to grow up. One can imagine Mark in the morning, running out from the house and looking up at the range of hills dominated by North Barrule. A glance over his left shoulder would have shown him the old Church, looking much as it does today. A village green lay between Vicarage and Church – as it does yet. In Mark's time it was larger than today, and usually the scene of greater activity. On one side of it there was a well to which the villagers, mainly the women-folk, came for water and a gossip. Quite near the entrance of the churchyard stood the famous pillar-cross which bears, on one face, a representation of the 'three legs' that is now the symbol of the Isle of Man. Twice each year the green was the site for St Maughold's Fair, held on 31 July and 15 November (old style). As a portent of what was to follow the November Fair was moved to Ramsey in 1798, though the Summer Fair survived until 1834.[97]

Education

At the time Mark was ready for primary education the Jalloo School was occupied by John Brideson, eighty-eight years old and clearly unfit for the post of schoolmaster. Consequently, young Mark attended the school in Churchtown, Maughold, that had been started in 1776 by the Parish Clerk, Edward Corkhill, and was conducted by him in a barn or cow-house. Clearly, he did well by Mark, who in later years remembered 'my old Master Corkhill' in a friendly way.[98]

Later Mark moved to Ramsey Grammar School, then under the direction of the Chaplain of Ramsey, the Rev Henry Maddrell, who served as Principal from 1790 to 1803, and was probably its only teacher. The Grammar School was quite a recent foundation when Mark joined it, having been established in 1762 by a grant of land from Charles and Jane Cowell to the Chaplain and Wardens of Ramsey. The original building (in which Mark studied) was situated just behind the position where Lough House now stands, and thus within a stone's

---

[97] J.W and C. K. Radcliffe, *A History of Kirk Maughold* (Douglas 1972) 32-7
[98] J W. and C. K. Radcliffe, *A History of Kirk Maughold* 124-7

throw of the school's second premises in Waterloo Road, which were built in 1864 and are now called the 'Old Grammar School.'

At the time Mark joined the school Ramsey had a population of about 900. The school applied a selective principle: only the sons of the clergy and professional people were accepted, so that the number of potential pupils was small. One gains an impression that the school was then in a phase of decline, so that its reputation reached a nadir in 1838 when only fourteen pupils were on the roll under the Rev Archibald Holmes (Principal 1825-43). Mark's only recorded reference to Maddrell gives an impression, in a somewhat oblique way, that he was insufficiently firm and a rather uninspiring teacher. Maddrell moved on in 1803, possibly because of the lapse of an endowment of £10 per annum. Having become Vicar of Kirk Christ, Lezayre he stayed there until 1842.[99]

In the manner of the times there would also have been extracurricular education at home. Tuition from his father, books for personal study, discussion and, in the evenings, reading aloud by a member of the family circle. He heard something of the administrative problems in his father's parish and came to realize the value of fitting the response to the situation: there being times for pastoral care and others when a firm hand was essential. For example, many Ramsey people attended Maughold Church, and we have seen that Thomas Cubbon was a petitioner for a bridge to be thrown over the Ballure River in order to ease their journey. Moreover, Ramsey people buried their dead in the graveyard at Maughold, and at that time the family of the deceased had the task of digging the grave. The habit had grown up of not beginning work until the corpse had actually been brought into the church, and the grave was often quite shallow.[100] The situation became wholly unacceptable so that Thomas had to take a firm stand and require that the grave should be dug before the corpse arrived, and to an adequate depth.

Mark had a horse, a mare, which he remembered with affection in later years and which probably kindled the passion for horses that he was able to indulge later in life. When Mark left the Island his father took over the horse and found it an excellent mount. There were other outdoor activities too, for Thomas was fond of hare-coursing despite the strong disapproval of his wife. In the way of the times, father and sons enjoyed both the sport and the companionship.

He had friends beyond the family, who were drawn from both school and the district about Maughold. There were the Logans of Dreemskerry and the Callows of Claughbane – and doubtless he bared his head to the redoubtable William Callow, Captain of the Parish and Member of the Keys. Outside the family but within the household there was one for whom he felt a special affection: 'Old Hester' who seems to have been the family's principal servant

---

[99] L. E. Williamson, *A Short History of Ramsey Grammar School*. (Douglas 1972) (MNHL D426/1/3)
[100] Constance Radcliffe, *Ramsey 1600-1800* 91

and who probably cared for him while his mother was occupied with the younger children.[101]

Mark had been born while the uncle for whom he had been named was still in India, and they did not meet until 1795 when Uncle Wilks, as young Mark called him, returned from India on sick leave.

His Uncle

Harriot and Mark took a house in St James's Place, London but spent much time on the Island, and their stay was certainly eventful! Mark purchased a substantial property, Ballafletcher in Braddan, and had to raise a mortgage. Their first child, Laura, was baptized by the Rev Cubbon in Maughold Church on 9 January 1797.[102] On 18 January 1798 the Cubbon's last child was born, and baptized privately on the same day; named James John, he survived only until September.[103] On 23 October 1798 a son was born to Harriot and Mark. Christened John Barry, he was always called Barry within the family as a tribute to Mark's great friend Barry Close, who was the boy's Godfather.[104] Then, on 8 January 1799 Mark's mother, Elizabeth, was buried at Ballaugh Old Church.

When its contents became known, Mrs. Elizabeth Wilks's last will must have caused some heart-burning among her children. It stated

> to each and every of my children who have any claim on me six pence legacy ... my son James Wilks, High Bailiff of the said town of Ramsey, [to be] whole and sole executor and residual legatee of my houses, lands, goods and chattels, mortgage monies, credits and effects.[105]

Since Mrs Wilks had been living in Ramsey the suspicion that James had influenced her decision is inescapable! He seems, moreover, to have had an eye for the main chance, having married a very well-connected widow named Catherine Moore (née Cosnahan). Nevertheless, both Mark and Harriot maintained a friendly correspondence with James.

Soon it was time to return to India, and Capt Wilks made arrangements for a passage with the Spring fleet. There were two young children, so it was agreed that Harriot would remain in England until they were old enough to be left in good hands and then rejoin Mark in India. This would entail a separation of three or four years – an arrangement that was usual at the time. Accordingly, Harriot and her infants were installed in St James's Place, and there Mark made his final preparations for the voyage. He joined a fleet of three ships, all about 700 tons, which sailed from Portsmouth on 24 April 1799 for the 'coast and bay.'

---

[101] MNHL MD 436 25/8
[102] Baptisms 1797: Maughold, Laura Wilks (MNHL MF/ PR 23, 1716-1849)
[103] Burials 1798: Maughold, James John Cubbon (MNHL MF/ PR 23, 1716-1849)
[104] Baptisms 1798: Maughold, John Barry Wilks (MNHL MF/ PR 23, 1716-1849)
[105] Archidiaconal Wills, Wilks, Elizabeth alias Christian (MNHL MF/ RB 593, No 59)

A strong bond must have been established between uncle and nephew – something greater than a simple family tie – because Capt Wilks did all he could for young Mark. He wrote to the boy's father about his plans.

London, 17 April, 1799

My dear Brother,
I have delayed until almost the eve of my going on board what I have to say to you on the subject of our friend Mark. From 15 to 22 is I find the age at present for the admission of Cadets, among which number I have put matters in as good a train as I at present can for having him enrolled so as to leave England in the Spring of 1802. Meanwhile speculating upon this as upon all human projects with a discreet measure of doubt; if you are of the opinion that a good education will in any event be no disadvantage, I could wish you to send him <u>immediately</u> to Mr Stowel's at Castletown as well because I believe that to be your best seminary, because the change of scene, and rubbing against the world will be useful as a preparation to the year in this country which is part of my plan. For the amount of Mr Stowel's bill I expect you will draw on my wife, who will likewise arrange for him to come over to England when we come to that chapter. I shall now give a hasty sketch of the outline I would recommend in his education while with Mr Stowel. The classes will of course maintain their rank and I have no wish to degrade them, on the express condition that they occupy not more than one half the time allotted to study. To speak and write our own language with purity and elegance, is a most important, though much neglected branch of education. My father's practice of making us write to him once a week, returning to us our own letters corrected, when necessary, and writing to us regularly in a style suited to our comprehension, is a part of instruction that you will particularly take on yourself. Mr Stowel will meanwhile put such English works into his hands as are suited to his age and capacity, which will expand his ideas somewhat faster than the mere study of words. Let him resume his Arithmetic immediately, and be thoroughly grounded in it, getting on as fast as may be with the Mathematics is a pursuit of the first importance to the success of his future views. And as far as is practicable, let him have both the theory and practice of surveying, and be expert in the use of the Theodolite. If there be a drawing master of any kind let him attend him, but in every event he should from the beginning of his Mathematical studies never hear a demonstration without being able to delineate the figure with neatness and precision. French if he can learn pronunciation from a Frenchman and not otherwise. Dancing always, whenever and as long as there is a Master; intrinsically it is not worth a farthing but it is a valuable passport to good company and as it assists at rubbing off the rough edges. Were I to go on the burthen of my song would still be Mathematics and particularly Trigonometry with its practical application to his future. But these he will pursue when he comes to this country and the time he spends with Mr Stowel will not admit of laying down a very extensive plan. Geography and the use of the globes, and as much Astronomy and Natural Philosophy as he is capable of learning and falls within the plan of the school, he will of course have an opportunity of attending to. The Modern Chymistry which (after Mathematics and the sciences to which

it is allied) is worth all the rest of the Sciences, and indeed nearly embraces them all, has I fear not made much progress in the Island; otherwise I should wish him to imbibe a taste for it.

Endeavour as much as you can to have him mix with people older than himself, and to acquire the habit of acting and thinking like a man. Colonel Cunningham's family I think will take some notice of him, and that sort of society will be of infinite use.

I have scarcely a spare half-hour between this and the time I leave town to embark, you have therefore got to the end of my preachments, and I have only to offer my best wishes for you and yours and to say that I am always

Your affectionate
M. Wilks

PS. Your letters may always be directed to Captain Wilks, Madras, send them by the post paying inland postage (otherwise they will be returned) whenever you hear of an opportunity which always occurs every spring and autumn whether you hear it or not.[106]

Only two months after her husband's departure Harriot herself had an unwelcome adventure. An epidemic of smallpox was ravaging these Islands, including the Isle of Man. She had therefore left London for Bath, but on 25 June 1799 felt compelled to move further afield and take a couple of rooms in a farmhouse five miles away. Laura had caught the chin-cough in Bath. She recovered quickly but Barry, eight months old and teething, had taken the sickness. As sometimes happens after whooping-cough he had developed tuberculous meningitis with violent convulsions – thirty and more spasms on some days. 'Water in the head' was diagnosed. For three weeks he seemed unlikely to survive, but then he was treated with salts of mercury and an unexpected recovery followed.[107]

Bound for India

But to return to Capt Wilks's letter and its outcome. What a prospect it opened for young Mark: a year of comparative independence at the best school in the Island, hobnobbing with the Cunninghams, a year in London! Alas, only part of the plan was realized.

The 'Mr Stowel' was the Rev Joseph Stowell who had opened a school in Castletown in 1795 and conducted it with great success. In 1799 he moved to Peel as Master of the Grammar and Mathematical Schools, so perforce Mark remained at Ramsey Grammar School. Moreover the pre-departure period was compressed, for Mark arrived at Fort St George in July 1801 – a year earlier that Uncle Wilks had planned and just before his sixteenth birthday.

One may speculate on reasons for Mark's early departure from these Islands. Several factors may have played a part: disenchantment with the

---

[106] MNHL MD 436 24/4
[107] Wilks Papers Vol 1 (BL Mss Coll Add Mss 57313) fol 16-17

education that Henry Maddrell offered, excitement over stories about India from Uncle Wilks and a desire to emulate him. Most important, however, was the need for Mark to become self-supporting, and even contribute to the family. The Island's economy was depressed at the time. Thomas and Margaret had nine surviving children, and three of the girls seemed likely to remain unmarried. Indeed, in 1792 Anne Collet had expressed concern to her brother about the prospects for her nieces

> I grieve when I think of their marrying a Manx heirey – a common labourer who is industrious can supply his wife more comfortably in Philadelphia than they in general can – if our circumstances would admit of making an offer that one of them might think it worth accepting of I should have done it before now for I know if she were prudent she might marry better here than in all probability she could at home.[108]

Moreover, young Mark's repeated reference in his letters, to sending money home – and the evidence that he did so – shows that he felt an obligation to assist as far as he was able.

Nevertheless, he spent some time in London. Crossing to Liverpool, he took coach to the capital spending two full days on the way and sleeping both nights in the coach. He received a warm welcome from Harriot, now back in St James's Place, and there he came to know his two young cousins – particularly Laura. At first he was dismayed to find that his box had been mislaid during the journey, but Harriot provided consolation by arranging for him to be fitted out with a suit of clothes 'in the fashion' and a pair of half-boots. After about a month at St James's Place, Mark went as a boarder to the Rev Macfarlane's School. This was a semi-military establishment intended to provide an appropriate education for young men destined for the army, other than the engineers and artillery for whom Woolwich was available. The fees were £100 per year. He was very happy, and enjoyed being the best scholar there. There had been a plan for him to visit his family in the Island before going to India, but this did not eventuate.[109]

Like his uncle before him, young Mark entered the Company's employ through nomination, or patronage. One of the more important duties of the twenty-four Directors was routinely to make appointments to the various junior posts becoming vacant in the Company's service. Between 1793 and 1812 the annual average of these posts was Writers – 40, Cadets – 240, Assistant Surgeons – 30. A monetary value could be attached to each post and, on this basis, the posts were divided into twenty-eight notional parts. Two of these were parts were allocated to the Board of Control as a courtesy, two parts each were allotted to the Chairman and Deputy Chairman, and one part to each of the twenty-two other Directors. Consequently, each ordinary Director might

---

[108] CKS U 1287 94/3
[109] MNHL MD 436 29/3

expect to have right of patronage over seven to eleven posts.[110] In February 1801 Mark was nominated Cadet in the Madras Army by one John Manship, a London businessman and long-standing Director.[111] He was a man of substance who has been called 'the stern, unbending father of the Direction.' He was antagonistic toward Henry Dundas, President of the Board of Control, and in some instances his judgement proved to be superior.[112]

As a nominated Cadet, Mark had to comply with procedures laid down in the Preparatory Instructions – and to be brisk about it! Everything was done at East India House in Leadenhall Street, originally a fairly unpretentious building but recently provided with a rather grand Ionic portico and an East wing. There he had first to produce an extract from the Maughold Parish Register of Births and Baptisms in a prescribed form, prepared by his father (as Vicar) and duly witnessed, as a proof of his age. He presented this document to the Committee of Shipping, and was given a card of Necessaries for Equipment, a List of the Shipping, and the Court's Regulations as to the sums to be paid for accommodation on board ship, which were fixed at not more than £95 for a place at the Commander's table or £55 in the Third Mate's Mess. Having decided upon the ship in which he wanted to sail, he had to secure, from the Shipping Office, a Certificate to the effect that he had passed the Committee of Shipping. This authorized him to move on to the Pay Office where he signed the Bond of Service and received the Company's gratuity of ten guineas. Next he went to the Private Trade Office to pay his passage money and receive the Order for Baggage – which was limited to a chest of necessaries, a liquor case, a hamper of wine, and a cot with bedding. Finally he made his way to the Secretary's office to obtain his Certificate of Appointment.[113] Only then was he free to relax while awaiting a call to embark.

It came soon enough. Then there were hurried farewells to Harriot and the children, and he was off on the great adventure. Early in March young Mark went aboard one of a large fleet of ships, all about 1200 tons. Like his uncle he sailed around the Cape because the sea-and-land route through the Mediterranean was not yet in being but, unlike his uncle, he has left us no account of his voyage.

---

[110] C. H. Philips, *The East India Company 1784-1834*, 14
[111] Cadet Papers of Cubbon (Mark) 7 Feb. 1801 (BL (OIOC) L/Mil/9//111 f 341)
[112] C. H. Philips, *The East India Company 1784-1834*. 61, 71, 336
[113] Preparatory Instructions to Persons who may be nominated Cadets in the Service of the Honorable United East-India Company. 3pp, approx octavo, nd. (NLW Clive Mss and Papers (2nd Series) A. Mss vols No. 2309)

CHAPTER SIX

Interlude 1795 - 1799

Mark and Harriot Wilks had left India early in 1795, and Mark had remained away for four and a half years. During this time the position of the Company in South India was transformed, with the impetus for change coming sometimes from developments within India itself, but often as a by-product of the French Revolutionary War going on in Europe.

Ceylon

Taking advantage of the freezing winter conditions of 1794-95 the forces of the young French Republic had invaded the Netherlands, driven the Stadhouder (Willem V, Prince of Orange) to seek refuge in England, and turned the people of Holland into citizens of a Batavian Republic allied to France and paying French taxes. Dutch overseas possessions thus became outposts of France, a position that was made quite clear when, on 31 December, the Vereenigde Ostindische Compagnie was formally dissolved and the Batavian Republic received its debts and possessions.[114] The most immediately important of these were the Cape of Good Hope and Ceylon. The former was promptly occupied by an expedition from Great Britain, but what of Ceylon? The Company decided on a prompt action. A force under Maj Gen James Stuart, Mark's former chief, was despatched to the island and accomplished its task with remarkable speed. Although the Dutch had constructed some splendid coastal forts the smaller ports were easily taken, the more so because their Dutch garrisons were completely demoralized by events at home. There was a further reason for Stuart's quick victory. The principal force defending Ceylon was the Neuchatel Régiment Meuron, and the British were able to bring about its transfer to the Company's service. The unusual events attending upon the transfer warrant a description.

The founder and colonel-proprietor of the Regiment was Charles-Daniel de Meuron, a native of Neuchatel, then a possession of Frederick II (the Great) King of Prussia and third Prince of Neuchatel. In 1755, when aged seventeen, de Meuron joined a private Swiss regiment which had the Chevalier de Hallwyl as it colonel-commander. In 1765 he became an officer in the Swiss Guard of the French king. Perhaps in emulation of de Hallwyl, he turned his hand to raising a private regiment in his native place, took service with the Dutch VOC in 1781 and was posted to Ceylon.[115]

---

[114] C.R. Boxer, *The Dutch Seaborne Empire 1600-1800* (London 1973) 336
[115] Guy de Meuron, *Le Régiment Meuron 1781-1816* (Lausanne 1982) 19-43.

Like its Dutch counterpart, the EIC had an established practice of recruiting officers and other ranks into its armies from the Protestant cantons of Switzerland, including Neuchatel: for example, 397 men from Switzerland joined the Madras Army between 1751 and 1754.[116]

The man who brought about the transfer of allegiance was Hugh Cleghorn, a young history lecturer at St Andrew's University who preferred a career in the British secret service. He was sent to Neuchatel, 'an excellent observation post,' and there became friendly with Charles-Daniel de Meuron; this was in 1791 when de Meuron had retired. As a result Cleghorn was able to report to London that de Meuron was disposed to leave the employ of the VOC for that of either His Britannic Majesty or the EIC. This was a welcome windfall for the British Government because the Regiment consisted of 1200 men with experienced officers and well accustomed to the climate of India. However, there was a delay until circumstances became favourable. These came about when France invaded the Netherlands. Acting independently of the EIC's Secret Committee, Henry Dundas authorized Cleghorn to offer de Meuron a handsome inducement to come over to the British.

Carrying letters of instruction from the British Government, Cleghorn left England on 1 March 1795 and travelled overland through Germany and Switzerland to reach Neuchatel on 24th. There he negotiated with Charles-Daniel de Meuron, advancing the argument that since the government in Ceylon no longer gave its allegiance to the Stadhouder, who had originally engaged it, the Regiment was no longer contracted to that government. Among the main points of the final agreement were: (i) the Regiment would be paid by the British from the moment its Colonel detached it from the service of the Dutch government in Ceylon, and this would continue for the same period as that for which it had engaged itself in the Dutch service; (ii) the British government would make up the back-pay due to the Regiment from the VOC; (iii) the Count de Meuron and his regiment would be accredited to the government of Madras to which he would give all necessary assistance and co-operation. De Meuron himself was appointed a Major-General in the British Army.

Cleghorn and de Meuron left Neuchatel together on 17 April and travelled to Venice. They sailed from there on 18 May, crossed overland through Egypt, took another ship and arrived in South India on 12 September. From there de Meuron wrote to his brother, who was in command of the Regiment in Ceylon, and all arrangements for the transfer were completed on 28 September. In October 1795 the Régiment Meuron embarked for South India and the service of the EIC.[117]

---

[116] W. J. Wilson, *History of the Madras Army* 5 vols (Madras 1882-89) vol 1 (1882) 62-3
[117] Guy de Meuron, *Le Régiment Meuron* 102-6

The Conquest of Mysore

During Capt Wilks's voyage to India the final act of Muslim rule in Mysore was being played out. It began in a way that had been seen before and that we have witnessed in our own times.

Cornwallis left India in mid-1793 and was succeeded by Sir John Shore, one who had made his career with the Company and possessed both a more restricted outlook and a stronger tendency toward appeasement than did Cornwallis. His tenure of the supreme office (1793-98) coincided with a period when France recovered from government by a vacillating absolute monarch and an unguided revolutionary regime to emerge as a dynamic power under the Directory (1795-99). In South India, the hoped-for period of tranquillity did not eventuate. Antipathies flared within the Maratha Confederation. Shore managed, at a stroke, to shake general confidence in the Company's good faith and, in particular, to undermine the Nizam's position. This was inept because French influence has long been strong in Hyderabad where, since 1786 15,000 Sepoys had been training under command of a French officer, Michel Raymond. This mismanagement deprived Shore of the confidence of both his own officers and the Directors, and he was recalled at the same time being created Lord Teignmouth.

Some remarkable men now came on to the Indian stage. First to appear was Lt Col Arthur Wellesley who arrived at Calcutta in January 1797 in command of H.M. 33rd Foot, a unit that came to be known as the Duke of Wellington's Regiment (West Riding). Arthur saw his posting to India as a chance to break with his former unsatisfactory life. The voyage had taken nine months and, having provided himself with a comprehensive library, he put the time to good use in serious study for the first time in his life: Indian languages, military science and history, economics, politics, and some volumes of Voltaire were all grist to his mill. Clearly, however, his cool appraisal of people and situations was already well developed: for example his summing up of Shore as 'a good man but cold as a greyhound's nose'[118] could hardly be bettered. Arthur was followed, unexpectedly, by his older brother Richard, Earl of Mornington, ten years his senior and one who had hitherto treated him with a disdain that bordered on contempt. On 26 April 1798 he landed at Calcutta as Governor-General, accompanied by his youngest brother, Henry, as private secretary. Last came Edward, Lord Clive, son of a famous father, to become Governor of Madras in August 1798.

Mornington was one of those Governors-General who played pivotal roles in the development of Anglo-India. He was Anglo-Irish and a member of the ascendancy in the country of his birth, intelligent, overwhelmingly sure of himself, but one whose self-assurance (at this stage of his career) was based on study and meticulous preparation. That he possessed immense *amour-propre* is revealed by Macaulay's observation of him, in 1833, as the seventy-three year

---

[118] Anthony Brett-James, *Wellington at War* (London 1961) 49

old Marquis of Wellesley 'such a blooming old swain I never saw…hair combed with exquisite nicety, a waistcoat of driven snow, and a star and garter put on with rare skill!'[119] Moreover, more than most men of his class and time he seems possessed of what Galbraith has called 'the lust for land'; the notion that 'territorial conquest was…the basis of both wealth and power.'[120] He was also quick and decisive. For example, within three months of arrival he wrote his appreciation to Dundas in London

> …the interest of the Company in India can never be secure while Tipu Sultan shall retain the ready means of intercourse by sea with the French Government. His remaining territory on the coast of Malabar is his most powerful instrument of war.[121]

For his part, the Sultan of Mysore sowed the seeds of his own destruction. Resentful though he was, Tipu might have remained reconciled to his lot if events in Europe had not given him hope of revenge. A faction in France under the Directory advocated a policy of 'revolutionary expansionism' which would bring 'sister republics' into alliance with it; and this faction turned its eyes toward Egypt and India. Since the First Coalition had collapsed in 1797 Great Britain had stood alone against Revolutionary France. Therefore, to Versailles and the Ile de France (Mauritius) Tipu sent his ambassadors, and there they were welcomed as affording help in forwarding French aspirations in India. Some of these envoys returned to Mangalore soon after Mornington's arrival in Calcutta, and they were accompanied by a small French contingent, which probably prompted Mornington's conclusion noted above.

Mornington embarked on a probing correspondence with Tipu, beginning with an offer to negotiate on his alliance with France, but becoming increasingly firm in tone. The Company was confronted with a simple comparison of resources: Tipu could call upon large reserves of men and supplies so that his strength was growing daily; the Company's own resources were limited and it had commitments elsewhere in the Sub-continent. Time, therefore, was of the essence. On 18 October Mornington learnt that Bonaparte had landed in Egypt, in accordance with his appreciation that '*La puissance qui est maîtresse de l'Égypte doit l'être à la longue de l'Inde*'[122]; and two days later Lord Clive was ordered to prepare for war.

In one respect at least the Company's position had been made more secure. As a result of negotiations in Hyderabad with the Resident, Major James Archilles Kirkpatrick and his new assistant, Capt John Malcolm, the Nizam agreed to disband his French-trained army and replace it with four Company's

---

[119] Thomas Pinney (ed), *Selected Letters of Thomas Babington Macaulay* (Cambridge 1982) 93
[120] J. K. Galbraith, *The World Economy since the Wars* (London 1994) 12
[121] A. S. Bennell, 'Wellesley's Settlement of Mysore, 1799' *Journal of the Royal Asiatic Society* (no vol number) pts 3 & 4 (1952) 124
[122] H. H. Dodwell (ed) *The Cambridge History of India* vol 5 327

battalions under terms of a subsidiary treaty that bound him to the Company. Various considerations underlay the Nizam's decision. On the one hand, his army had been overwhelmed by the Marathas in March 1795, so that he had to accept a humiliating treaty and loss of territory: was that army worth keeping? Moreover, Kirkpatrick had already established the intimate relationship with the Nizam's inner circle that led to his marriage (1800) to Khair un-Nissa, a great-niece of the Diwan. Finally, there were the undoubted skills of the Resident and his assistant.

The story of the war itself may be told briefly. On 3 February 1799 Lt Gen George Harris, the Commander-in-Chief, began his march toward Seringapatam from Vellore. His Adjutant-General and virtual Chief of Staff was Col Barry Close. Maj Gen James Stuart with a contingent of the Bombay Army moved north-east from Kannanur. Lt Col Arthur Wellesley commanded a force advancing from Hyderabad, which was made up of the Nizam's troops and his own 33rd Foot.

Harris's army of 50,000 men was an astonishing formation. It moved as a huge rectangle almost 10 km long by 5 km wide with, inside it, a mass of people and animals. There were 150,000 camp-followers: water-carriers, cooks, grooms, grass-cutters, sweepers, farriers – indeed all the trades needed to support the combat troops – and the wives and children of these men; 60,000 animals: camels, horses, bullocks, elephants, and the remounts for the cavalry; the siege-train and ammunition wagons. It moved perhaps 8 km a day. Visualize the scene: the various uniforms of the soldiers and costumes of their followers, the shouts of men and shriller cries of women in half-a-dozen languages, the even more various calls of the beasts, the animal smells almost unknown today in the West; and above and around the whole moving multitude a cloud of fine red dust raised by thousands of pairs of feet. How different was the reality from the small, neat rectangles used to represent armies in text-book plans of campaigns.[123]

Tipu was defeated twice in the field, on 8 and 27 March. He then prepared to make a stand at Seringapatam. The Company's army was concentrated around the island, and began its siege on 17 April. There was little time to lose for the season was far advanced toward the monsoon so that supply lines were failing as they had in 1791. By 3 May a breach had been made in the walls. At 1300 h. next day the assault was launched, with Maj Gen David Baird leading the 4000 strong storming party, and Col Wellesley in charge of the reserves. By evening the place had been taken, Tipu was dead, two of his sons (the former hostages) had surrendered, and doubtless Baird felt his long imprisonment had been avenged. Next day Tipu's eldest son, Fateh Hyder, also surrendered together with the force he commanded. These three young men and the rest of Tipu's family were held at Seringapatam pending a decision about the final settlement.

---

[123] C. H. Philips, *The Young Wellington in India*. The Creighton Lecture in History 1972. (London 1973) 26

The Régiment Meuron had taken part in the Seringapatam campaign: 76 of its personnel became casualties of whom 16 were killed. They and others who died during the Régiment's garrison duties at Seringapatam are buried in the British cemetery there together with the wives and children of some members of the Régiment.

The Peace

Mornington had made his plans for the peace, which included a restoration of the Wadiyar family to the throne of Mysore. Already, on 22 February, he had given Harris instructions for his political conduct toward the population of Mysore, and for its future government. On 4 June a Commission for the settlement of Mysore territories was appointed. What an assemblage of talent! Its members were Lt Gen Harris, Col the Hon Arthur Wellesley, the Hon Henry Wellesley, Col Barry Close, and Lt Col William Kirkpatrick; and it secretaries were Capt John Malcolm and Capt Thomas Munro. It met at Seringapatam with the objective, in the medium term, of securing those conditions of safety and tranquillity that would allow the Indian genius to express itself, so that farmers and artisans could begin creating modest prosperity in the land. Its immediate task, however, was to establish a government for Mysore. The Governor-General held decided views about the latter matter, and those views formed the basis for a treaty. Given the complexity of the situation Mornington reached his decisions with remarkable speed. The settlement was to be: (i) a part of Tipu's territories would be divided between the Company, the Nizam, and the Marathas so that only the central tableland remained to the new kingdom of Mysore, which was cut off from the sea and possible contact with the French; (ii) the Wadiyar dynasty would be restored with, as Diwan, a talented Brahmin administrator named Poorniah, who had held senior posts under both Hyder Ali and Tipu Sultan.[124] His plan had to be carried out in such a way as to maintain the alliance with Hyderabad and the Marathas, and to avoid encouraging those who were still loyal to Tipu's family from rallying round it. Timing, therefore, was critical.

It was decided to apportion the existing territory of Mysore according to its yield of revenue; not an easy task because accurate information was lacking. The eventual proposal was that the Company and the Nizam should each receive lands yielding about Rs24.4 lakhs, the Marathas about Rs9.1 lakhs, and the new state of Mysore some Rs47.3 lakhs (see glossary for rupee and lakh). So as to separate Mysore from the west coast, which Mornington believed to be essential, the Company's portion included the districts of Malabar and Coimbatore. Perhaps fortuitously, the revenue from these districts turned out to be the highest among all the forfeit lands.[125]

---

[124] A. S. Bennell, 'Wellesley's Settlement of Mysore 1799' 128
[125] A. S. Bennell, 'Wellesley's Settlement of Mysore 1799' 129

Now the sensitive matter of timing came into play. On 19 June 1799 Tipu's sons, and other close members of his family, left Seringapatam and were escorted to the fine old fort at Vellore, where they remained for several years. The movement could hardly have been done surreptitiously for the record of detainees at Vellore a few year later showed Tipu's ten oldest sons, a brother and two nephews; and these personages would have been accompanied by servants.[126]

On 22 June a treaty that gave effect to the land settlement was signed by representatives of Hyderabad and the Company and was ratified in the following month. Quite soon, however, some land changed hands again for the Nizam fell into arrears with payments under his subsidiary treaty and, in lieu, made over to the Company the districts of Kurnool, Cuddapah and Bellary – this last being part of his gains after Seringapatam. These constituted the so-called Ceded Districts, and were placed in the charge of Major Thomas Munro.

But who would be the new Prince? It is often stated that he was a close kinsman, even a grandson, of the deposed Hindu ruler. However, having investigated the question carefully while responsible for Mysore's affairs Wilks gave a somewhat different account, and one that is worth repeating. When Hyder Ali usurped power in Mysore, he retained the Maharajah, Chikka Krishnaraja Wadiyar, as a figure-head. He was given districts that yielded Rs3 lakhs as his privy purse and, at the great annual Dussera festival, was displayed to the people on the palace balcony with Hyder Ali in the position of Chief Minister and Commander-in-Chief. In April 1766 the Maharajah died, and Hyder Ali then went through the ceremony of paying his respects to the eighteen-year-old eldest son – as would a subject to his sovereign. The young man, Nunjeraj Wadiyar, soon tried to assume some authority and thus provoked Hyder to remove his income and surround him with spies. About five years later Nunjeraj made another bid for power, whereupon Hyder had him strangled and installed a brother, Cham Raj, in his place. When, about 1775, this young man died and the male line became extinct, Hyder set about finding a successor by means of a remarkable charade. He ordered the male children from all eligible branches of the Wadiyar family to be brought together. Then the floor of the audience hall was strewn with a variety of attractive objects: fruit, toys, money, ornaments, sweetmeats – and the boys were invited to choose what they liked best. During the ensuing mêlée one boy picked up a small dagger in his right hand and a lime in his left. Hyder announced that this was evidence of the child's concern for both military and civil affairs, and embraced him as the future Maharajah. He, too, took the name of Cham Raj and became the father of the boy who eventually was restored as Maharajah.[127]

On 30 June 1799 this five-year-old boy was placed on the gaddi, with the title of Maharaja Sri Krishnarajah Wadiyar Bahadur III. It had been decided

---

[126] Clive Mss and Papers, 2nd Series B Letters Nos. 545-6 (NLW)
[127] Mark Wilks, *Historical Sketches of the South of India.* vol 1 294.

that this should be done in the old capital, Mysore City, but the situation there made it difficult to mount an adequate ceremony, for Tipu had demolished both palace and fort, and used the materials to begin building a new capital to be called Nazabad. When he was defeated the site remained a mess with a few huts for workmen scattered about upon it. To the best of these the young Maharajah was conducted, and in front of it he was enthroned.

Relations between the new Mysore and the Company were regulated by a second treaty, the Subsidiary Treaty of Seringapatam. Broadly, its provisions were that the new State should have no independent foreign policy, and it should support a subsidiary force of Company's troops. The subsidy was set at Rs24.5 lakhs which might be increased at the Company's discretion. Provision was made, therefore, to station elements of the Company's Army within the State. Moreover, the Company had the right to take over the government of all or part of the State if there were reasons to suppose that the subsidy might not be paid.[128] In addition, the Company's Resident in Mysore was given wide powers to supervise and advise. Finally, against the advice of Arthur Wellesley, supervision of Mysore was given over to Fort St George – a provision would have long-term repercussions.

The Subsidiary Treaty was signed at Seringapatam on 8 July 1799, and the Commission was dissolved on the same day. On 9 July Arthur Wellesley became commander of the troops remaining in Mysore after the bulk of Harris's army had marched away. Col Close became Resident in Seringapatam. Soon afterwards another of Arthur's friends, Capt Colin Mackenzie, was appointed to direct a Survey of Mysore – the first such to be undertaken in India.

For a time Arthur lived at the Daria Daulat at Seringapatam but, the place being low-lying and unhealthy, the Company's headquarters were removed to Mysore City. Much building was in progress there, including construction of a new palace on the lines of the former structure. Some 2 km north of the palace Wellesley built an unpretentious house to accommodate the Commission. It seems to have been run up quickly, and Issar has described it as being derived from the 'factory' builders of the EIC rather than any special style of architecture[129]; indeed its only embellishment was a staircase with two wings that met at first-floor level.

Thus, Mysore State had been transformed since Mark Wilks left it in 1795, and it had now assumed the geographical form it was to retain until Independence in 1947.

---

[128] A. S. Bennell, 'Wellesley's Settlement of Mysore 1799' 131-2
[129] T. P. Issar, *The Royal City* 56

CHAPTER SEVEN

Together under Mornington's Regime
1799 – 1805

Mark Wilks returned to an uncertain future in the Madras Presidency soon after the Mysore settlement. The defeat of Tipu had removed a threat that had hung over it for many years. A peace dividend was being sought from among those who had served the Company well, and with little thought of the consequences. Wilks himself had served for seventeen years in the Madras Army, but the last four-and-a-half of them had been spent at home. Many friends had retired or moved on, and others had taken their places. Although his reputation was good he had become a somewhat shadowy figure, and when he was posted to the 2nd Battalion of his old Regiment it was with the prospect of a long period of regimental duty.

Fortune, however, smiled upon him. Lord Clive was attracted to this officer of good repute who had returned to duty a few months after his own arrival and at a time when he needed sound advice and help. There is little surprising in the fact that Clive and Wilks got on well together. Clive had spent some years in Italy, was interested in the antiquities of that country, and handled an artist's pencil with facility. Though not a quick-witted man, his interest in intellectual pursuits predisposed him toward someone like Wilks who could reveal much of the rich tapestry of art and architecture that South India had to show. In September 1799 the office of Military Secretary to the Governor was created, with a salary as for an aide-de-camp and an additional allowance of forty pagodas (Rs120) per month for clerks. Capt Mark Wilks was the first appointee. This placed him firmly at the centre of affairs in Madras and enabled him to make arrangements for the reception of his nephew. Soon afterward he was given the additional post of Barrack Master of the Presidency Division at Fort St. George. Moreover, in that same September Col Close became Resident in Mysore, and was succeeded as Adjutant-General by Lt-Col Patrick Agnew, who had been a witness to Mark's marriage.

By the middle of 1800 Mark's ill-health had recurred. As a remedy he was sent off by Lord Clive on a leisurely tour through Madras Presidency and Mysore; and his Lordship drew an official veil over his considerate action by enjoining Wilks to inform him about the conditions of the country through which he passed. On 14 August Wilks wrote from Kistnagherry

> I sit down to obey your Lordship's kind injunction to give you some account of myself without having anything very decided to communicate: that the journey has not disagreed with me I consider a proof of returning strength and with the exception of some slight feverish symptoms at Arcot I have since had no reason

to regret having met with no medical man to whom I should be willing to apply. This country is studded with hill-forts, a number of which have been evacuated without having been destroyed and the remainder are being used as quarters for troops. Most of them contain enough powder to blow up the gateways and reservoirs ...[and] Capt Davis with his party of Pioneers could demolish the whole in a few months.[130]

He went on to estimate that Col Wellesley could clear the Baramahal and Salem districts of dissidents in about a year, and he considered the former tract to be quite prosperous and its inhabitants well clothed.

In mid-September he wrote to Clive from Seringapatam, saying that he had received a request from Col Close to meet him at Cheneropatam, asking Lord Clive's approbation for a plan that would delay his return to Madras by a few days, and remarking 'I have indented on the stores for camp equipage for which the Military Board should order me to be hanged. I trust your Lordship will sign my reprisal.'[131]

Lt-Col Agnew had not been allowed to remain undisturbed in his office chair, for he was soon called upon to deal with trouble in the far south, nearly 650 km from Madras, as a result of actions by the poligars of Tinnevelly. These feudal chieftains were at once oppressive upon the cultivators over whom they held power and antagonistic toward the Company; and they used the resources exacted from the cultivators to support numerous armed retainers who were perceived as a threat by the Company. After the fall of Tipu a military force was sent to Tinnevelly. It was opposed by the poligars but, after some fighting, many of them were confined there. On 2 February 1801 the imprisoned poligars escaped and were joined by about 4000 armed men. This force established itself in the rebuilt fort at Panjalamcoorchy. A mixed force of the Company's soldiers attacked the fort over difficult ground on 31 March, but was repulsed with the loss of 50 killed and 267 wounded. The Governor-in-Council immediately appointed Lt-Col Agnew to command the troops in the field.

He arrived at Panjalamcoorchy with reinforcements on 21 May and captured the place three days later.[132]

As a result, when Mark Cubbon arrived at Madras in July 1801 he found his uncle in a position of influence and Agnew, with the laurels of victory fresh upon him, even better placed to help his friend's young kinsman.

---

[130] Clive Mss and Papers (2nd Series) B Letters Correspondence from Capt M. Wilks to Lord Clive 14 Aug – 15 Sep 1800 No 2345 (14 Aug 1800) (NLW)
[131] Clive Mss and Papers (2nd Series) B Letters No 2346 (19 Aug 1800) (NLW)
[132] W. J. Wilson, *History of the Madras Army* vol 3 (1883) 37-44

Mark Cubbon

Mark's first experience of Madras was much the same as his uncle's nearly twenty years before. The artificial harbour had still not been built so he, too, transferred to a massula boat that carried him more-or-less to the shore.

It was essential that a cadet join his regiment as soon as possible after arriving in India because his seniority and pay began only when he had done so. Mark's commission was signed by the Rt Hon Edward Lord Clive on 9 March 1802: it appointed Mr Cubbon, Gentleman, to be Lieutenant in the 5th Madras Native Infantry from 20 July 1801 when he was aged 15 years 11 months. Later he was to receive a second commission, from Geo. Hewett, Lt General, Commander-in-Chief of all King's and Company's Forces in the Indies, which appointed him Lieutenant in the King's Army from 20th July 1801 — but signed on 7 March 1811.[133]

In 1800 there were eighteen Regiments of Madras Native Infantry, each with two battalions. Mark's battalion, 1st Bn 5th MNI had been raised in 1759 and seen action at Sholighur 1781, the Carnatic 1788-91, and Mysore 1788-91. Its Sepoys wore tight white drawers and red coats, with black facings. The uniform of British and Indian Officers consisted of loose white trousers and red coats, with black facings and gold lace. Later the Sepoys were issued with the same kind of white trousers as their Officers.[134] In those days an Infantry battalion was much bigger than today: 1042 fighting men including 22 European and 20 Indian Officers, together with a band, 160 boy recruits and 20 water-carriers.[135]

Inevitably, questions arise about Mark's training for a career in an Indian Army. The first requirement of a young officer was that he should acquire a sound knowledge of Hindustani, the lingua franca of the Company's armies. We may be sure that Uncle Wilks had encouraged Mark to study the language assiduously during the voyage so that he needed mainly practice to secure a working knowledge. Once in Madras this was facilitated by daily exercises with the ubiquitous Munshi — four hours a day, transcribing Hindustani into English and back again.

Much had to be done before actual military training could begin: measurements and fittings for uniforms, and essential equipment to be obtained. The latter was wholly practical: already he had a camp cot with bedding and pillows, but he needed a mosquito net, and water containers to take the legs of the cot — to prevent nocturnal visits by those vicious little red ants, and there was a folding camp table, a more-or-less easy chair, and a brass wash-basin on a tripod stand. Finally, a horse had to be secured. The going rate for a country-bred animal, suitable for a junior subaltern, was perhaps Rs200, but later evidence suggests that Mark spent rather more than that. No doubt his

---

[133] MNHL MD 436 27/1
[134] Boris Mollo, *The Indian Army* 14, 29-35
[135] W. J. Wilson, *History of the Madras Army* vol 2 (1882) 290-1, vol 3 86

first time astride a horse, since leaving his own mare in the Isle of Man, was pure bliss!

Having attended to all of these things, Mark was in a fit and proper state to report to his temporary Commanding Officer who would arrange for his preliminary military training as a subaltern of infantry. Since 1798, cadets of the Company's ordnance branch had been trained through the ten specially-provided places at the Military Academy, Woolwich. Cadets destined for other branches, including the infantry, went directly to India without any preliminary training – except for what establishments like Mr Macfarlane's school could provide.[136] Basic training was therefore necessary. Mark was posted temporarily to a regiment of Native Infantry quartered near Madras, probably at Pallavaram, about 30 km from Fort St George, where a cantonment had been established some twenty-five years earlier. Pallavaram was a medium-sized cantonment, able to accommodate four infantry regiments. It was unpleasantly hot because a hill some 150 m high between it and the coast cut off any cooling sea-breezes.[137] Training was supervised by the Adjutant. It began with about a month devoted to foot-drill, followed by instruction in minor tactics, musketry, and regimental paper-work. It was not all work for there was the possibility of a gallop morning and evening, and of shooting small game such as partridge, hare and snipe. Important sites within the region could also be visited, such as the complex of monolithic temples and rock-carvings, dating from the 7th century, at Mahaballipuram some 80 km south of Madras. To young Lt Cubbon's eyes they must have seemed wonderful, as indeed they are. After several months of training Mark was posted away to his own battalion, 1/5 MNI, which was stationed at Sankery Droog, under the command of Lt-Col Alex Cuppage.

These activities had been planned by Uncle Wilks, who wrote about them, and other matters, from Fort St George on 28 December 1801 to his brother James in Ramsey

> The departure of Lord Clive will produce some changes in my plans in this country – the history of the transactions which have led to this determination is too extensive for a letter, and would scarcely be intelligible without a knowledge of the characters – in relation to myself it amounts to the impossibility of my desiring to be confidentially employed by his Lordship's successor… It is probable that my future residence will be in Mysoor a climate more congenial than this to my constitution. Mark Cubbon has had a slight attack of a bowel complaint from which he has perfectly recovered. I will shortly send him off to join his corps, at least as well equipped as his neighbours – my accounts of him continue to be good and I shall hope that the protection under which he will require at his age to be placed and which I have provided for him in his Lt Col

---

[136] T.A. Heathcote, *The Indian Army* 130

[137] L. F. Rushbrook Williams (ed), *A Handbook for Travellers in India, Pakistan, Nepal, Bangladesh and Sri Lanka* (22nd ed London 1975) 509

will hereafter make him good for something. I am with love to your fireside and that at Maughold Head ever affectionately yours.[138]

Wilks's letter of 28 December has an addition, written on 17 February 1802

> You will see from the date of the above that it was intended for an opportunity which sailed without it – from the Malabar Coasts: I found after I had written it that the ships would not remain a sufficient time for my letter to cross the Peninsula – Since that period Lord Clive had made his public Declaration to resign the Government [and] had transmitted his actual resignation to the Court of Directors, and was within three days of actual embarkation for Europe: when the Private Secretary of Lord Wellesley arrived post on the special mission to prevail on his Lordship to remain until the Government at home should have provided for the contingency of his resignation: this case was made on public grounds which rendered it irresistible and his Lordship now awaits for his successor, or at farthest till January 1803. Till that period I shall probably remain as at present Private Secretary to Lord Clive – Town Major of Fort St George, and Barrack Master of the Presidency Division, constituting altogether the best situation in his Lordship's gift.[139]

There were good reasons why Mornington did not want a political vacuum in the southern Presidency. By now Fort St George controlled extensive territories and considerable wealth. Capt Colin Mackenzie's survey had reached a 'Rough Estimate of the British Dominions in India in January 1802 by Concession or Conquest according to the latest treaties' at 272,800 sq km. In fact, this was the Company's territory in the India Peninsula alone.[140] Moreover, the Madras Government's annual receipts exceeded Rs490 million, with the largest contributions coming from land revenues, payments from the Nawab of the Carnatic and the Maharajah of Mysore, and profits on trading. The surplus in 1801 was Rs852,000.[141] Clearly, management of this estate was not a task for prentice hand. In the event Lord Clive stayed on for eighteen months before being replaced by Lord William Bentinck, who came ashore at Fort St George on 30 August 1803.

In November 1801 an intriguing task came Capt Wilks's way. He served as secretary of a highly confidential 'examination' into the conduct of the Company's Resident in Hyderabad, Major James Archilles Kirkpatrick, carried out by Lord Clive on the instructions of the Governor-General. Only Clive and

---

[138] Wilks Papers vol 1 (BL Ms Coll Add Ms 57313) letter 6
[139] *ibid*
[140] Clive Mss and Papers (2nd Series) A Mss. Rough Estimate of British Dominions in India (NLW Mss No 1044, Jan 1802)
[141] Clive Mss and Papers (2nd Series) A Mss. Comparative Statement of Receipts and Disbursements of the Madras Government 30.4.1800-1.5.1801. (NLW Mss No 383)

Wilks were present when evidence was being taken under oath from the main witnesses.[142]

About this time also, Wilks received an interesting letter from Arthur Wellesley

> I have been to the palace to visit the [Tipu's] ladies and I find they look forward to a residence with their sons [in Vellore] separate from the other women as a source of so much happiness to them, that it would be worse than improper to separate them from their sons even for a short time.[143]

Late in 1801 Capt Wilks had been appointed Town Major of Madras. He was permitted to retain the post of Barrack Master but resigned as Military Secretary to Lord Clive. The change gave him a handsome addition to his income. There was also good news from home: Harriot's malady, which had given her so much dreadful pain, had been diagnosed as small kidney stones passing to the bladder – renal colic in fact. Treatment had followed diagnosis and she was almost free from pain by May 1802. Preparations were in hand for her to return to India, leaving England in August. Meanwhile, as she told James Wilks in Ramsey

> I am ordered to drink the Tunbridge water and shall spend as much time there as my preparations for my voyage will allow me ... My children are, by your Brother's desire, to be left in the care of Mrs Hume, a friend of ours who is lately returned to England. She is a very amiable woman and the mother of a large family – I lived two years in her house before I was married. Barry [aged 3 years] is ... at a preparatory school ... where two of Mrs Hume's sons also are – I prefer this to his being left in here in a house with only little Girls – he is a fine, manly little creature and I would have him continue so.[144]

By this time a new route from Britain was available: by ship to Egypt, overland to Suez, and thence by ship to Madras. Harriot probably took this quicker 'overland route' in preference to going around the Cape.

Ever since he left England Capt Wilks had paid attention to affairs at home. The principal of the purchase money for Ballafletcher had been paid off by December 1801, and Mark hoped that the accumulated interest and a loan from Major John Taubman could be discharged using the rent obtained from the farm. There were other calls on his purse, as shown by a letter to brother James on 6 September 1803 following the death of sister Deborah's husband

> I have received yours of 13th of April. The first thing to be done is to provide for the future comfort of our sister: the girls having been kindly taken care of by

---

[142] William Dalrymple, *White Mughals* (London, 2002) 3-7
[143] Wellington, 2nd Duke (ed), *Supplementary Despatches, Correspondence and Memoranda of F.M. the Duke of Wellington* (London 1858-64) Vol 2 385.
[144] Wilks Papers vol 1 (BL Ms Coll Add Ms 57313) letter 21

Mr R. Gelling and Mrs Moore. I shall consider the care of the widow to belong exclusively to myself. I beg you to communicate this intention to Mr Gelling and Mrs Moore and express to them the high sense I entertain of the affection and liberality of their conduct....I remit to Major Taubman by this opportunity £700 with the following instructions.

1st To desire the Douglas bank to discount £50 of this sum and pay it <u>immediately</u> to Mrs Richard Gelling.

2d To pay off the balance due by me on account of Balla Fletcher & to get Mr Stowell to cancel it in form.

3d To pay the remainder whatever it may be to you.

The object of this is thus – I intended that the rents of Balla Fletcher should enable you to clear off the debt of £350 which you have incurred on account of the brewery, but the balance which on a settlement of account appeared to be still due to the Major prevented this arrangement from being of use...I conclude that after paying <u>immediately</u> to Mrs Gelling £50 and clearing off the mortgage there will remain more than £350 to enable you to discharge the mortgage on the brewery.....I shall be obliged to you for the information you allude to regarding Ballabroie, and the detail by which a transfer or sale made here would be valid there...Harriot is delicate but not more so than in England, the misfortune of a miscarriage which has always been serious with her, has increased the tendency to be delicate.[145]

There is much more about how to assist Deborah and their brother Thomas, all of which reveals Mark's abiding sense of responsibility for his family.

In August 1803, after some months of regimental duty, Lt Cubbon was given his first independent command, comprising a small detachment at Hooly Onoor. His uncle told James about it in the letter of 6 September, part of which is given above.

Mark Cubbon is well and commanding a small post of communication with a few native troops. He is acquitting himself well and the situation will render him manly and habituated to think and act for himself. He also gives me a good account of his progress in the language – having no white faces along with him he can scarcely fail.[146]

One can visualize the young subaltern coming to know his men: how they saw the world, the matters that troubled them, their relationships with families at home in their villages, and the various interactions between groups in the detachment. In all these matters he would be guided by the Jemadar and senior Indian NCOs who were part of his small force. At that time Mark was rising eighteen years old and had been commissioned a mere two years before. Here is an example of a gift that India conferred upon those who served her – responsibility at an early age.

---

[145] Wilks Papers vol 1 (BL Ms Coll Add Ms 57313) letter 23
[146] *ibid*

Mark learnt more than Hindustani and the techniques of command. Removed from large town or cantonment he was brought into close touch with rural India. Perhaps for the first time he saw the beauty of the slow dawn of each day, and the rapid coming of night with no preceding twilight. Sunrise and nightfall brought flights of bright green arrows passing overhead as flocks of rose-ringed parakeets made their way to and from their feeding-grounds – often the villagers' crops and orchards.

An important task of the detachment was to represent the Company Bahadur in the countryside – to show the flag. This entailed riding to villages in the district, talking with members of their panchayats, and taking the pulse of the communities. In the process Mark learned much about life in the villages that were the heart of Indian society. During the more prolonged of these tours he and his escort would live under canvas, or he would possibly stay in the village rest-house. In either case he could observe the daily routine of the village from a very early rising to their retiring at about nine at night. There were leisurely discussions about crops, cattle, prices and the like, held either in the open or its near-equivalent – the koodam or wall-less outer hall of a well-to-do villager's house. These meetings usually took place after the midday meal when the men would take their ease and chew pan to aid their digestions.

He was also able to learn something about the intricate structure of the village community. According to Pandian a large village had representatives of sixteen trades and eight professions, and possessed several public officials including a magistrate and a watchman. Some tradesmen, like the carpenter and blacksmith, were familiar from the Isle of Man but others had no direct equivalent – the oil-presser and the potter for example. Probably the most ubiquitous tradesmen were the carpenter, blacksmith, and the dhobi or washerman. The main task of the dhobi, and of his wife, is obvious. But he did more than wash clothes. He provided sheets of cloth to decorate the roof of marriage pavilions, and he used the rags from worn-out clothes (which were his perquisites) to make torches for use during festivals and marriage processions. Part of the carpenter's work was familiar enough, such as forming rafters, door-posts and bed-frames. In addition he fashioned images for various purposes, spoons, and the wooden parts of agricultural implements such as ploughs. At this point his work interacted with that of the blacksmith, who made and repaired plough-blades and hoes, together with axes, knives, hinges and locks.

Mark observed also the toty or sweeper, the most menial servant of the village, who worked under direct control of the watchman. He swept the communal areas, fed cattle in the pound, carried letters, and undertook other minor tasks. For all these he received nominal payment from the government and a small annual sum from the villagers. He was, of course, a member of the 'backward classes' and, as such, was unable to enter the villagers' houses or go personally to the village well lest his presence cause pollution. Indeed, Mark may have heard a thirsty toty calling for water, which some compassionate villager would pour into the man's cupped hands.

Then there was the kavalkar or village watchman. Being at some distance from one another, and internally fragmented by divisions of caste, the villages were easy game for the petty thief, or the dacoit bent upon more serious crime. Consequently, every village employed one or more watchmen to protect lives and property. He did not wear a uniform, but carried a staff of office nearly three metres long. Several times each night he made a round of the village and visited the cultivated fields. Every householder made a contribution toward his wage, in the form of grain and money. The post was often hereditary within a family and doubtless certain tricks were passed on. Certainly the office carried with it an opportunity for extortion so that villagers were careful not to offend their watchman, while having little respect for him.[147]

Mark Wilks in Mysore

In June 1803 Mark Wilks resigned his post as Town Major and applied to join the army in the field under command of Lt Gen James Stuart, with whom he had served in the war of 1790-92 and who now requested his services. Higher authorities decreed otherwise however, for he was posted to Mysore City. Barry Close had been Resident in Mysore from 1799 until 1801 when he was sent as Resident to Poona. He was succeeded briefly by Josiah Webbe and then by another of the great men of British India, John Malcolm. For much of his tenure, however, Malcolm led a peripatetic existence as he was moved about the country on various special missions. At the beginning of 1805 he took up the post of Resident for what he hoped would be an extended period, but in March was called to Calcutta before being sent on a mission to Sindia of Gwalior. In April 1807 he returned to Mysore and stayed long enough to marry Miss Charlotte Campbell in August!

From 1803 to 1808 Major Wilks was Acting Resident – officially called Political Resident – and worked closely with Diwan Purneah. Malcolm himself described the situation in a letter of 1807,

> ... all communications with this State are conducted through the Resident, whose duty it is to aid with his advice without interfering with the management of the country. The connexion between Mysore and the British Government owes much to the ability and integrity of Sir A. Wellesley, Col Close, the late Mr Webbe, and Major Wilks whose talents have been successfully employed in its improvement and cultivation.[148]

In addition to his responsibilities for Mysore Major Wilks had the task of regulating relations with the Rajah of Coorg.

In Mysore he set about some material developments that remain today. One such was to begin building a new Residency in place of Arthur Wellesley's

---

[147] T. B. Pandian, *Indian Village Folk: their Works & Ways* (London 1898)
[148] J. W. Kaye, *Life and Correspondence of Maj Gen Sir John Malcolm* (London 1856) 381 footnote.

simple house of 1799. The result, now called 'Government House', is an elegant building having an open central courtyard separated by columns from a surrounding arcade. At the north end of the house is a large projecting portico designed to provide shelter for a horse and carriage, and this opens into the drawing-room. To the south, on the ground floor, is a three-bayed banqueting hall – the largest room in South India – which has a ball-room beyond it. Immediately about the house is a formal garden, and the whole is surrounded by an extensive park that initially extended to about forty hectares.[149]

Some essentials of life were unavailable in Mysore so that, on 24 March 1804, Mark Wilks found it necessary to seek the help from Madras

> My dearest Agnew –
> If the Cooley with the books has not left Madras, when this letter reaches you, I wish you to execute another commission for me, and as it is one quite in your way I expect that you will do it handsomely. You must send me a wig not of your own formation, but that of the best Knight of the Comb with whom you are acquainted. I do not know how to measure my head but I recollect that it is rather larger (and probably thicker) than yours – I enclose a lock to shew the colour – my hair has fallen off so much that I have been obliged to cut it short, yet it continues to fall off and very soon will save me the necessity of shaving my head, which I am advised to do as the only means of recovering it. The Wig is Wilks's Whim, & if the Cooley has set off you must send another with Wig by itself. Wig or there will be no possibility of pacifying him. I imagine you will find great store in Mr Collins's shop......We proceed on our journey tomorrow toward Seringapatam where General Wellesley is hourly expected – Malcolm is gone or going to the Coast in search of health, and talks of returning to Mysoor. I shall be very well pleased when he arrives and leaves us at liberty to revisit Nundy. God bless you my dear Agnew, give my love to Margaret & my brother
> ever your affectionate
> M. Wilks[150]

Mark Cubbon's Progress

In June 1804 Mark Cubbon had his first bad bout of fever and, like sufferers before and since, passed from symptom to symptom while wondering what would come next. He received some consolation, however, in the form of a gift of Rs250 – possibly because Uncle Wilks knew what was in the wind and wanted him to be out of debt. He arranged also for his trusted factotum, Rama Sawmey, to deliver a compass as requested. Mark was eager to improve his surveying skills and had asked for a theodolite as well– which was more difficult to provide.[151]

By 9 July from Wilks in Mysore had good news for his nephew

---

[149] T. P. Issar, *The Royal City*. (Bangalore 1991) 54-5
[150] BL Wilks Papers vol 1 (BL Ms Coll Add Ms 57313) letter 27
[151] Letters from Col Mark Wilks FRS to his nephew Lieut Mark Cubbon. (CKS U1287 C95) letter of 26 Jun 1804

> I have good reason to believe that you are by this time appointed Adjutant of the 2ᵈ Bn 5ᵗʰ Regᵗ in the room of Lieut Marriot promoted. I give you this intimation in order that you may be making your little arrangements, but however certain I consider the event, it is always most prudent to say nothing on a subject of this nature until it appears in orders.
> I can give you an introduction to your new Commandant which may be useful. When you join, complete all your little equipments and let me know how you stand, in order that I may take the charge of your starting quite clear in your new career. Ever affectionately yours,[152]

At this point, there are a few jotted notes, and Wilks then proceeded to mention a matter that seems to have worried him – and apparently using a new pen.

> Adverting to your late letter to me on the subject of the late transaction at Nuggur, I hope you are more guarded in your conversation and still more in your correspondence with others, free opinions unfavourable to the personal character are more apt than you may imagine to be noticed in a way that is injurious to their author. With regard to the opinions themselves I recommend to you for some years to come to hold a guard over forming very strong ones two general propositions
> 1ˢᵗ That <u>opinions</u> are in their very nature fallible, and
> 2ᵈ That it is more probable you should form an erroneous judgement than that an Officer of high character should do a very foolish or very criminal thing. … even with these guards in forming your opinions, I would still most urgently recommend another general rule – viz to speak and to write freely when you have anything favourable to say – But when your opinion on a character is unfavourable <u>to be silent</u>.
> You may believe me that an observance of these cautions will obviate more uneasiness and secure more real comfort and satisfaction in your progress through life than all other prudential axioms put together.
> You will never hear from me prudential motives merely as such placed in a very high rank (sic). – but those which I now suggest to you are direct corollaries from the purest principles of morality.[153]

Sure enough, next month the young man was appointed adjutant of the 2ⁿᵈ battalion of his regiment. The new appointment had come through while Mark was still at Hooly Onoor. He and his uncle, who was in Mysore City, had hoped to meet in Seringapatam, but this would have meant a detour of 320 km and therefore was not feasible. However, to ease the young man on his way, Uncle Wilks despatched two drivers with eleven bullocks, eight coolies, and a tent! And he invited 'any further commissions' saying that the excellent Rama Sawmy would execute them.

---

[152] MNHL MD 436 26/- (this folio contains a large number of letters)
[153] *ibid*

But where precisely was 2/5 MNI? It had been at Hyderabad, but was it there still? So Mark wrote to Col Agnew and received a prompt and succinct reply

> I advise your proceeding without delay to Bellary where you will either meet your Corps, or ascertain the directions of its march so as to join it. The corps left Hyderabad some time since, and has been ordered to march on Bellary.[154]

By January 1805 Lt Cubbon had been with his new battalion for some time, and was working hard to master the duties of adjutant. The countryside about Bellary is a plain, but nearby are two of the barren, rocky hills that are characteristic of the Deccan. Fort Hill (150 m above the level of the plain) had been extensively fortified over many years. In Mark's time there were upper and lower systems: a citadel around the summit with supporting lines of defences outside it, and a lower fort on the eastern side of the hill. The two forts were connected by a single winding path. Just outside the citadel were deep tanks for holding water. The town of Bellary was also on the eastern side of Fort Hill, but the cantonment – Mark's home – lay to the west of it.

His work apart, the cantonment was not calculated to stimulate the intellect. He had time for reading, however, and asked his uncle about some books. The response, written from Mysoor on 13th January 1805, was characteristic

> My dear Mark,
> I have your letter dated the 6th and shall no longer postpone sending you a few books.
>
> | | |
> |---|---|
> | Buffon | 15 vols octavo |
> | Arrian | 2 |
> | Montesquieu | 2 |
> | Glenz, State of Europe | 1 the best performance extant. |

These are not exactly the sort of books you desired with the exception of the first. Arrian if you have not read him will instruct and amuse you. Montesquieu in spite of his having been most unjustly stigmatized as the first mover of revolutionary principles in France, goes to the bottom of his subject, and you have only to guard occasionally against his systematizing too much – I doubt particularly all his facts regarding the unequal births of males and females, on which he theorizes: the polygamy of Mohammedans and the plurality of husbands among the Nairs.

I have not here any book on metaphysics, but in toping over my old papers I lately found a Persian exercise which I have bound and sent. It is a curious specimen of the literature of the 13th century in Persia: in its parade of enumerating all the sciences with which it has nothing to do, it resembles the practices of European authors very long after the revival of literature – but where the law of the Koran does not deter the author and force him to take refuge in obscurity I do not know that he has been exceeded in acuteness by any metaphysician from his own day till the present....

---

[154] MNHL MD 436 26/1

You do not tell me whether you are doing anything at Persian. You see there is in it more matter for investigation than you perhaps suspected it to contain … I have had a severe attack of dysentry – but am better. Mrs W. had not arrived when the overland despatch left England…The books go off tomorrow.[155]

Young Mark must have come to grips immediately with the books, because on 22nd January Uncle Wilks wrote

I have your's of the 18th
You need not be afraid of the exercise, it is *from* Persian into the plainest English that such a subject admits…I sincerely mourn with you over the state of intellect in your vicinity. You will not suspect me of insincerity, however you arraign my partiality in ranking your own understanding in a very high class: and I am proportionately anxious that you should come into contact with kindred minds….
The quantity [sic] of mind which one finds in rather the best society in this country is but sparingly distributed, and exclusive of other considerations I should on that account alone be delighted if the routine of the service should bring you this way.
        Ever most affectionately yours

PS. Tell me in due time how you like Montesquieu – it is a great object to read such books as you relish – disquisitions which have few charms now may be more agreeable hereafter. If you have not seen Adam Smith: Wealth of Nations I recommend to you to *try* whether it is one of the subjects that interest you but do not force within your judgement or your taste. You will derive most knowledge from works which you read *con amore*.[156]

Clearly, Uncle Wilks was pleased with his nephew's progress for he wrote to the Rev Thomas Cubbon on 31 July 1805

My Dear Brother,
Mark's character is now sufficiently formed to enable me to speak of it with considerable confidence, and you and his mother may rest assured that if he is spared to his friends he will do credit to them all.…He has not neglected the improvement of his mind that his opportunities have admitted. He possesses a degree of steady sound judgement not common at his years…with straightforward honorable principles…his conduct comes up to my best expectations.
With best love to my sister and your fireside, believe me always
            Your affectionate
            M. Wilks[157]

---

[155] MNHL MD 436 26/-
[156] MNHL MD 436 26/-
[157] MNHL MD 436 24/6

On 24 July young Mark, in Camp at Bellary had reported to his father in different terms which, however, conveyed a similar confident message

> My Dearest Father,
> I have received your letter of 14 January. I am ashamed and very distressed at the anxiety which my silence has occasioned…and am determined to allow no ship to sail without writing to you or my good Mother.
> That the war has created great distress in the Island is no matter of wonder, but we are engaged in a just and necessary war and with Mr Pitt at our head can feel confident of rising superior to all opposition…and should we have to fight for India on Indian ground against any European Power, we shall prove that this Empire is not to be shaken.
> I have been Adjutant of the 2nd Bn 5th N.I. for about a year, and am in hopes of getting some good appointment in a year or two more, and it is probable I shall be a Captain in four years more if not in three. Whenever I am able I will certainly take a trip to the Island to see you – please God I will be in the Island in six years more.
> In your next letter I hope to hear from you how your finances stand because should you be in the least want, I will have the greatest pleasure in sending you what will enable you to get on very comfortably. If I get a situation on the Staff I will continue to send you 2 or 300 pounds every year which in the Island will save you a great deal of trouble.
> Major Wilks is in good spirits and acting Resident in Seringapatam…his character stands one of the first in the country for abilities and integrity. I have found him a second father and look upon him with veneration. He has loaded me with favors since I arrived in India.
> I have been in good health for these three years. I am now 5 ft 10 ½ inches in height and I dare say will be 6 feet soon. The climate agrees with my constitution remarkably well, and I hardly feel the heat when other officers are broiling.
> The Marquis Cornwallis has arrived in India much to the regret of the Army. We had many famous prospects under the Marquis of Wellesley who proposed to make a large addition to the Madras Army. Peace is made with the Mahrattas, but good or bad I cannot say; indeed no authentic intelligence has yet arrived regarding the Peace.
> You would be astonished to see the great number of servants we are obliged to keep, no man will perform two offices, you must have one to take care of your clothes, one to clean your shoes…two men to every horse. I have now about 30 servants as I keep 4 horses each worth £100, one of which I shall sell and send you the money. The servants' wages amount to half an officers' pay and the other half does not go far when Europe (sic) articles are required….
> A Sepoy battalion would be a fine sight in England. There is a European officer to each Company. The Sepoys are better behaved, more orderly and better disciplined than any Europeans in India, and just as good soldiers also, they have a wonderful affection for their officers and will follow wherever they lead…
> They will advance after being many times repulsed … They are all pre-destinarians, which is the most excellent doctrine for a soldier, and their steadiness in battle proceeds in great degree from that cause.

> I was engaged in no scene of action in the late War, and have no prospects of seeing any fighting.
> This battalion is considered the best disciplined on the coast and Gen Sir John Cradock told us on our own parade that we should take the field if a new War broke out; this was a very high compliment...
> How is Mr Maddrell getting on? I wish he had taken more pains to thrash latin into me than he did, there is no place where a fine education is respected so much as in India.
> I have lost the greatest part of my Manx. I expect you will send me through Mrs Wilks some Manx books and all the old ballads you can collect; also a Bible and prayer book.
> The failure of the herring fishing is a bad thing for the poor people of the Island, the next year will I trust make up for it.
> [There is much more about mutual acquaintences].
> I remain, my Dearest Father,
> Yrs. most affectionately
> M. Cubbon[158]

This letter reveals much about the twenty-year-old Mark. Among other things, there was his immense optimism, and that pride and confidence in his men that is essential for a European who aspires to be a successful leader of non-European troops.

The 'late war' that Mark mentioned was a conflict between the two, fundamentally incompatible, powers remaining in South India: the Company and the Marathas. It began partly as a result of inter-clan feuding within the Maratha Confederation and partly from Mornington's misunderstanding of the way that Confederation was organized.

The Maratha Confederation was a loose association of five great families: relevant here are those of the Bhonsla, Holkar, Sindia, and the Peshwa or hereditary Chief Minister in Poona. Mornington saw the Peshwa as the supreme authority and assumed that control of him would secure control of the Confederation as a whole; but by 1800 the Peshwa was the least powerful figure among the Marathas.

A feature of the Confederation was the way its various parts fell into antagonism against one another. Latterly this had taken the form of a contest between the other Princes for control of the Peshwa; and in 1801 Sindia reached an accommodation with him. Perhaps counting on this measure of security the Peshwa committed a series of vicious crimes that alienated Holkar. As a result, on 25 October 1802 the Battle of Poona was fought: Holkar won a resounding victory over Sindia and the Peshwa, and installed a puppet Chief Minister. In desperation the Peshwa took refuge with the Company at Bassein where, on 31 December 1802, he accepted a subsidiary treaty as an outcome of negotiations with Col Close. This envisaged his reinstatement to office in return to agreeing to pay for a force of at least six of the Company's battalions to be

---

[158] MNHL MD 436 25/5

stationed within his territories, to exclude from his service all members of European nations hostile to Great Britain – notably the French – and to abstain from negotiations or hostilities with other states except in consultation with the Company. Thus the treaty effectively separated him from the other Maratha leaders.

Restoration of the Peshwa was now undertaken. By a series of forced marches over some 800 km Maj Gen Wellesley reached Poona, forced Holkar to retreat northwards and, on 13 May 1803, reinstated the former Peshwa. This campaign contrasted sharply with Harris's march on Seringapatam four years before: needless people or comforts were rigorously excluded, close attention was given to the supply lines which included employing many of the 'trotting bullocks' from Tipu's stud, and excellent arrangements were made for both gathering intelligence and carrying information. The future Duke recorded his appreciation

> In consequence of the regularity of the system of government established by the Diwan in Mysore, and the improvements in the country, its resources enabled him to provide for all the calls made upon him. The supplies were furnished with a facility and celerity hitherto unknown in this part of India.[159]

Once restored, the Peshwa regretted the treaty that made him dependent upon the Company, while the other Maratha Princes were angered by both the treaty itself and the presence of Company's troops at Poona. Sindia and the Bhonsla took up the challenge in the south, but were comprehensively defeated by Arthur Wellesley at Ahmadnagar (12 August 1803), Assaye (23 September) – where his 5800 men overthrew 40,000 with 102 guns, Argaum (29 November) – and by capturing the hill-fort of Gawilgarh (15 December). Both Princes were brought to accept subsidiary treaties in December 1803 on instructions from the Governor-General, and despite protests from Arthur Wellesley, who saw them as conflicting with the 'scrupulous good faith' that he believed essential to upholding the Company's position in India. In the north, the Company's fortunes were mixed but, by April 1805, treaties had been signed. An outcome of the conflict was to turn many members of the Maratha armies into masterless men who, as we shall see, would bring misery to the Deccan. This was foreseen by John Malcolm who stressed in his 'Hints for a memorandum on the present state of India' (6 April 1804) the importance of employing (in the forces of the Company or Mysore) as many as possible of the bands of irregular horse such as had served lately with General Wellesley because 'it will at once reduce the number of "plunderers" and help to suppress the remaining "plunderers"'.[160]

---

[159] Gurwood, Lt Col (ed), *Selections from Despatches and General Orders of Field Marshal the Duke of Wellington*. (London, 1841) Extract No 173

[160] Clive Mss and Papers (2nd Series) A Mss (NLW Mss No 1818)

Mark Cubbon may not have served with Arthur Wellesley but, arguably, learnt much from him. At that time it was clear that the British were becoming the dominant power in India. How should Indians be governed by the new power? The Governor-General and his brother held different views on the subject. As Philips has pointed out, Arthur and those around him had become aware of their own minuteness within Indian society, and had come to the conclusion that a power which could not work through the existing institutions of that society must prove destructive so that despotism would be the outcome.[161] Consequently, as we have noted above, he warmly commended the new government of Mysore for providing the supplies that had made his campaigns possible; and in a letter of March 1804 to Malcolm he revealed the very core of his ideas for the government of India

> I would sacrifice Gwalior [Sindia's country] or every frontier of India, ten times over, in order to preserve our credit for scrupulous good faith....What brought me through many difficulties in the war, and the negotiations for peace? The British good faith and nothing else.[162]

In due course Mark was to apply that principle in the State for which he became responsible.

War with the Marathas brought about a change in the government of the Company's territories – a change in both personnel and direction. The Governor-General had pursued a 'forward policy', which involved going to war with both Tipu and the Marathas in five years. Wars cost money, and he had taken bullion from ships of the Company's China Fleet in order to support his forces. Both the Board of Control and the Directors were distressed to see the Company's profits disappearing through the barrels of their soldiers' muskets. They were alarmed by the rapid increase in the Company's debt. They doubted their own abilities to manage their new territories profitably. Closer at hand they saw a growing threat from Napoleon I, whose position had been consolidated by victories at Ulm, Austerlitz and Jena.

In mid-1805 Mornington was recalled and a retreat from his 'forward policy' ordered. Arthur, exhausted by continuous campaigning, had already left India in March of the year; but his correspondence shows that he did not forget his friends in South India, particularly John Malcolm and Mark Wilks.

---

[161] C. H. Philips, *Young Wellington in India*. 36.
[162] Gurwood, Lt Col (Edit), *Selections from Despatches and General Orders of Field Marshal the Duke of Wellington*. Extract No 176

CHAPTER EIGHT

Together with a Government Adrift
1805 – 1808

To Mornington's place as Governor-General came the Marquis Cornwallis, now sixty-seven years old and in indifferent health; but one who, as a soldier, would follow the orders given him by Government and Company. On 19 August 1805 Major Wilks, in Goomnaigpolliam, replied to his nephew's enquiry saying that the recent change of government was too delicate to write about but that he was 'sorry to see the new reign commence by disabling us for ever before peace is made.'[163]

Cornwallis was not long in post. On 5 October 1805 he died at Ghazipur, some 80 km west of Patna, and was buried there. His place was filled by Sir George Barlow, with consequences that will be seen later.

Back in Mysore, Uncle Wilks wrote to Mark on 9 November

> I am glad to hear that you keep...clear of the rage of gambling of every description. Once, pretty early in my career I had such a lesson – I possessed a few hundred Pagodas in cash and in horses, and I lost to the last Pagoda that I could possibly pay and had the firmness to resist the liberal offers of lending which assailed me from all sides of the table...How comes on the Hindustanee? And the Persian? In the former I fancy you must now be a good practical scholar: have you looked into the latter? You will find the beauties of its poetry amply to repay your labour after getting on a little.[164]

Mark's period of comparatively good health ended with 1805, and on 4 February 1806 Uncle Wilks wrote

> I am grieved at the account you give me of your health. I have talked over the case with Doctor Ingledene and he concurs with me in the opinion that you ought as soon as possible to quit Bellary provided your medical adviser on the spot concurs in the necessity or propriety of the measure. The approaching [hot] season is oppressive everywhere but worse at Bellary than almost anywhere else...with your complication of disorders and misadventures your constitution may be ruined for ever if you can not get away for a while...[In Mysore] Dr Ingledene and your old friend Rama Sawmey would soon set you on your legs. Show this letter, with my best remembrances, to Col Martin who I am sure would be happy to facilitate your views, and peace being now concluded with

---

[163] MNHL MD 436 26/- (Folio contains originals of many letters to Cubbon, mainly from Wilks)
[164] CKS U 1287 C95, Letter 3

both Sindia and Holkar you can have no scruples about being absent from your Corps…You will, of course, draw upon me if you have any wants.[165]

Quite quickly, however, young Mark's health took a decided turn for the better, so that Wilks could write on 13 February

> You will readily conceive the gratification which I derived from your letter dated 4th after the unpleasant history contained in your former. I think you will do well to reconsider your project of a visit in July when the climate of Bellary is as good as this in favour of a change at the present season when we have so much the advantage of you. Capt Durand seems to think that you are diffident regarding your attainments in the Persian language; but however this may be you need not have the least apprehension of my looking grave on that subject, on the history of your misadventures or on any other. Very early in the day I certainly had some doubts how you would turn out, but I have long been entirely satisfied that your principles and dispositions are radically of the right breed. [several pages of a philosophical nature follow before a practical matter is reached.] The Arab horses which you heard of were sent to me by Bruce and Fawcett of Bombay, as stallions to be distributed in Mysoor. They are in such miserable condition that it is as yet difficult to say how they will turn out. Some of them will certainly be fine horses. I particularly desired that they might not be tall. Horses of a decent size now cost as I understand from 1000 to 1200 rupees taking your chance of them as they land at Bombay, expenses from thence perhaps 200 more, and the probability is that not one in ten turning out exactly as you wish. I understand it is quite a science to know a fine horse when in the skin and bone state in which they usually arrive and the persons in Bombay who are initiates of the mystery make a profitable traffic of it. Any of your military friends from the subsidiary force visiting Bombay and knowing something of the matter would execute your commission cheaper than a house of agency. I can send you a credit on Bombay for your portion of the concern….I have personally a small account with [Bruce and Fawcett] which will enable me to manage your commission.[166]

On 20 February Uncle Wilks wrote again.

> I am happy to find by your letter of 15th that you continue to recover. The ships lately arrived at Madras bring me letters from Mrs Wilks as late as 28th September. [Since her health continued to give concern and she was pining for her children, Harriot had left India early in 1805.] She is still complaining, but I hope on the whole likely to improve in her health as soon as she has recovered from the effects of a hurried journey [to Bath] from Weymouth where she landed and of a cold which she caught in the pilot boat coming on shore. Of the children I have the best possible accounts. Laura reads and speaks French like a Parisian and dances like a little Parisot, she remembered her mother perfectly and from the moment of her arrival has never consented to leave her for a

---

[165] CKS U 1287 C95, Letter 3; also MNHL MD 436 26/- (part only)
[166] MNHL MD 436 26/-

moment excepting for the purpose of going to her masters. You know I fancy that she was during her mother's absence with our friend Mrs Hume and educated with her children. She never has been and never shall be at a boarding school, an establishment which seems to qualify young misses for being excellent mistresses, and very bad wives accordingly to accounts I have lately received of such seminaries. Barry is a sturdy, good humoured little fellow, uncommonly quick as you may imaging from his having at 6 ½ years old made progress in his Latin greater than his master thought proper to encourage. His mother says he reads English better than she does, in which account you will recognise the mother.

I have not done justice to Montesquieu in sending his work without reminding you of the terror under which he must have ventured even obliquely to plead the cause of liberty. Imagine to yourself the horrors of the bastille, and the secrets of that prison house haunting the imagination of the author, and you will be furnished with a clue for distinguishing between the genuine sentiments of the author and those with which he occasionally shields himself against the imputation of desiring to subvert the institutions of his country. As the subject seems to interest you I shall put into the next batch Beccaria's celebrated little work on crimes and punishments [The Marchese de Beccaria's *Dei delitti e delle pene* which denounced both torture and capital punishment]. You will probably have heard that the theory of this Italian Marquis [a country and a rank not the most favourable for the growth of good principles of government] was induced to practice by the late Emperor of Germany [Leopold II] when Archduke of Tuscany [1765-90] with entire success. In Mysoor where the establishments are not sufficiently regular to afford a fair trial, some of the principles have been tried, and answered for a time, but our lenity has brought us such an influx of thieves since they began to hang in the Company' territory, that I fear we shall be compelled to be as savage as our neighbours.

On Mysoor I shall also send you a memoir by a Major Wilks of the Madras establishment, printed by order of the Governor-General in Council without leave from the author. I do not wish to increase its publicity and had I foreseen the imprimatur would probably have kept it in my bureau. I have no objection to it being perused by Capt Marriot who I understand from Capt. Durand to be the associate of your studies – whenever you come to see me I shall be very happy if it be convenient for him to be your associate in that project also.[167]

Major Wilks had good reason to be pleased with much that was recorded in the memoir. In reorganizing Mysore, Diwan Purneah had sought to attach the population to the Maharajah's government, and had therefore engaged in the State's service at least one individual from every family of the military class. They had been paid half in money and half by a distribution of abandoned land. Their duties were essentially to secure the safety and security of their villages and districts. In making these arrangements Purneah had tried to respect ancient local usages – which would have gratified the Hindu population after years of Muslim rule. The revenue of the State had risen from Rs64.5 lakhs in 1799-1800 to Rs77 lakhs five years later. Debts had been cleared and there was

---

[167] MNHL MD 436 26/-

an accumulated surplus of Rs15 lakhs. Wilks himself strongly recommended centralizing all departments of government at Mysore City, not least to enhance the status of the Maharajah.[168]

Literature was not the only article provided by Uncle Wilks. On 3 March 1806 he wrote 'the accompanying contains the means of curing your horse if he is still alive and the best salastry in India has not mistaken his complaint from the description you give'.[169]

Three days later he mentioned the only serious misunderstanding to arise between himself and his nephew. It came about through a misrepresentation of a letter he had written to a Major Macpherras. After requesting from Macpherras such help as might be useful to a lad still of tender years, Wilks mentioned an imprudent tendency of Mark's to speak too freely in public. Wilks felt sure that maturity would cure the fault, but that if in the meantime Macpherras should detect it, he would be doing Mark a signal service by giving him some private advice. Unfortunately, someone in Macpherras's office had conveyed a twisted version of the letter to Mark.

In seeking to put the matter right, Wilks began with a gentle reminder that drew upon his nephew's military knowledge.

> An experienced officer in breaking in a young soldier or a young corps seeks to find a succession of slight affairs attended with certain success as exercise to qualify it for a hazardous enterprise. Your zealous friends have made a notable history of my letter to Major Macpherras [wherein I asked him] to exercise such good offices as might be useful to a boy scarcely emerged from his childhood, [because] I noticed a tendency which had sometimes alarmed me of your getting into scrapes ...namely that of speaking with too little reserve of facts, incidents and characters... Such is the substance of the communication which has been tortured to represent me as destitute of understanding as of feeling. These misrepresentations arise less frequently from malice than from error, and very often indeed from incapacity to understand a simple proposition...I exhort you to disbelieve the opinion of Col Agnew being in any respect inimical to you or adverse to your advancement. I will answer for his being next to myself the person in the whole service who will be most happy to contribute to your advancement. (I am) desirous of guarding you against officious friends and the consequent office of becoming your own tormentor...'a foolish friend is more dangerous than a powerful enemy.'[170]

By the beginning of the next month matters between the two men were back to normal, and young Mark was asking his uncle's opinion about the qualities needed for advancement. On 15 April Wilks replied

---

[168] Mark Wilks, *Administration of Mysore* (Fort William 1805, by Order of the Governor-General-in-Council)
[169] MNHL MD 436 26/-
[170] MNHL MD 436 26/-

> With the exception of one Department of the service which I shall presently notice, the fundamental qualifications seem to me to be nearly the same: professional knowledge necessarily stands first, embracing, of course a respectable tincture of history as well as the principles of the art. A mind well stored with useful knowledge of a general nature, and with all that relates to the history of our transactions in this country in particular seems to come next; such a mind is prepared to direct its powers to the successful execution of any duties with which it may be charged. But these qualifications aided by the most brilliant talents will be either inert, or depending on the efforts of others in this country without such a knowledge of the languages as renders their possessor capable of transacting business directly, and without the intervention or aid of a third person...
> I have made an exception above, and it relates to the Quarter Master General's Department which has become highly respectable and important and by fixing the staff of divisions, holds out a gradation of solid prospects in that line. In this and the Departments connected with it, a practical knowledge of surveying and added to your mathematical knowledge of sketching works as well as country would be an accomplishment highly desirable...I have seen Col Agnew in many situations attract the most distinguished notice by this accomplishment, which he possesses in an eminent degree...
> I have had the pleasure of seeing Sir J. Craddock at Seringapatam two days and at this place [Mysore] where he passed a day and night. I took up his posted bearers to Bangalore to pay my respects to Lady William Bentinck where I saw him for three days more, and entirely concur with you regarding his appearance and manners. ...
> I shall be glad to receive your list of books – I observe that the collection bequeathed to me by the late Mr Webbe has many of which I have duplicates, and such of these as are not on your list shall go to augment your collection.[171]

On 29 April Wilks took up another matter

> You have been so long intent on getting a great dashing steed that I am glad you have found one to your fancy. ...I will honor the draft for 800 rupees with pleasure. The money however must be payable at Seringapatam – not Madras. I send a letter which will explain itself. I think you know James [Collet, son of Mark's sister Anne], at all events it will be proper for you to write to him [in Madras]. I have requested Col Agnew to attend to his wants and if he sees right to put him on board another ship.[172]

Mark's education continued to occupy his uncle, as shown by a letter of 9 May 1807

> I advise you above all things not to allow your classical education to slip through: in Greek you had perhaps not made sufficient progress to hold your own with facility, and although the finest of languages it may go if you find it

---

[171] MNHL MD 436 26/-
[172] MNHL MD 436 26/-

troublesome to recover. With latin this can scarcely be the case, the Roman authors furnish standard models of taste and elegance:... resolve to give even <u>two hours in the week</u> and you will not only recover but acquire.
I shall look for you with the <u>very</u> <u>first</u> of the cool weather.[173]

Moreover, Wilks did his utmost to secure Craddock's interest for his nephew. For example, on 28 May 1806 he wrote to Mark and, unusually, endorsed his letter 'Private.'

> I have availed myself of Sir John Craddock's great kindness toward me in the several communications I have had with him, to take an opportunity of mentioning your name in such terms as I hope and believe you deserve, and I have reason to believe that he is disposed to take an early opportunity of advancing you...you will see the propriety of keeping this contribution absolutely to yourself...But you can without the appearance of any other object than seeking to be well informed in the various duties of the service, easily make yourself acquainted with the routine of the respective departments of the Deputy Quartermaster General and Adjutant General ...and if you can get a little practical exercise in surveying and sketching a country...[174]

Nor was Wilks neglecting his official duties, for on 1 June he was leaving Mysore on a tour of four or five weeks to Bangalore and Nundidroog. On the 13th he was in Yevalanca, and praised Mark warmly for an unspecified action.

> What you have done and what you have forborn to do in the case of Lieut Forward is generous, graceful and prudent, such conduct can only proceed from the best principles and the purest feelings...
> If I had the honor of being known to Mrs Lewis I should return her my best thanks for the <u>fascination</u> which you pretty warmly describe. As there seems little chance of my seeing you in Mysoor while there is such 'attractive metal' at Bellary I think I must contrive to pay you a visit and solicit you to present me to this divinity. ...You will indeed owe much to Mrs Lewis if she gives you a taste for the higher order of female society.[175]

Who was the lady, and what were her attractions? Was she lovely enough to make a man ride a hundred kilometres over rough ground to look upon her; or were her qualities of a more intellectual kind? And could she have been the same 'Mrs Lewis' who appears in a painting of the Maharajah's European Durbar in the mid-1840's, when Cubbon was a Major General and Commissioner for Mysore? Unlikely!

Major Wilks had matters at home to concern him as well, as shown by a letter of 24 July

---

[173] MNHL MD 436 26/-
[174] MNHL MD 436 26/-
[175] MNHL MD 436 26/-

> I have a letter from Mrs W by the overland despatch dated the 6th of March, she she writes in good spirits but the symptoms she describes do not excite any hope beyond the mere possibility of one of those unexpected blessings which the Almighty sometimes condescends to bestow.[176]

But hopes were vain. Harriot died on 2 May 1806. She was only thirty-three and left two young children whose father was 13,000 km away. Her husband did not receive the news for several months. He wrote to his nephew in January 1807

> I consider it very fortunate that very soon after a late mournful event, my mind was forcibly aroused to the performance of some important public duties. [I was] excused from any share in the investigation [into the Vellore mutiny] at Seringapatam, except of that of administering beef and claret to the judges Messrs Theckerley and Peile who are still with me. …although I have been so fortunate as to obtain the approbation of the Supreme Government, I hope there is no chance of my succeeding Col Close; because I hope [he will] accede to the request of the Governor-General to remain another year in India. Although in good general health I have been for the last two years afflicted with chronic rheumatism which has increased so as to nearly cripple me in one limb and prevent me from taking any kind of exercise. Whenever Col Malcolm shall arrive I shall wait the time requisite for delivering over my charge in a satisfactory manner [and then] proceed to somewhere below the ghauts to melt out the rheumatism. I do not believe that Bonaparte is killed, that peace is near at hand, nor that you need disturb your sleep with the dreadful effects of emigration, or consolidation of farms. I recommend that you get <u>Malthus on population</u>. He is the first author who has ever let in the clear blaze of day on a question where all his predecessors have floundered in the dark.[177]

Then, on 24 April 1807 Uncle Wilks wrote about some information that young Mark had discovered

> The subject of the first part of your letter is of great delicacy, and I shall state the facts so that you will have a motive for silence or very great reserve whenever it is introduced in your presence. Macleane [Harriot's father] was a natural son, and according to the law of England has neither relations nor heirs; in such cases the estate of an intestate goes to the Crown, which never appropriates it, but on the memorial of the connections of the deceased allows it to go nearly in the same manner as if the defect in birth did not exist… [Macleane's will had at one time been in Harriot's possession but, when she returned to India in 1802, he recovered it in order to make some alterations] If there be no will in England, application will be made to the King in the usual manner on behalf of my children – I imagine the net amount will be near 10,000 pounds.

---

[176] MNHL MD 436 26/-
[177] MNHL MD 436 26/-

I have accounts of Laura and Barry and indeed little letters from themselves so late as the latter end of July only, they were both perfectly well. I shall be very anxious before I go [leave India] to see you in some situation where you may have some better means of recommending yourself than in your Adjutantcy. It was only for the first two or three interviews [with Craddock] that I attached much importance to the offers and promises which I once thought would be of service to you.[178]

Mutiny at Vellore

In 1806 Lt Cubbon was deeply disturbed by a calamity that befell the Madras Army. Sir John Cradock, had spent much of his career in Ireland, the West Indies and the Mediterranean but at the end of 1803 he was appointed Commander-in-Chief in Madras with the local rank of Lieutenant General. This was a time of peace after a long period of warfare, and minds were turned to 'improvement' of the Sepoy. Probably Cradock was unaware of local sensitivities, and his personal background would, in any case, have made him hostile to them. Equally, there seems little doubt but he was badly advised; it is recorded that Major Pierce (Deputy Adjutant-General) drafted the new regulations and that they were approved by Col Agnew. In April 1805 Cradock issued the new orders for dress. In future Sepoys were not to wear beards, display 'painted marks' (showing their position within Hinduism), nor wear jewellery such as ear-rings; in place of a turban they were to wear a round hat which would have a leather cockade with a feather, and they must wear leather stocks. While these imposed changes were the principal source of grievance, gossip made matters worse: for example, a ship-load of Padres had just arrived from Britain to convert them, and the new uniforms including the wearing of cross-belts.

Objections were expressed by the 2/4 MNI in Vellore; some soldiers were disciplined and the battalion itself was moved to Madras. Seemingly, by May 1806 Cradock was ready to withdraw the offensive regulations, but the Governor of Madras, Lord William Bentinck – aged 32 years – did not agree. The matter came to a head in July, at Vellore. Four sons and other family of Tipu Sultan were held in the fort there. Their custodian and commander of the fort was Lt Col Thomas Marriot, whose quarters were close to their palace. The garrison comprised 380 British soldiers of HM 69th Foot and about 1500 Sepoys drawn from 1/1, 2/1 and 2/23 MNI. At about 2 a.m. on 11 July the Sepoys, led by the Indian officers, shot down their British officers and penned the men of the 69th in the barracks, where 82 were killed and 91 wounded. The survivors escaped and forced their way to the ramparts where they defended themselves under the command of two young military surgeons. Meanwhile, the Sepoys raised the Tiger Standard of Tipu.

At Ranipet, 22 km distant, was a large cavalry cantonment. A British officer, who had been outside the Vellore fort, rode there post-haste with the news.

---

[178] MNHL MD 436 26/-

Cavalry units, both Indian and British, were on the move immediately under command of Col Rollo Gillespie. At Vellore, he climbed up the ramparts on a rope, and led the troops there to clear a space around the inner gate of the fort. Light field guns came up and blew open the gates, the cavalry charged in, and the mutiny was soon over – but with the loss of 350 mutineers' lives and 129 British.

A thorough review followed. The offensive regulations were cancelled within a few days, but the three battalions that had mutinied were disbanded. Lord William Bentinck and Gen Cradock were recalled by an order of the Court of Directors issued in April 1807. The new Commander-in-Chief, Lt Gen Hay McDowall, arrived in September. Bentinck was replaced temporarily by the senior member of the Madras Council, and succeeded as Governor by Sir George Barlow in December.[179] The Government of India absolved Tipu's sons from any part in inciting the mutiny.[180]

Lt Col Thomas Marriott had been implicated in the affair because he had not taken firm action at the start of the revolt. By July 1806 young Mark had been caught up in some scheme to challenge the authority of the Company to dismiss Col Marriot. On 26 August Wilks put to Mark, by way of comparison, the authority of a Commander-in-Chief to recommend promotion, or of the authority given to the EIC (by Act of Parliament) to dismiss an officer. He went on 'I therefore conjure you on no account to have anything to do with these representations, and to dissuade all your friends from taking any part in them.' Two days later he dismissed a paper (said to be from Bellary) on the right of the government to stop promotion as 'verbal quibbling and puerile misrepresentation,' and hoped that Mark did not admire it.[181] In the event Marriott escaped dismissal and went on to command the force that captured Kurnool in 1815.

Worse still, measures had been taken against Col Agnew, young Mark's best friend and adviser next only to Uncle Wilks. In June 1807 Agnew and Pierce were removed from their appointments and ordered home. Mark was shocked by this, and sought the advice of his uncle about how to proceed; that letter has been lost, but Wilks responded rather cryptically (Madras, 4 September 1807) with

> If I were in the secret myself I should also let you into it: I know nothing of Col Agnew's departure, nor does he, but from the public rumour …there are few men in India who think more highly of Col Agnew than does Lord William Bentinck and none who speak of him with greater respect. Mrs Agnew's passage is taken in a part of the ship over which the Government have no control if they were disposed to exercise it, and Col Agnew's is not taken at all. You have been wrong, I fear, in assembling a Committee without the sanction of Government.

---

[179] W. J. Wilson, *History of the Madras Army* vol 3 235-65.
[180] Clive Mss and papers (2nd Series) B Letters No. 545, 546 (NLW).
[181] CKS U 1287 C95, Letters of 26 and 28 Aug 1806

I would particularly advise your circulating nothing without the requisite sanction. Application has been made by Col Agnew for the sanction of Government to a meeting of the Officers at and near the Presidency, and I suppose this will be granted.[182]

Wilks had his own idea of how the matter should be resolved. Like others who have worked with institutions like the old Government of India he knew very well that they can be persuaded and guided, but not driven! On 4 November he wrote again to assure Mark that Col Agnew was not ordered home. Such an order had been issued by the EIC in London but had been stopped by a higher power, presumably the Home Government. Agnew and Pierce returned to duty, but were not restored to their appointments on the Staff. In April 1808 Agnew departed on leave to Great Britain and remained away until 1810; on return he was posted as Commandant of 21 MNI.

Wilks went on to report that he had 'heard today of a peace between Russia and France, and that a general continental peace was expected…The consequences will probably be a very disadvantageous and very insecure peace, or rather truce, for England.'[183] Presumably this was the Treaty of Tilsit that followed Napoleon's victories over Prussia and Russia, and after which he introduced his Continental System. History shows Wilks to have been correct.

Wilks leaves India

By November 1807 young Mark had once more managed to accumulate debts, and Uncle Wilks sent him the means to discharge them – a draft made payable to Mark himself so that none need know how he came by the funds. The debts 'would have been a weight which you could not in half a lifetime have thrown off,' but the uncle had no doubt that he would learn from the unhappy experience. Wilks's benign delicacy was encapsulated in his last words on the subject 'The pleasure of having relieved you of it and the persuasion that these consequences will ensue are to me an abundant repayment.' He was soon to return from Madras to Mysore State, with his headquarters at Nundidroog; and he hope for a visit so that his nephew could see the progress that had been made in 'a literary work of fearful size.'[184]

By January 1808 Wilks was seriously unwell at Nundidroog. He had recovered from one illness but was now experiencing such frequent attacks as to make him determined to leave India in the following October. On 29th January he was going to Bangalore with

> Mr Grant of your Corps whom I asked to be my fellow traveller (without any interest regarding him except the recollection that at his time of day I should

---

[182] MNHL MD 436 25/6
[183] MNHL MD 436 25/7
[184] MNHL MD 436 26/-

have been thankful for similar attention). He seems to be a correct young man…I beg you to secure him a kind reception.[185]

However, by mid-April Wilks was back in Mysore once again, to take charge of the Residency. Young Mark was 'on the march' along the left bank of the Toombuddra and preparing for field service. Uncle Wilks assured him that some active service would be very advantageous because 'nothing can be more inconvenient on many accounts than to become an old officer without having seen any.'[186]

This is an opportune place to summarize a long letter from young Mark to his father, for it goes some way toward reviewing his experience in India to date. It was written on 26 February 1808 'from Bellary in the Ceded Districts.'

> It is now two years since I have heard a word from the Island [which may be due to] the rascality and mismanagement prevailing in the postal department in India. Many letters are destroyed to give the native writers the postage which is always paid in India.

He had now been more than six years in India and had been adjutant of 2/5 MNI for 3 ½ years. There was a rumour of an increase in the establishment of officers in each battalion to make it the same as in His Majesty's Regiments; if this happened he would be a captain immediately. He pointed out, however, that promotion to major or lieutenant colonel was not of half so much consequence as Staff post, and remarked that he

> would have been provided with a good staff appointment if Maj Gen Sir John Cradock, our late Commander-in-Chief, had kept his word, but like all courtiers he forgot it…This general has done all in his power to ruin our army, and to destroy the British influence in India. The Natives are beginning to view us with suspicion and dread, all occasioned by his treasonable but secret acts of folly [which] I have degraded all the British and at the same time rendered them objects of hate and contempt. …Officers are compelled to enforce his orders and ridiculous innovations respecting the beards, whiskers and turbands of the Sepoys, orders which accelerated if they did not wholly occasion the massacre at Vellore. It is prudent to overlook the little prejudices of such good and faithful subjects – as brave soldiers as any under the British Crown…the current ideas in England about the disaffection of the Madras Army is due partly to the credulity of some of our oldest officers. It is the custom to reward informers handsomely and latterly any vagabond who came with a horrid story is believed. Officers have profited by experience and do not now destroy their constitutions by debauchery and dissipation. I have to thank God for excellent health for many years. …I am sometimes laid up with colic to which I am subject, but it soon goes off.

---

[185] CKS U 1287 C95, Letter of 28 Jan 1808
[186] CKS U 1287 C95, Letter of 8 Apr 1808

Fort Hill, Bellary, surmounted by the citadel and with a wall around its base. Cubbon was here as a subaltern with 2/5 MNI. (SLT, 1992).

Uncle Wilks was now in Nundidroog but

> his health I regret is not so constantly good...it is very precarious depending on heat and cold ...and has determined him to leave India in October of this year. I am now to visit him in Nundidroog and to stay some months with him. I shall probably accompany him to Madras and see him quit India never to return. It is the greatest pride of my life to be related to such a man [who] possesses high character, talents, integrity of every achievement and virtue that can render a man estimable...while he was with Lord Clive he was always considered to be the real Governor...since his time all has been on the decline.

He speculated on whether matters would revive under Sir George Barlow, and concluded it might well do so 'provided he does not listen to advice of old, superannuated and interested Madras Civilians'.

Despite his reading of Beccaria's 'celebrated little work on crimes and punishments' Mark was none too pleased by the Courts of Justice, for only murderers were hanged but thieves were confined and fed by the Government.

> Hence when food is dear (as in 1807) men will try to steal...if they are caught they are confined and fed, which is what they want most. [He estimated] the cost of guards, food and the like is about 800,000 Pagodas – a sum which will pay 17,000 fighting men: Shame! Shame!
> We have taken possession of the Danish settlements in India and are forming an administration and are casting a jealous eye upon Persia...I would not be surprised to be upon the banks of the Indus in 9 months time....We could bring together 45,000 men in three weeks and we could bid defiance to any force

Buonaparte may choose to send....Col Agnew goes home in this fleet – an excellent and very clever officer and much regretted...
Pray when next you write let me know my age and on what day I was born.[187]

In the months that followed, uncle and nephew continued to move about the country; and clearly Wilks did not allow his uncertain state of health to tie him by the leg. On 9 May he was in Hyderabad, and by 13 June in Seringapatam where he had just recovered from bilious fever; he hoped for a meeting with Mark in Madras, after an interval of 3½ years.

That Mark Wilks remained open to influence and instruction is revealed by an account he wrote to his nephew in July. He described a meeting with Sir James Mackintosh during which he experienced 'the most correct, profound and extensive knowledge I have ever encountered in my passage through life.'[188] Meanwhile, at home Laura was still under the care of Mrs Agnew at Bath. He was determined not to spend another hot season in India. His health had not been good, and he urged Mark to make another application for leave so that they might meet. By August the relapses had become so frequent, and the last attack so severe, that he could no longer trifle with himself and was determined to leave India in October.

True to his word, Lt Col Wilks left India for the last time in October 1808. The passage to Cape Town took twelve weeks and two days, and included every disaster short of going to the bottom – a hurricane, three ships of the fleet missing – he had suffered much from sea-sickness but was still working on his book. A month in the Tavern of the India Ocean had greatly improved his health.[189] He then moved on to London, where he arrived in May 1809. He put up at the Albion Hotel in Jermyn Street, and wrote from there to the Rev Cubbon 'merely to tell you of the welfare of the two Marks.' He had himself

> returned to England with a small competency, forced by severe ill-health to flee for my life...although I regret being unable to accomplish the moderate projects in my contemplation. Mark is in principle all that your most rigid wishes could exact, and in talents one of the best and most promising young men of the establishment to which he belongs.

The two men had not met for several years, until about a month before Mark Wilks's departure, but then 'I found him equal to my best expectations, and hope that I have laid a train for his introduction into a line in which he may and I hope must force himself forward.'[190]

A short account of Mark Wilks's subsequent career may serve as a background to the desultory correspondence with his nephew after he left

---

[187] MNHL MD 436 25/8
[188] CKS U 1287 C95, Letter of 2 Jul 1808
[189] CKS U 1287 C95, Letter of 17 Feb 1809
[190] MNHL MD 436 27/4

India. Certainly he did not vegetate. Indeed, he could be said to have led a double life: in the Isle of Man as a land-owner, pioneering gentleman-farmer and politician; and as a distinguished scholar and colonial administrator in London, Bath and St. Helena.[191]

He had extensive properties in the Island. Kirby remained in his possession, and at one time or another he owned Castleward, Ballanare, Ballahot (in Malew), Ballachrink and Erinville in the vicinity of Bishop's Court, and probably the Mitre Hotel (in Kirk Michael). For good measure he owned or held a long lease on a house Portland Place, London (which passed to his daughter) and a house in Bath for Laura's sake.

The farms, especially Kirby, were managed actively, for example he initiated a comparison of green manure (called 'weed manure') and farmyard manure on the growth of root crops. In August 1812 he was elected Vice-President of the Isle of Man Branch of the Workington Agricultural Society.

As a scholar his magnum opus was 'Historical Sketches of the South of India in an attempt to trace the History of Mysoor' – a title that is now shortened to the first six words. When the first volume was published in 1810, he sent a copy to Lady Wellesley for his friend who was then in Portugal. The future Duke wrote to say that his wife had told him of the gift and that he was 'longing to read it;' and he commented, also, on the 'poor Madras Establishment'[192] – presumably in reference to the so-called officers' revolt. Sir James Macintosh called the work 'the first book on Indian history founded on a critical examination of testimony and probability.' Moreover, Marx used 'Historical Sketches' as a source of information on the organization of small Hindu communities as part of his discussion of the division of labour and manufacture in his das Kapital (published 1867).[193]

As a scholar, the climax of Wilks's career came when he was elected a Fellow of the Royal Society on 23 February 1826. Among those who nominated him were Sir Thomas Stamford Raffles of Singapore fame, and one Henry Harvey whom we shall meet as Agent for Public Cattle in 1809.[194] He was also a Vice-president of the Asiatic Society for several years.

Wilks was elected a Member of the House of Keys in 1811, but on 20 November 1812 he was appointed Governor of St. Helena, then a possession of the EIC. A Governor needs a Lady so, on 16 February 1813 he married Dorothy, youngest daughter of Major John Taubman SHK of Bath. Governor, Lady and Laura arrived in St. Helena on 22 June 1813: there his emoluments were a salary of £1800 per annum, a furnished house and his table servants. In June 1814 he was promoted to full Colonel in the Madras Army, his

---

[191] Partly based on E. I. Carlyle's entry for Wilks in Dictionary of National Biography.

[192] Wilks Papers vol 2 Correspondence as Governor of St Helena and later, 1813-23 (BL Mss 57314) letter 55

[193] Karl Marx, *Capital – a critique of political economy* vol 1. (translated by Ben Fowkes, London 1976) 477-9

[194] Royal Society: Certificate of Election, Col Mark Wilks.

commission being signed by the Prince Regent. For more than two years he was able to immerse himself in the affairs of the Island and gave particular attention to measures for improving its agriculture, but on 15 October 1815 the Emperor Napoleon arrived as a prisoner under the care of Admiral Sir George Cockburn. Wilks continued as Governor and had several interviews with Napoleon, some of which are recorded and published as 'conversations.' Seemingly they got on very well and the deposed Emperor was disappointed when Wilks was replaced by Sir Hudson Lowe. The reason for the change was simply that, in the opinion of the British Government, protocol required Napoleon to be under the charge of a General Officer in the British Army. Wilks was, of course, only a Colonel in the EIC's Army. Lowe had commanded the Corsican Rangers for several years, spoke French and Italian, and had clearly been groomed to become Napoleon's guardian. He arrived in St. Helena on 14 April 1816 – also with a new wife – and the Wilks family left immediately afterwards. Years later the Duke of Wellington expressed strong disapproval of this move, and it was perhaps due to him that Wilks was offered the Governorship again in 1822.

His return to the Isle of Man was attended by both pleasure and grief. There was pleasure in the shortness of the period before his re-election to the House of Keys, in August 1816; but on 5 September his son, Barry, died. The boy had entered the EIC's Haileybury College during the previous year with a view to joining its civil service. He was interred with his mother in Grosvenor Chapel, Mayfair. Perhaps there was consolation in seeing Laura married to John Buchan on 22 July 1817, in Bath. Buchan was a soldier who had commanded a Portuguese brigade with some distinction during the Peninsular campaign. Later he was promoted Lieutenant-General and appointed KCB, and he seemed to get on well with his father-in-law.

There had been an unlikely addition to the ex-Governor's establishment as shown by the inscription on a gravestone in Braddan Old Churchyard, a stone's throw from Kirby House:

> Samuel Ally
> An African and native of St Helena
> Died the 28th of May 1822 aged 18 years.
> Born a slave and exposed to the corrupt influence
> of that unhappy state, he became
> a Model of TRUTH and PROBITY to
> the more fortunate of any country or condition.
> This stone was erected by a grateful
> Master to the memory of a faithful Servant
> who repaid the boon of Liberty with unbounded attachment

To close this brief account of Wilks's career after he left India, it is pleasing to record that he was elected Speaker of the House of Keys on 2 July 1823, in succession to his old friend and father-in-law, the late Major John Taubman.

CHAPTER NINE

Mark Cubbon Alone 1808 – 1834

Mark ended his tour as Adjutant of 2/5 MNI on 2 January 1809 and was replaced by Lt John Beaumont, who had been a Cadet in the same intake as himself. However, he did not spend much time as an ordinary regimental officer but, later that year, was appointed Assistant Agent for Public Cattle. His immediate superior, the Agent for Public Cattle, Lt Henry Harvey of 20 MNI, was appointed at the same time. The posts were attached to the Commissary-General's Department but were not quite of it; but this was Mark's first step toward a post on the Staff. The Agency's duties were to supervise the breeding and training of the famous trotting bullocks.[195]

The 'Officers' Revolt'

Also in 1809 Mark suffered his most harrowing experience to date, and one in which he was more closely involved than with the episode at Vellore. This was the so-called officers' revolt.

The affair was some years in the making, and began with the death of the Marquis Cornwallis in October 1805. Sir George Barlow, senior member of the Council in Bengal, automatically became acting Governor-General and was confirmed as temporary Governor-General by the Court of Directors in February 1806. However, the British Government revoked the appointment a few days later, having decided upon Lord Minto. By way of compensation Barlow was sent as Governor of Madras in place of Lord Bentinck, as we have already seen. He arrived in the southern Presidency in December 1807, bringing with him an unenviable reputation as a result of his behaviour while acting in the supreme post. This was the man who would stir the pot of discontent.

A variety of ingredients had accumulated in that pot. Among them was a disparity in the allowances received by officers in the Armies of Madras and Bengal. Then there was the way that preference for Staff appointments, which carried significant additional emoluments, was given to King's officers over those of the Company's Armies. In 1808 the 'tent allowance' was abolished, to the detriment of senior officers. This was an allowance with which they were expected to find camp-equipment for their men. Its withdrawal impugned their honesty as well as affecting them financially. Finally, the new Commander-in-Chief, who had replaced Cradock, was aggrieved for a personal reason. Lt Gen Hay Macdowell had not been appointed to a seat on the Madras Council. Instead, a Civilian filled the place and collected the handsome allowance; and this too, it seems, was a decision of Sir George Barlow.

---

[195] Madras Almanac 1810

Early in February 1809 Macdowell and other senior officers secretly prepared a memorial, critical of Barlow, for the Governor-General. In the event they decided not to send it, but Barlow managed to obtain a copy. On 1 May he recommended that thirteen officers, mainly lieutenant colonels and majors, be punished in various ways, and suspended them from duty pending a decision by higher authorities. Among them was Lt Col Alex Cuppage, Commandant of 5 MNI and Mark's first Commanding Officer. When Barlow's action became known most of the arraigned officers made clear their opposition toward the Madras Government – which was tantamount to mutiny. Moreover, officers at Hyderabad, Seringapatam and elsewhere expressed their sympathy and resolved to make voluntary contributions in support of their suspended comrades. The resolution was signed by 158 officers, foremost among them being those stationed at Hyderabad. Both Henry Harvey and Mark Cubbon became involved.

In this serious situation Col Barry Close, then Resident in Poona, was appointed to command the troops at Hyderabad. A few days after his arrival on 3 August, and despite many frustrations, he persuaded the disaffected officers to return to their duties and submit to the Governor-General. Those at other stations followed the lead of Hyderabad. Disciplinary action was taken against some senior officers but most were restored to their posts.

Finally, the affair was played out with the appointment of Lt Gen John Abercrombie as Governor at Fort St George in December 1812 and the departure of Barlow in May of the following year. Throughout the whole affair, the Indian officers and men remained loyal to the Government.[196]

Mark had been closely involved in this sorry business, and there was no-one from whom he could seek advice because both Uncle Wilks and Col Agnew were far away. On 10 August 1809, clearly distressed, he wrote seven pages from Mysore to his uncle in London.

> My Dearest Uncle,
> I have just heard that a ship sails for Europe on the 13th and have but a few hours left me for writing. I shall therefore confine myself to a concise description of the state of affairs in this miserable Country without entering into causes or particulars…You will have heard from other sources of the total disregard shown to the memorials and remonstrances of the Army, of the suspension of most of our oldest and best officers, and finally of the gradual approach of the Army to the…regime in consequence of those tyrannical proceedings.
> After all petitions had failed the Hyderabad Subsidiary Force came forward to the Army and pledged itself to obtain by force what was denied to representation … and the whole of the Army pledged itself to support them … Rather than concede a little Sir George Barlow has resolved to bring on a civil war, and oppose Europeans to Natives. He has assembled 4000 Europeans under Col Hare and got the Royal Artillery from Ceylon, and that Force is going

---

[196] W. J. Wilson, *History of the Madras Army* vol 3 236-96

to march against the Hyderabad Force, but to weaken the Army as much as possible he has proposed a pledge to all officers for signature to obey all his orders and support his Government or be removed from all Military functions…Our only hope now is that Lord Minto will extricate the country from its present ruinous situation, he will be in Madras in a few days and must be convinced of the necessity of conceding a little. The suspension of all the officers to be abrogated and a general amnesty would be gratefully acknowledged by the Army and set all matters to rights, but unless he does that there can be no hope of escaping ruin for the Army is so desperate that it will fight to the last, of which advantage will be taken by the Native Powers. Harvey and I have been obliged to resign our appointments and are now proceeding to the coast where all the recusants are to reside.

To Lt Col Davis
Sir,
I have received the declaration proposed by the Government for signature of officers, but as approving the required pledge required the necessity of acting against my Brother Officers I beg leave to decline it.
M. Cubbon

I have thus perhaps given up all my hopes and prospects in India, and unless Lord Minto reverses everything must return again to my Corps as soon as this disturbance will be composed.…With respect to my particular conduct, if you do not approve it I do not think you can condemn it. I cannot bring my feelings to act against my Brother Officers nor will I for mercenary considerations afford assistance in executing measures I detest, against Officers whom I love. Hardly one Officer of responsibility has signed that paper and the King's Officers of Cavalry Regts have sent a Paper to Sir George Barlow begging him to pause and reflect upon the destruction that appears to hover over us…I have conversed with the best informed Natives at this place, and their opinion is that if the Officers choose to speak to the Sepoys it would be difficult to separate them – whether the Officers should do so is another matter. Our fate is dreadfully obscure *genus humanum dominat coligo futuri* [?]… Harvey has desired his father to show you his letter which was finished before I heard of the opportunity and the haste in which I have been obliged to write will plead my excuse for this scrawl. Give my love to Barry and Laura and for heavens sake do not omit to send me your Picture and theirs also…I had your letter from the Cape and was overjoyed to find you in such good health after encountering so many disasters.

My dearest Uncle,
Most affectionately yrs.
M. Cubbon

PS: Poorniah says: Oh, that Major Wilks were in India, nothing like this would have occurred.[197]

---

[197] MNHL. MD 436 25/9

In response to this cri de coeur Uncle Wilks wrote from London on 16 April 1810 to damn the whole affair as

> misgovernment on the one hand, and on the other rashness, madness, imbecility, incapacity, folly and guilt. Harvey has committed a great error, but it was an aberration of an honourable mind. In all similar cases the best men are always the victims, while the real authors if the mischief escape unhurt. I shall be impatient to know what has been done in his case and yours. His letter to the Quartermaster-General must I fear prevent his return. You stand only in the general mass of recusants, and I suppose will be restored.[198]

Then he turned to family matters: Laura was still with Mrs Agnew, and Barry was doing well at school – first scholar out of eighty-four.

Harvey had indeed served himself badly by writing an impolitic letter to the Quartermaster-General of the Madras Army and might expect the worst. However, contrary to the worst fears of Mark and his uncle, the authorities in Madras bore no lasting grudge against the junior officers who had joined the revolt. Both Mark and Henry Harvey were returned to their posts in the Department of Public Cattle under the Commissary-General, Col Morison. Amid this turmoil, Mark seems to have kept out of debt but another part of his behaviour displeased his uncle, who wrote on 31 January 1811

> I have received all your budgets up to April and am obliged to you for them. No opportunity has passed without your writing to me; but on no opportunity have you written to your father. I passed some weeks at the (Maughold) Head and if you had seen the big tear start into your mother's eye in relating the date of your last letter, you would not think a month's labour ill bestowed in drying it up. Twenty minutes twice in each year would prevent this most unseemly appearance of estrangement from those who have every human claim on your affections.[199]

Wilks had taken a house in Bath. He informed Mark that Laura was under his care; many had predicted he would spoil her, but he had resolved not to do so. She had a good governess and he would instruct her himself

> …on subjects on which few females are informed. I shall take special care that she shall not become a pedant, but I shall endeavour to furnish her with resource against ennui, and with the means of looking with intelligence and interest at all those operations of nature and human contrivance which afford neither amusement nor instruction to the uninformed. I cannot form to myself the idea of a more intelligent pupil, or one more anxious for instruction – nor have I ever been engaged in an occupation which afforded me more pure satisfaction.[200]

---

[198] CKS U 1287 C95 letter of 16 Apr.1810
[199] CKS U 1287 C95 letter of 31 Jan. 1811
[200] CKS U 1287 C95 letter of 31 Jan. 1811

Wilks had used a young kinsman to deliver the long letter of which the foregoing are parts, James Mark Cosnahan, the son of John Cosnahan of Douglas and nephew to his brother's wife. Now in his seventeenth year, James was on his way to join the Madras Army and had spent a few days with Wilks so as to learn what he might expect.

By the middle of 1811 Wilks was in the Isle of Man and busy with his farming. He retained a house in Bath, partly for the sake of Laura and Barry and partly on account of his own interests. We shall not pursue further this long correspondence between uncle and nephew. There is, however, something like a coda in a passage of a letter written in 1813 when Uncle Wilks was Governor of St Helena. Having counselled Mark on the need to provide support for his ageing parents and three unmarried sisters, he wrote 'you will of course always have a will by you.'[201]

While on furlough in Great Britain Col Agnew had seen a good deal of his friend Lt Col Wilks in Bath and had met some of the Cubbon family. By October 1810 he was back in India as Commandant of 21 MNI, which was quartered in Madras. He promptly renewed contact with Mark and, taking up the task of adviser, wrote in his downright way on 1 November 1810

> I am glad to see you selected by Government for any office after the part both you and Harvey took in the unlucky events of 1809. I do not mean to enter into the merits of that line of conduct; but have observed that the same oblivion has not been drawn over the acts of all who participated with you in it.

Agnew then went on to warn Mark about one Vencaty Royaloo, formerly Principal Servant in the Department of Cavalry Supplies, saying

> I have always heard of him as a very clever fellow, and useful to those who wish to make a profitable thing of the department, but I doubt much if he has some other qualifications that are at least as necessary.[202]

This and other letters show Agnew's concern that Mark should curb his impulsive tendencies and ensure that he made his way in the Service.

The remark about Vencaty Royaloo must have disturbed Mark, for he was soon asking Agnew to find him a reliable assistant – like Uncle Wilks's manager in the Barracks Department. Agnew was unable to recommend a person immediately, saying that he had himself never required more than a matey boy or at best a writer. A few days later, however, he wrote 'Sashachellum, formerly Col Corner's Dubash when employed in an office somewhat similar to yours, is

---

[201] CKS U 1287 C95 letter of Jul. 1813
[202] MNHL.MD 436 26/1

willing to undertake the situation' and Agnew believed he was likely to be 'particularly correct in all his accounts'.[203]

Minto's Expedition to Java

A new prospect now opened before the East India Company and especially before Col Agnew. As in 1795, events in Europe determined the Company's actions and led it to acquire territory, albeit temporarily on this occasion. In 1806 Napoleon I had decided to set up his brothers and a sister as monarchs over some of his peripheral conquests. Accordingly, the Batavian Republic was converted into the Kingdom of Holland for his brother Louis. The new king did not behave as expected. He learned Dutch and refused to adopt measures that harmed his subjects' interests, among them the embargo on British goods imposed under the Emperor's Continental System. Napoleon responded in 1810 by annexing Holland and incorporating it fully into his Empire. One result of this action was to bind Dutch possessions in the East Indies even more closely to France than Ceylon had been at the time of the Batavian Republic.

Lord Minto, Governor-General of India, therefore resolved to complete some unfinished business by bringing the East Indies under control of the Company. An expeditionary force of about 10,800 fighting men was assembled in Madras and Bengal under command of a first-class officer, Sir Samuel Auchmuty, the Commander-in-Chief at Madras. He had already recognised Col Agnew's qualities by appointing him his Military Secretary, and he now made him Adjutant-General to the force. Lord Minto sailed with the expedition, taking with him the young Thomas Stamford Raffles. After some severe fighting the Dutch forces yielded and, by a treaty of 17 September 1811, Java and its dependencies were surrendered to the Company. Early in October Agnew was sent to London with despatched describing the campaign. Raffles was made Lt Governor of the newly acquired territories. He remained in post until 1816, when he was forced to retire and recruit his health in Great Britain – before taking up the appointment that gave rise to Singapore.[204]

Mark's imagination had been gripped by this enterprise. He made enquiries of Col Agnew about his prospects for joining it. Agnew replied on 30 January 1811

> As I find that the Commissariat department of the expedition is to go from Bengal, I see no hopes of your going, even would that be advisable. Under existing circumstances I think it would <u>not</u> be so – and as you would, by leaving the line at present, forfeit your claim to promotion in it, I advise you by no means not to think of it. Poor Shaw is dead, and, if I have not mistaken Morison, he considers you as first for promotion. This will give you a good thing, as matters <u>now stand</u> in our Service, and all the <u>credit</u> you or any of us would get by any intent of exertion on the expedition would not be worth one

---

[203] MNHL.MD 436 26/1
[204] W. J. Wilson, *History of the Madras Army* vol 3 323-30

1: St. Mary's Chapel, later the Grammar School, at Castletown, seen from the south-west. The arches are part of an arcade between the 13th century nave and an aisle (now demolished). The wing with chimney was added in early 18th century, mainly to provide for the new Academic School. (SLT, 1995)

2: Maughold Church, where the Rev Thomas Cubbon was Vicar. The pillar-cross stands on the left of the gate-way (A Heaton Cooper, 1909: Courtesy of the Director, Manx National Heritage).

3: Landing over the surf on to the open beach at Madras, as experienced by both Wilks and Cubbon (Lt. R. Thompson ca 1850, Courtesy of the Director, National Army Museum, London).

4: The former Residency in Mysore City, from south. Built by Mark Wilks and completed in 1805, it was later known as Government House (SLT, 1992).

5: Within the fort at Mercara, Coorg: statues of Vira Raja's elephants (SLT, 1992).

6: Nandidrug from Nandi village, about 48 km north of Bangalore. In the 18th century Hyder and Tipu constructed extensive fortifications around its summit; and within these Mark Cubbon built his house (SLT, 1992).

7: Gateway in the outer wall of fortifications on Nandidrug. In Cubbon's time the hill was ascended by means of 1,175 steps (SLT, 1992).

8: Front of Mark Cubbons's house near the summit of Nandidrug (SLT, 1992).

Fanum to us for any useful purpose. I have <u>rather late</u> gained my experience on this point, and therefore warn you against the Rock on which I have been wrecked. Had I been a <u>bullock agent</u> or a <u>Bullock Driver</u> instead of a Staff officer for the last 20 years, I would now <u>laugh</u> at the injustice under which I suffer. Let the expedition take its course, and hold fast by your Commissariat claims.[205]

This was sound advice but, by late February, Mark was put out by, as he believed, being overlooked by Morison when arrangements were being made at Madras to load stores for the Expedition. Agnew set about smoothing his ruffled feathers with information and advice. Two weeks later Agnew had reason to write to Mark about his conduct. Seemingly he had been signing himself 'Sub-Assistant Commissary-General' – in an inaccurate and somewhat ironic reference to his post of Assistant Agent for Public Cattle. Col Morison had remarked on it to Agnew, clearly thinking it singular behaviour and not entirely sensible. Agnew pointed out that Morison spoke well of Mark's general conduct, and asked why a <u>whim</u> should be allowed to spoil an otherwise good impression. He reminded Mark that some in the Service were not favourably disposed to either him or Harvey 'for remembrance of what it may be duty to forget, but which duty it is sometimes difficult to perform.' This advice had an avuncular tone to it which was continued in the remark 'I hope you have written to your Uncle and your <u>Sisters</u> who complain much of your silence.'[206]

In April the relationship between the two men was reversed. One of Agnew's closest relatives had come drunk on to parade. On 13 April, in great distress he wrote to Mark in Bangalore

I have heard that Bertram, who is now in Bangalore …has again been induced to besot himself with beer and to distinguish himself with gross vulgarity of language. You know him and can speak to him…I beg you as a friend to do so, and charge you as a gentleman not from mistaken kindness to him not to conceal his conduct. I despair of his reformation but if you can save him by promoting his reform do. What can I say more? [207]

Soon afterwards Agnew joined the fleet for Java, and it is unlikely the two men met again. However, Bertram's later record suggests that Mark exerted himself successfully on Agnew's behalf.

Toward the end of 1811 Mark came to a turning-point in his career. On 24 January 1812 he wrote to his father from Bangalore that he had, in October 1811, been

…advanced to the situation of an Assistant Commissary-General, one of distinction and of considerable present and prospective advantage. It is,

---

[205] MNHL.MD 436 26/-
[206] MNHL.MD 436 26/-
[207] MNHL. MD 436 26/-

however, so far above my rank or claims on the Service that it must be attributed entirely to Sir George Barlow's consideration of the eminent public services of my Uncle Wilks. I have been appointed to the most delightful cantonment and the most healthy in all India, and attached to the largest Field Force in this Presidency. And as I enjoy <u>better health</u> than I have been blessed with since my arrival in the Country, I must consider myself one of the most fortunate young men, although I am unlucky in my Regimental promotion.[208]

He went on to report that his distant kinsman, James Mark Cosnahan, had been staying with him for some time before joining his regiment and was making such rapid progress in Hindustani as would soon earn him a bonus of £200; and that he liked the younger man very much. Mark wished to add to his father's little estate, near the mills in Kirk Maughold, and promised a remittance of £200 next October, and £500, perhaps £600, a year later.

Lt Cubbon was the junior of five Assistant Commissary Generals – but no longer 'Sub-Assistant Commissary-General'. Henry Harvey was given a similar appointment and promoted to captain. Perhaps this new post raised the question in Mark's mind for he asked his father, when next he wrote, to tell him his exact age saying 'I have forgotten it and make myself only 26 on 21 July 1811' – which was not far from the mark. Soon a warm regard began to grow between Morison and Mark, and with it increased responsibility for the younger man, who was promoted captain in 1816.[209]

The Pindari War

In 1817 the Commissariat of the Madras Army was tested to its limit by a campaign against the Pindaris and the final war with the Marathas. These conflicts sprang directly from the lack of a clear settlement to the war of 1803-04. In February 1804 Maj Gen Arthur Wellesley wrote 'I think we run a great risk from the free-booter system…it increases daily …no inhabitant can or will remain to cultivate unless he is protected by an armed force stationed in his village.'[210]

He was proved right because the following dozen years were marked by disorder throughout Central India and Rajasthan. During much of this time disharmony and internecine warfare were the main attributes of the Maratha Confederation. Indeed they were united only by hatred of the British, because this foreign power alone prevented them from becoming supreme from Kanya Kumari to Punjab and perhaps beyond it. Yet those at Home who controlled British power, the Directors and the Board of Control, were unsure of themselves and their best course of action – as had happened before and would do so again.

---

[208] MNHL. MD 436 25/12

[209] Information on promotion of Cubbon and other officers is from Madras Almanac.

[210] Army Dept. India, *The Mahratta and Pindari Wars* (Simla 1910) (Wellesley quoted)

Two groups of free-booters shared the territories of the Marathas. One, the Pindaris, was their offshoot and often served as their auxillaries. In so far as they had a base it was at Nemawar on the Narbada river – the northern boundary of South India. Their military strategy and tactics were based on those of the Marathas, but had been refined to the utmost degree. They have been described by Sir John Malcolm in a telling passage

> Pindaris were neither encumbered by tents not baggage…the party, which usually consists of two or three thousand good horses with a proportion of mounted followers, advanced at a rate of forty or fifty miles a day, turning neither to right nor left till they arrived at their place of destination. They then divided and made a sweep of all the cattle and property they could find, committing at the same time the most horrid atrocities and destroying what they could not carry away. They trusted to the secrecy and suddenness of the irruption for avoiding those who guarded the frontiers of the countries they invaded; and before a force could be brought against them they were on their return.…If pursued they made marches of extraordinary length. …If overtaken, they dispersed and reassembled at an appointed rendezvous; if followed to the country from which they issued, they broke into small parties. Their wealth, their booty and their families, were scattered over a wide region.[211]

The other free-booters were bands of Pathans, who operated in parallel with the Pindaris though their origin was different, as was their military structure which included infantry and artillery. Nominally in the service of Holkar, in fact they exercised themselves in their own interests and that of their most notable leader, Amir Khan.

In 1813 Lord Minto was succeeded by one who would soon become the 1st Marquis of Hastings: fifty-nine years old, with a respectable if unspectacular army career behind him, lacking any direct experience of India, a friend of the Prince Regent, and in need of recruiting his finances. As is sometimes the case he proved himself the man for the hour.

The Directors of the Company were at last provoked into taking a decision by actions of the Pindaris themselves. In 1812 they raided Mirzapur within the Company's own territory. In 1814-15 they twice rode through Hyderabad to plunder the northern districts of the Madras Presidency, carry away Rs10 lakhs in plunder and leave devastation behind them. In September 1816 Hastings was ordered to eliminate the evil.

This was to be no minor skirmish. The forces of the five Maratha Princes and Amir Khan amounted to 91,000 cavalry and 66,000 infantry with 569 guns; the Pindaris mustered 30,000 men, made up of cavalry and infantry in equal numbers, and 20 guns. Arthur Wellesley had already noted this tendency of both Marathas and Pindaris to incorporate infantry and artillery into their forces, and had condemned it for negating their advantage as fast-moving light horsemen. Moreover, he saw it as essential in operations against the Marathas

---

[211] W. J. Wilson, *History of the Madras Army* vol 3 365-6 (Malcolm quoted)

to have sufficient supplies in camp to be able to move at will for as long as one wished. Thus he foresaw the modern maxim that amateur military commentators speak of strategy, but professionals of logistics! And making logistical arrangements for the Army was the province of the Commissariat.

As a first step Hastings had to neutralize the Peshwa and Sindia. He recognised also that any reverse in dealing with the Pindaris could bring the entire force of the Marathas down upon him. Accordingly, he assembled 110,000 men – more than double the number Harris had taken to Seringapatam. This force had two parts. One was the Army of the Deccan, which comprised seven divisions commanded by Lt Gen Sir Thomas Hislop. The other was the Grand Army, consisting of four divisions including reserves, under command of Hastings himself. Among the formations in the Grand Army was 2/5 MNI.

The Army of the Deccan provided a blocking force between Poona (the Peshwa) and Nagpur (the Bhonsla), thus separating these two Princes and preventing the Marathas from assisting the Pindaris. The Grand Army drove the Pindaris northward across the Chambal river, so that by the end of January 1818 their organized bands had been destroyed and their leaders were either dead or bound to the Company. This hunt for the Pindaris became merged into a last Maratha War, which was brought about by the folly of the Peshwa and Bhonsla. These Princes separately attacked the Company's Residencies in their respective capitals. Both were defeated. The office of Peshwa was declared extinct and the reigning Bhonsla was deposed in favour of a young kinsman. Holkar and Sindia also yielded, but Amir Khan managed to secure the principality of Tonk for himself and his descendants! The whole operation was over by June 1818.[212]

Hegemony by the Company now offered the only prospect for stability in the Indian sub-continent south of Punjab. A comprehensive settlement was put in place. The Peshwa's territories were annexed to enlarge the Bombay Presidency. The Rajputs accepted the Company's supremacy as a welcome relief from the Marathas – who were themselves treated with consideration by the Company's representatives. But the social consequences of the settlement were even more rewarding. Malcolm, who had been given the task of settling the region, described it as 'All is peace, and a great impulse has been given to render India tranquil for a long period; but it is as yet only an impulse.'[213]

By this time the Company's writ ran from Kanya Kumari to the Sutlej river. One assessment suggested that it directly controlled nearly 1.5 million square kilometres and 87 million people; its tributaries and allies amounted to 43 million people in a somewhat larger area. For comparison, the population of Great Britain and Ireland was less than 21 millions. A modern British historian has suggested that rule by the Company Bahadur was seen by Indians as the

---

[212] Army Dept. India, *The Mahratta and Pindari Wars*.
[213] J. Malcolm, *Memoir of Central India* 3rd Ed. (London 1832) vol 1 430-1; also J. W. Kaye, *Life and Correspondence of Maj Gen Sir John Malcolm* (London 1856) vol 2 308

only acceptable situation. A return to the previous unrest and internecine strife would have been wholly unacceptable. The Company was not loved, but other powers were feared. Only the Company, with its various vices and virtues, could offer the stability they craved. An Indian historian has called this period 'the seed time for new India.'[214]

Last Years in the Commissary-General's Department
In mid-1825 Major Cubbon became seriously ill, and was shipped off to the Cape for several months to recruit his strength. Seemingly recovered, he returned to his post in Madras but suffered a relapse after a few months and therefore betook himself to the Nilgiris. In the chilly, invigorating climate of the hills his condition quickly improved. He and Rama Sawmy had kept in touch over the years, and it was Rama Sawmy who reported Mark's illness to Uncle Wilks, saying ' He was so kind as to write to me on his first arrival there and consequently I requested my friend Mr Sullivan to afford him everything he might require'.[215] This remark gives an intriguing view of the relationship between some Indians and British at the time, for John Sullivan was a senior man in the Service: Principal Collector and Magistrate of Coimbatore.

By this time Major Cubbon of 16 MNI was senior among the eight Assistant Commissary-Generals. In 1826 he became Deputy to Morison and was transferred to 41 MNI. Two years later Morison was appointed Resident in Travancore-Cochin and Lt Col Cubbon succeeded him as Commissary-General.

The new Commissary-General did not confine himself to his office, for Cubbon liked touring in order to see for himself the land over which troops might have to operate and be supplied. In October 1833 he was on just such a trip when he fell in with a young officer of 48 MNI, Lt Colin Mackenzie. It was in the north-west of Mysore, where Mackenzie and a companion were visiting the impressive Gersoppa Falls. They joined Cubbon's camp and were entertained magnificently as they travelled through the forests and bamboo thickets of the region. One day Mackenzie was out shooting when he missed his horse and was faced with a walk of several miles back to camp in the heat of midday. He had not gone far when he came across a dacoit trying to rob an old woman. He apprehended the fellow, his horse came up, and Mackenzie 'conducted [the robber] in triumph to the awful presence of Colonel Cubbon, who [in vulgar parlance] settled his hash'.[216]

In the course of the next few years Mark lost the three people most dear to him. In 1828, his father died. The Rev Thomas Cubbon's Will directed that Mrs Margaret Cubbon should be executrix and residual legatee. There were bequests to William and his wife, and to his three unmarried daughters; moreover, these

---

[214] Jadunath Sarkar, *India through the Ages*. (Hyderabad 1993) 63
[215] Wilks Papers vol 1 (BL.Add Mss 57313) letter 19
[216] Colin Mackenzie, *Storms and Sunshine of a Soldier's Life 1825-81* (Edinburgh 1884) 30

ladies were to receive the interest arising from moneys remitted from India by Captain Cubbon. There was no other mention of Mark: no thanks, no good wishes, no blessing, nothing![217]

Next year Mrs Cubbon followed her husband. Her Will also made bequests to William and her three unmarried daughters, who also inherited all her effects. She treated Mark more graciously than had her husband

> Feeling sensible as I do of the dutiful, kind and generous conduct of my son Major Mark Cubbon now in the East India Company service and that no pecuniary legacy in my power to leave him would be an object worth his acceptance I therefore leave him a gold mourning-ring containing his father's hair and mine. And I request his acceptance of the same in remembrance of those on whom he so liberally conferred his bounty with the intention of adding to their comfort in declining years.[218]

There, indeed, is a warmer heart!

On 19 September 1831 Col Mark Wilks died at the home of his son-in-law, Kelloe House, Berwickshire. Several months elapsed before Mark had word of it. What recollections must then have passed before him: the lean sensitive face, courteous but firm demeanour, quiet words of guidance in time of need, wry sense of humour; above all the strong intellect and good understanding.

There were four trustees to the Will including 'Henry Harvey Esq of Somersetshire.' Wilks had remained precise to the end of his life, as one paragraph of his Will reveals

> It is requisite to notice in this my Will that in the course of conducting some remittances from Major Mark Cubbon for his parents the Reverend Thomas Cubbon and Margaret his Wife the sum of £1494. 4. 9 was invested. ...These transactions were for convenience sake carried on in my name and if at the time of my death the said investment should be found standing in the public books in my name I hereby declare that the same is not my property but that of the Reverend Thomas Cubbon and Margaret his Wife or their assigns.

The Will also established a trust from which, *inter alia*, the provisions of his own marriage settlement (to his second wife) and that of his daughter should be met, 'also to pay to Jane Satterthwaite of Cockermouth the nurse and faithful servant of my first wife an annuity of thirty pounds during her natural life.'[219] All of which was characteristic of the man.

In 1832 the Commissary-General's Department was caught up in one of those inter-departmental arguments that occurred rather too frequently in governments run entirely by Public Servants – Civil or Military – no matter how

---

[217] Archidiaconal Wills, Rev Thomas Cubbon 1828 (MNHL MF/ RB 639)
[218] Archidiaconal Wills, Mrs Margaret Cubbon 1829 (MNHL MF/ GL 746)
[219] Archidiaconal Wills 2nd Book , Col Mark Wilks (MNHL MF/ GL 747) ; also MNHL. MD 436 24/11 annotated 'Uncle Mark's Will.'

capable. Seemingly, Maj Gen Sleigh had reported adversely on the condition of horses in three regiments of cavalry and as many troops of horse artillery, stating some country-bred horses that had joined since the previous inspection were 'inferior', and hinting that the Commissary-General's Department may have been responsible. Lt Col Cubbon's comprehensive response, supported by seven analytical tables, showed that his Department was in no way at fault; and he reiterated the importance of securing blood horses for military purposes, from the Arabian Gulf for example.[220] It was an excellent piece of report-writing, but one must regret that talents and energy were wasted on such matters.

Indeed, it has been said that when Morison and Cubbon worked together in the Commissariat the former attended to the routine work while the latter assembled and wrote the brilliant reports for which the unit became respected.

At this time, Mark's financial affairs were looked after in Madras by a Mr Moses. His general practice was to invest blocks of Rs5000 in the Company's Bonds, accumulate the interest in his bank account until it reached Rs5000, and then invest it. Mark was also joint trustee with Arbuthnot & Co for the estate of a Capt Fyfe who had died in 1830 leaving a widow and three young children. Moses kept an eye on that matter also, and ensured that Mrs Fyfe received regular payments.[221]

News of what lay ahead for Lt Col Cubbon must have got about for, out of the blue, came a letter from Henry Harvey. He was long out of the Service, married, the father of four little girls, and wrote from London on 17 March 1834. He was a Director of the newly-formed London and Westminster Bank, which had its offices at Waterloo Place, Pall Mall. His letter contained what would now be called a tremendous sales-pitch. He asked Mark to solicit some of the wealthiest men in Madras, including John Arbuthnot, scion of the banking family, to make deposits, saying he would be 'happy to receive large remittances from them and to turn them to account.' As a recommendation he recounted how he had withdrawn £2000 from Coutts on account of Col Wilks's estate and placed it at 2% and seven days notice of withdrawal! And he suggested that Mark 'my good friend' might use 'some of your savings to buy shares in the bank.' The remarkable epistle was rounded off with 'Heaven bless you my friend, Yours ever affectionate.'[222] One may speculate on what Mr Moses thought of the proposal. He need not have worried, for the Bank continued under its original name until 1909, and then underwent several mergers and name-changes before settling as the National Westminster in 1970.

Before going on to the last and most productive stage of Mark Cubbon's career, it is worth recording changes to the way India was being governed. Over the years, successive governments in London had sought to bring the Company's activities under its own ultimate control. The Charter Act of 1833

---

[220] MNHL MD 436 28/1
[221] MNHL MD 436 25/13
[222] MNHL MD 436 25/14

carried this process an important stage further. It did away with the Company as a commercial entity in India, where it was restricted to acting as the political agent of the Crown. It was still able to trade with China but lost its monopoly there. Moreover, the Act gave the Governor-General of India in Council power to pass Legislative Acts for all British India, and to do so with the sole help of a fourth (Law) member of the Council. This new post was to be filled by a person who was not in the Company's Service; and the first so appointed was T.B. Macaulay.[223] Although lacking first-hand experience of India, he had acquired much information from his membership of the Board of Control (from June 1832) and as its Secretary (from December 1832).[224]

---

[223] V. A. Smith, *The Oxford History of India*. 526
[224] C. H. Philips, *The East India Company 1784-1834*. 338-9

CHAPTER TEN

Prelude To The Commission: Mysore And Coorg 1799 – 1834

Mysore

When the Wadiyar Dynasty was restored in Mysore (1799) the new Rajah was a child of five years, and Diwan Purniya virtually Regent. There was also a Company's Resident to provide advice. The first Residents: Barry Close, John Malcolm and Mark Wilks as Political Resident, were men of exceptional abilities; but thereafter seeds of discord were sown. Indeed, Lewin Bowring [who succeeded Mark Cubbon in Mysore] wrote that 'the fundamental source of difficulty between the Company and Raja Krithnaraj arose because 'that able officer Major Wilks was succeeded by a Mr Cole who was a weak man unable to control the Raja...who fell into the hands of designing scoundrels.'[225] Among the Rajah's earliest counsellors was one Ram Rao, a Brahmin who had served the Muslim regime as a cavalry commander and subsequently in Purniya's civil administration. This man planted his relatives in positions of reward and influence. Others followed his lead.

Much of this had been foreseen by Arthur Wellesley. From his vantage points in Mysore City and the Maratha country he had turned his calculating eye upon the Madras Government and its dealings with Mysore State. Alarmed by what he saw, he stated, in January 1804, that

> only by placing Mysore under the immediate superintendence of the Governor-General-in-Council can general tranquillity and security be ensured. The consequence of the existing system [under Madras] will be that the Rajah's government will be destroyed by corruption and calumny.[226]

As he foresaw, Fort St George was incapable of providing precise direction to the Resident, and this fact was tacitly acknowledged by the Governor-General, Lord William Bentinck, in September 1831.[227]

Other factors were also at work. For all his administrative skills, Purniya gave the young Rajah little or no training, and the boy's education was neglected. Even more serious was the deteriorating condition of the Ryots, which was due mainly to a contraction in the market for their produce. Years before, the military successes of Hyder Ali and his son had brought plunder to Mysore in the hands of their soldiers, who were so many consumers of what

---

[225] L. B. Bowring, *A Memoir of Service in India* (BL (OIOC) Ms Eur G 38) 185
[226] Gurwood (Lt Col), *Selections from the Despatches and General Orders of F. M. the Duke of Wellington.* Extract 145
[227] K. N. V. Sastri, *The Administration of Mysore under Sir Mark Cubbon.* (London 21)

the Ryots had to sell. After 1799 the soldiers of the Company, who were paid regularly, ensured that this situation continued in Mysore. However, from about 1805 the number of troops was reduced so that demand for the Ryots' produce diminished and prices fell.

Nevertheless, all remained tranquil in the State until 1810. In November of that year, serious differences arose between Purniya and the Rajah, who assumed the government. A year later the Diwan retired, leaving the sixteen-year-old Rajah supreme but without any reliable Indian advisers. As early as December 1811 the resident, Mr Cole, reported that the Rajah was on the one hand wholly incapable of managing the affairs of his State and, on the other too jealous to delegate authority to the new Diwan. Among charges levelled against him were that he had acquired 'habits of extravagance and sensuality, had no regard for truth or faith, and disregarded the advice of the Resident.'[228] In 1817 Thomas Munro described the Maharajah to Lord Hastings 'he is indolent, prodigal and has already dissipated…the treasure laid up by the Diwan. He is mean, artful, revengeful and cruel.'[229] In 1825 a serious attempt was made to secure the Prince's reform. Sir Thomas Munro, now Governor of Madras, visited Mysore in order to reason with him. He failed to secure any improvement, but recorded some of the State's ills. Revenue was declining rapidly, not least because of gross mismanagement of the means of collecting it; expenditure was increasing; almost all the reserves amassed by Purniya – about Rs255.5 lakhs – had been dissipated; almost every department of government was in arrears.[230]

In his far-reaching analysis of the disturbances in Mysore, Stein concluded that a principal cause of them was the Maharajah's repeated demands for more revenue at a time of falling prices. From about 1814 this resulted in the reintroduction of a system of tax-farming under which most Amildars accepted contracts obliging them to collect each year a higher revenue than in the previous year; if they failed to do so they had to make up the deficit.[231]

The Ryots showed astonishing patience but, by 1830, they had become restive. In April of that year an attempt was made to set up a separate, independent regime at Nuggar and the movement extended into the north-western taluks of the Bangalore Division. The Diwan went to the region but was unable to conciliate the Ryots or otherwise control the situation, whereupon strong reinforcements of Mysore's own cavalry and infantry were

---

[228] Thomas Hawker et al, *Report on the Insurrection in Mysore* (Bangalore 1833) 7

[229] J-D. B. Gribble, *Two Native States, being letters from Hyderabad and Mysore* (Madras 1886) 100-1

[230] W.G.L. Rice, *Mysore and Coorg – a gazeteer* 3 vols (Bangalore, vols 1 and 2 (1876-7) deal with Mysore, vol 3 (1878) with Coorg), vol. 1 299, and J-D. B. Gribble, *Two Native States*. 96

[231] Burton Stein, 'Notes on "peasant insurgency" in colonial Mysore'. *South Asia Research* Vol 5 No 1 1985 14-5

Prelude to the Commission: Mysore and Coorg 1799-1834 115

Maharajah Krishnaraja Wadiyar III in 1827, when his personal authority was at its height. (S. W. Reynolds after A. Stuart: Courtesy of BL (OIOC))

sent to him. In January 1831 the Maharajah took command of his troops: fifteen people were executed by his orders in the Nuggar district and a further eighteen were disfigured by mutilation of ears or nose.

The Company had avoided assuming direct rule for as long as possible, but when unrest became serious and widespread their forces were ordered to intervene. On 19 October 1831 the Government of India assumed direct responsibility for the affairs of Mysore. This was done by the Governor-General, Lord Bentinck, acting on Articles 4 and 5 of the Subsidiary Treaty, which specified obligations of the British Government toward the State of Mysore. He informed the Maharajah by letter that he intended to transfer the entire administration into the hands of British officers and for that purpose had appointed two Commissioners who would proceed immediately to Mysore. During the suspension of the Rajah's rule the Commissioners were to exercise all the functions and perform all the duties of a Regency. Moreover, the Governor-General appointed a Committee to enquire into the insurrection and report to him under the heads: its origin of the insurrection, its progress and suppression and, its consequences. The Committee comprised:

Maj Gen Thos. Hawker	(Commanding Mysore Division) Chairman.
Lt Col W. Morison CB	(Resident in Travancore and Cochin)
J. M. Macleod, Esq.	
Lt Col M. Cubbon	(Commissary-General, Madras Army)

It met in Bangalore and, on 12 December 1833, submitted its 'Report on the Insurrection in Mysore' to the Governor-General-in-Council.[232] Parts of the Report confirmed the fears of Arthur Wellesley and others, for example

> The great faults of the Rajah's Government appear to have been that throughout it was venal and corrupt; that no efficient control was exercised over district officers; that the people were fretted and vexed by unjust and arbitrary acts of those officers and could obtain no redress; that there was no security of property; and nothing that was fit to be called the administration of justice.[233]

From June 1832 the Commissioners became directly responsible to the Government of India; but from 31 October 1931 until June 1832 they had worked under the supervision of the Government of Madras with a consequence that will be seen later.[234]

As we have seen, two Commissioners were appointed to administer the State. The senior was nominated by the Governor-General and the junior by the Governor of Madras. From the start this arrangement was bedevilled by

---

[232] W. G. L. Rice, *Mysore and Coorg* vol 1 302
[233] Thomas Hawker et al, *Report on the Insurrection in Mysore*. 62
[234] W. G. L. Rice, *Mysore and Coorg*.. vol 1 303

conflicting ambitions and power-politics. Those most closely involved were Lord Bentinck, in the supreme post but far removed from Mysore, and Sir Stephen Lushington, Governor of Madras, subordinate to Bentinck but relatively close at hand. Moreover, Lushington was well-connected: his father-in-law was Lord Harris of Seringapatam fame, and his elder brother, Gen Sir James Lushington, was a member of the Company's Court of Directors. A younger brother, Charles, was making his way in the Madras Civil Service and Sir Stephen was ambitious for him.

Bentinck had prepared the ground before announcing assumption of the Mysore Government. On 10 October 1831 Col John Briggs, Resident at Salsette, received a private letter from the Governor-General requiring him to return to Madras and there take up an appointment as Senior Commissioner for the Government of Mysore. This did not please Governor Lushington who saw the appointment of a military man as an intrusion upon the pastures that should properly be reserved for his senior civil servants. Indeed, when Briggs arrived in Bangalore on Christmas Day 1831 he found Charles Lushington already there as Junior Commissioner. He had brought from Madras such Indian civil servants as he had thought necessary, and had appointed as Diwan a Brahmin named Vencataramaniah who had been recommended by the Resident. Lushington returned to Madras after only a fortnight and was replaced by G. D. Drury, another up-and-coming Madras civil servant. Before departing Lushington publicly recorded his opinion, in reflection of his brother's, that the Diwan had full powers as actual head of the administration and the Commissioners were merely advisers in the same way as the Resident. All this was, of course, wholly contrary to the Governor-General's intentions. In addition, Governor Lushington vetoed almost all proposals for reform put forward by the Senior Commissioner.

In Briggs's view the result was to cut off the Commissioner from all meaningful contact with both the Rajah and his people, and to prevent him from interfering with any measures of a Diwan whom those people knew to be both ignorant and corrupt. In the bazaars the Senior Commissioner was spoken of as one who lacked any authority and who incurred only the displeasure of the Governor of Madras. No wonder Briggs described his life as a 'fiery ordeal and purgatory.'[235]

Valiantly did Briggs put up with his ordeal for nearly two years, and achieved some improvements. In May 1832 a new Junior Commissioner was appointed, and in June control of the Commission was transferred from Madras to the Supreme Government. In November, Briggs was replaced by the Resident in Travancore and Cochin so that the Commissioners became : Senior – Lt Col W. Morison CB as from 13 November 1832; Junior – J. M. Macleod, Esq. as from 26 May 1832. J. A. Casamaijor continued as Resident at Mysore City.[236]

---

[235] T.E. Bell, *Memoir of General John Briggs* (London 1885) 139, 142, 152-162.
[236] W. G. L. Rice, *Mysore and Coorg* vol 1 303

An arrangement where the Junior Commissioner was in place well before his senior colleague arrived but that colleague had the power to over-rule his junior was unlikely to work: it did not! Consequently, in April 1834 a decision was taken to appoint a single Commissioner. William Morison became an Extraordinary Member of the Supreme Council of India, and Third Member in the following year. In June 1834 Lt Col Mark Cubbon took charge as sole Commissioner for Mysore.

There is a story that three names for the post were placed before Lord Bentinck: Mr John Thomas of the Madras Civil Service, Col J. S. Fraser, and Lt Col Mark Cubbon. One might expect that Thomas, tarred with the Madras brush, would be ruled out immediately. Fraser, however, was a considerable man and honest to the core. In the event, Morison's influence with the Governor-General ensured a decision in Cubbon's favour; but his arguments were soundly based because Mark knew the Maharajah and his people, and so was particularly well fitted to rule the State in accordance with the Native system.[237] This was important because, in his first instruction, Bentinck wrote 'the agency under the Commissioners should be exclusively native; indeed that the existing native institutions should be carefully maintained.' The Court of Directors reinforced this instruction by stating it was 'desirous…not to introduce a system which cannot be worked hereafter by a native agency.' Bentinck's plan was to transact public business by a Native agency under European superintendence, and obviously he looked forward to a restoration of Indian government in Mysore when conditions were right. For the time being, however, supervision of the government of Mysore was undertaken at the highest level by Cubbon and four Superintendents – one for each Division of the State.[238]

When the Maharajah was set aside he was given an allowance of Rs3.5 lakhs plus 20% of the gross revenue of the state – often referred to as his 'fifth share'. He retained the right of sentencing convicted criminals, but was so indolent in discharging this duty that the gaols became overcrowded with prisoners awaiting sentence; whereupon the Commissioner himself took up the task of confirming sentences handed down by the Huzur Adawlut or Senior Native Court.

Coorg

In due time the delectable little state of Coorg became Cubbon's responsibility. Set upon the inland slopes of the western Ghats it was only 4097 sq km in extent.

In 1651 the capital of Coorg was moved to Mercara, a small town about 125 km west of Mysore City. The place is dominated by a low hill, and a mud-walled fort was built around its summit. Within this the Rajah had his palace.

---

[237] K. N. V. Sastri, *The Administration of Mysore* 22
[238] W. G. L. Rice, *Mysore and Coorg* vol 1 170, 303-4.

The country had long been in the hands of the Lingayat dynasty. The Linga Raja (?1710-1780) had at least three sons, and was succeeded by the oldest Vira Rajendra who, in later years seems to have become insane. Certainly he ordered the execution of his immediate relatives, principal officers of state and others who had displeased him in his father's time. During his reign the tiny country was not well used by its large neighbour. It was over-run by Hyder Ali in 1773, and again in 1782-83 by Tipu, who replaced the Mercara fort with a much more substantial structure having stone ramparts 2.5 m thick and 4.5-6.0 m high on the outer side. However, as an outcome of his defeat by Cornwallis, Tipu was forced to grant independence to Coorg in March 1792. Recalling his experiences it was no wonder that Vira Rajendra evinced immense satisfaction when he witnessed the defeat of Tipu by Gen James Stuart at Sedasere on 8 March 1799.[239]

When Vira Rajendra died his younger brother, another Linga Raja usurped the throne, but made up for it by ruling comparatively well until his death in 1820. Linga Raja's own son, Vira Raja, came to the throne early in life and soon displayed a sadistic character. For example, Rice records that he had two cousins, daughters of Vira Rajendra, whom he forced to plunge their hands into boiling ghee before having them strangled.[240] Another story, possibly apocryphal, throws further light on his character and may explain the presence of two life-sized stone elephants within the fort. In the morning Vira Raja liked to be awakened by two elephants trumpeting beneath his windows. However, one evening he sent a message to the elephants' mahouts that they should not perform next morning – but the message was not delivered. Next morning the elephants awakened the Rajah as usual and, flying into a rage, he ordered that they and their mahouts should be killed. Then remorse overcame him, and he ordered that stone statues of the trumpeting elephants be made: this was done, and the elephants are there yet, at one side of the open space within the fort. Their mahouts have no memorial.

Whether this tale be true or not, Vira Raja's behaviour became less tolerable as time went by. Various attempts were made to reform him, including a visit by Casamaijor in 1833; but they were fruitless. Next year the people sent a complaint to the Company, asking that action be taken. In March 1834 Col J.S. Fraser was appointed Political Agent of the Governor-General in Coorg, and a proclamation was issued deposing the Rajah. An army of 6000 men entered the State. On 4 April Mercara fort was taken and the Rajah became a prisoner of the Company. On 7 June Fraser wrote to Bentinck 'In my opinion he has forfeited every claim to indulgence, and I think that his atrocious character would render it discreditable to the British Government to concede more to him than was granted to him – life and honourable treatment' His advice was followed and the State annexed 'in consideration of the unanimous wish of the inhabitants of Coorg to be taken under the protection of the British

---

[239] H.H. Dodwell (ed), *Cambridge History of India* vol V 341
[240] W. G. L. Rice, *Mysore and Coorg* vol 3 164-7

Government…and the Territory…transferred to the Honourable Company.'[241] Fraser became Commissioner for the Affairs of Coorg with his office in Mysore, but the territory was not incorporated into Mysore. For a time the Rajah was confined at Bangalore and met Macaulay there. He then retired to London where he moved freely in the best society and again met Macaulay, at the house of Lord Ellenborough. He died in London in 1862.

Military Men in Charge

By 1834 both Mysore and Coorg were controlled by soldiers. Five years later Bevan wrote approvingly of the practice of employing military officers in civil administration. He pointed out that a member of the Civil Service, who had begun his career as a Writer, felt himself fettered by a mass of precedents and authorities. Free from this bureaucratic baggage, the soldier could see clearly what was before him and go forward to his objective.[242]

---

[241] W. G. L. Rice, *Mysore and Coorg* vol 3 189
[242] H. Bevan, *Thirty years in India 1808-38* (London 1839) vol 2 198

CHAPTER ELEVEN

Commissioner for Mysore 1834 – 1843

Lt Col Cubbon took up the post of Commissioner in June 1834. He held supreme authority in the State but was *de facto* Regent for the present Maharajah or a successor. The Resident, Mr Casamaijor, probably none too pleased, was consoled by an appointment as Resident in Travancore and Cochin. Cubbon then acted as Resident for a few months before Col J.S.Fraser took over. The Maharajah's principal palace was in Mysore City. The Resident also lived there, in that elegant house built by Mark Wilks thirty years before; and in Bangalore there was another fine house and offices for him at a little distance from the commercial quarter.

The Commissioner's headquarters were also at Bangalore, 360 km from Madras and 120 km from Mysore City: far enough to escape day-to-day surveillance by either Fort St George or the Maharajah. As we have seen, the city had been founded by Kempe Gowda I, and passed through the hands of the Wadiyar family to those of Hyder Ali. He built a new stone fort, oval in shape, immediately to the south of Kempe Gowda's mud-walled structure which then formed the site for the pettah or commercial quarter. Cornwallis took the city in 1791, and from 1809 the Company developed an adjoining site as a military station, thus taking advantage of its altitude of 1000 metres, excellent climate and fine surroundings. A plan of the place in 1834 showed the fort, 730 m from north to south and 550 m across. Tipu Sultan's palace was a half-kilometre to the south and, having been constructed of wood, it was already showing signs of decay; eventually it would be reduced to the audience hall and durbar hall. The pettah had expanded greatly, and around it much residential development had taken place; the whole was surrounded by a thorn hedge that remained until 1898. To the south-east was an extensive garden, the Lal Bagh. Satellite hamlets were coming into being, and the cantonment was being developed further away, to the north and east of the fort.

Soon after Bentinck's assumption of the Mysore Government, the Commission had set itself up in an ancient palace within the fort. Built by Hyder Ali, it was described – wholly misleadingly – by an inscription let into one wall as 'The Admiration of the Heavens.' From these austere quarters Cubbon controlled Mysore throughout his tenure.

And where did he live? A single-storey house had already been built or purchased for the previous Senior Commissioner. It was well placed at almost the highest point of the town – so that water had to be carried to its large garden! Here Mark Cubbon lived for twenty-seven years, and adapted the place to his own needs. His successor, however, saw it with a jaundiced eye, describing it as 'tolerably commodious for a bachelor but not remarkable' – so an upper storey was added in 1867. The best parts were the out-offices, especially the stables which could accommodate fifty horses in support of Cubbon's interest in breeding them. In front of the house he raised a magnificent flag-staff, probably even grander than the one at Fort St George. It was made of teak and had a platform twenty metres above the ground and from this one could mount higher still. From the platform a good view could be obtained of all Bangalore and the surrounding country – so that, perhaps, it was not a mere whim.[243]

Early Visitors

However, neither stables nor flag-staff were yet in place when Lt Col Cubbon received his first important guest. Thomas Babington Macaulay had been appointed Law Member of the Supreme Council of India in December 1833. The voyage out gave him an opportunity to do an astonishing amount of reading; suffice it to say that it included all *seventy* volumes of Voltaire. He was accompanied by his sister Hannah but, at Madras, was called to meet the Governor-General who was recuperating in the Nilgiris. Consequently, Hannah sailed on alone to Calcutta while her brother travelled by dhooli to Ootacumund. By mid-June 1834 he was at Bangalore, as he related in a letter from Ooty to sister Margaret at home.

> Bangalore is one of the greatest military stations in India. The Company has at least five thousand excellent troops here, stationed in the neatest cantonments I ever saw, - quite unlike English barracks. They are quite low white houses, of one storey only, with red tiles, very clean, with trees planted before them and an immense area in the middle covered with grass and railed in. Adjoining to these cantonments, which have something of the look of very neat almshouses, are the villas of the principal officers surrounded by small gardens. Here and there a shop has been established with a European name over the door. Through this very agreeable scene I passed to the house where I was to be lodged, the house of Colonel Cubbon, Commissioner of Mysore.

> The Rajah resides in his Palace with royal state. But he has no powers beyond the walls of his residence. The whole civil government of Mysore is administered by Colonel Cubbon who reigns, - for that is the proper word, - at Bangalore, over a country probably as large and populous as Scotland. He is a very fit man for so high a post. I had heard him highly spoken of at Madras; and even the civilians, though jealous and displeased that a military man should have been appointed to so important a political situation, allow that he was a person of eminent abilities. Still I was surprised. I had seen several superior men at Madras. But neither at Madras nor in England have I met with a person who struck me more. Not only did he seem to be thoroughly master of his business, and familiar with every part of the military and civil administration of India; but, although he left England at fifteen and has passed thirty years in the East

---

[243] L. B. Bowring, *A Memoir of Service in India* (1878) (BL (OIOC) Ms Eur G. 91).

without once visiting his native country, he was perfectly familiar with European literature and politics, had evidently been an indefatigable reader of good books and was in short, as Dominic Sampson said of another Indian Colonel, 'a man of great erudition considering his imperfect opportunities.' His ignorance pleased me even more than his knowledge. Such a listener I never saw. His eager curiosity, his earnest attention, his quick comprehension, were delightful. We passed three days together.

[Bangalore] fort was formerly considered one of the strongest in India....It was, when I was there, interesting on another account. One of the petty princes of the country, the Rajah of Coorg, sovereign of a district perhaps as large as Derbyshire or a little larger, had the audacity to go to war with us. He was indeed a more formidable enemy than you might imagine. ...But the truth is that every enemy is formidable in India. We are strangers there. We are as one in two or three thousand to the natives. The higher classes whom we have deprived of their power would do anything to throw off our yoke. ...At Coorg we were very near meeting with a serious check. After some hard fighting, however, the Rajah's heart failed him, and he surrendered. He had been a horrid tyrant, - had murdered every relation that he had, and had filled his dominions with noseless and earless people. ...He talks of his atrocities with wonderful coolness. He said to Colonel Cubbon 'I had a great mind to crucify the messenger you sent to me with a flag of truce. What would you have done if I had?' 'We should have hanged you to a certainty' said the Colonel. 'Exactly' – said the Rajah – 'I thought so. That was the reason why I did not crucify the man.'

... after breakfast on 23rd (June) I took leave of Colonel Cubbon, who told me, with a warmth which I was vain enough to think sincere, that he had not passed three such pleasant days for thirty years; and I proceeded on my journey through Mysore.[244]

Little wonder that Cubbon enjoyed Macaulay's visit. For years he had been unable to test his opinions against another well-stocked mind which had recently been at the centre of affairs. In such circumstances even a reasonably well-informed visitor would have been a source of pleasure, but Macaulay was far more than that. He had been called 'a book in breeches' by a detractor, and Greville wrote of him 'All that he says, all that he writes, exhibits his great powers and astonishing information, but I don't think he is agreeable.'[245] Perhaps this is a reasonable judgement from one at the centre of public life but, having no such advantage, Cubbon found Macaulay's 'astonishing information' decidedly agreeable.

This meeting, which gave so much pleasure to Mark Cubbon, is linked to a similarly enjoyable encounter, in 1808, between Uncle Wilks and Sir James Macintosh, then Recorder of Bombay. Macintosh had an ambition to write a

---

[244] Thomas Pinney (ed), *The Letters of Thomas Babington Macaulay* (Cambridge, 1974-7) vol 3 48-50.

[245] Christopher Hibbert (ed.), *Greville's England: selections from the diaries of Charles Greville 1818-1860.* (London 1981) 111

history of England from 1688 to 1789 in order to demonstrate how the Whigs had achieved the Glorious Revolution and saved Great Britain from a catastrophe like that which befell France after 1789. He did not live to accomplish the task, which was taken up by Macaulay.

Macaulay enjoyed Cubbon's company, and he like Bangalore. After two months at Ooty he returned to Madras by much the same route as that of his outward journey

> At eight o'clock in the morning of 3d September I was comfortably seated at Colonel Cubbon's house in Bangalore. With him I passed three or four very pleasant days. I described him to you in a letter from the hills. I think him one of the ablest and most pleasing men that I have found in India. …If I had to chuse my place of residence in this part of the world it should, I think, be Bangalore…I have been there both in June and September, and found that even in those months, which are very hot in most parts of India, I was able to take exercise at all times except in the very middle of the day. The situation is central. In forty-eight hours you may be on the tops of the Neilgherries for health. In forty-eight hours you may be at Madras for business. So ready is the communication from Bangalore to every other part of Southern India that in one of our discussions in Council, Lord William, Sir Frederick Adam, and Colonel Morison, all distinguished military men, agreed that who holds Bangalore holds India south of the Kistna from sea to sea.[246]

During one of Macaulay's visits an intriguing facet of Cubbon's character showed itself. Macaulay had reacted against his experience at an Evangelical school by becoming completely devoid of a religious sense and, having adopted conventional conformity, expressed amused disdain for all kinds of Non-conformity. This extended to other branches of the Faith and especially to those that treasured the Sacraments. Cubbon had already drifted away from orthodox western Christianity so that the two men probably shared opinions. Among the Commission's officers, however, were several practicing Christians, notably Capt Chalmers – a fervent Evangelical – and Lt Dobbs who later wrote about the event. One evening after dinner at Cubbon's house Macaulay set out to amuse his fellow-guests, and himself, with ribald stories about English Bishops. Knowing that this would cause deep offence to some of his officers, Cubbon showed by his manner that he did not approve and Macaulay quickly changed the conversation. At the time Macaulay was of the Supreme Council, with the power to make or break careers, while his host was only a lieutenant-colonel. Nevertheless, Cubbon was willing to defend his junior officers' sensitivities instead of flattering Macaulay and, to give him his due, Macaulay bore no malice.[247]

---

[246] Thomas Pinney (ed), *Selected Letters of Thomas Babington Macaulay* (Cambridge 1982) 132-3

[247] R. S. Dobbs, *Reminiscences of Mysore, South Africa and Burma* (Dublin 1882) 12-22

Soon afterward Cubbon received another visitor, one with whom he could be completely relaxed. This was the Lt Colin Mackenzie whom he had met while touring the region around the Gersoppa Falls a few months before. Since then Mackenzie had taken part in the campaign in Coorg. Thereafter he lived for a time in Cubbon's house, and recorded his opinion of his host and some fellow-guests 'Old Seton and Cubbon are such fine fellows, and Colonel Fraser is as little chary of his carcase (sic) as any *preux chevalier* of old.'[248]

The Maharajah

One of Col Cubbon's first official duties was to make an official call on the Maharajah with whom he wished to work as amicably as possible, although already there must have been doubts in his mind on that score. There is no record of the meeting but a general outline may be guessed with some certainty. In order to respect the Maharajah's beliefs, an auspicious day would have been selected — well in advance of the meeting. The journey to Mysore City was probably accomplished in a fairly leisurely fashion, and he would have stayed over-night at the Residency before going to the Palace to pay his compliments to His Highness.

After 1799 the Palace had been rebuilt within the fort, about two kilometres from the Residency. It was an extensive structure designed in the Hindu style and facing almost due east. The gaily decorated façade rose to four storeys, on the second of which was an open gallery, the Dussera Hall, where the Maharajah, seated upon his throne, showed himself to his people on great occasions. The main entrance to the Palace opened under the Dussera Hall and gave on to a passage leading to a courtyard. The left side of the courtyard was taken up with various offices including the armoury and library; straight ahead on the western side of the courtyard was a door leading to the zenana; on the right side were apartments occupied by the Maharajah himself. The principal room in this part of the Palace was the Amba Vilasa, an upstairs chamber twenty metres square and three metres high with the ceiling raised in the centre. Its floor was of polished chunam, and the only touch of grandeur was the doors which were overlaid with richly carved ivory and silver. Most of the Maharajah's other apartments, including his private chapel, opened off this chamber.[249]

Accompanied by his small Staff and an escort of the Company's cavalry, Cubbon would have ridden to the fort, through the gateway and along the broad drive to the Palace itself. Having left their escort outside the main entrance, Cubbon and his Staff were conducted to the Amba Vilasa. The Maharajah was seated in a part of the room separated from the rest by a wooden railing. After introductions, an exchange of compliments, and a brief general conversation the meeting was brought to a close by the Maharajah.

---

[248] Colin Mackenzie, *Storm and Sunshine of a Soldier's Life 1885-1881* (Edinburgh 1884) 40
[249] T. P. Issar, *The Royal City* 23-5

Often thereafter was Cubbon to meet His Highness in this room: at least once a year in a formal 'European Durbar' and sometimes in private to try to solve a problem.

The Wadiyas were Kshatriyas, but the reigning Maharajah had been brought up under the influence of Hindu priests and, during his early years, of his Brahmin Diwan Purniah. Moreover, the whole family was marked by piety within the Hindu faith, so it was unthinkable that he and his European visitors should eat or drink together.

From the day the Company had assumed responsibility for Mysore, the Maharajah resented their action, and his resentment manifested itself in various ways, sometimes of a petty kind. Over the years he proved difficult to hold to an agreement. An example from July 1841 concerned his obligation to provide accommodation for the Superintendent of Ashtagram Division and his staff. The alternatives he offered were shown to be quite unsatisfactory including Seringapatam which long ago had been found unhealthy. The Commissioner therefore wrote to His Highness, through the Resident, rehearsed the various alternatives, and concluded that the best solution would be to build new quarters and charge the cost to the Maharajah's fifth share.[250]

Later that year the Maharajah expressed his repugnance at having to serve on some of his relatives and courtiers summonses to appear and give evidence in the Adawlut Court, and he invoked the notion that the near relatives of a sovereign, and members of his court had always been exempt as a mark of respect to himself. His contention had the support of the Resident, Major Stokes. In November Cubbon commented in detail on His Highness's contention, as follows:

(i) the Adawlut Court is the Commissioner's Court and thus the highest law tribunal in the State; to suggest that it would be degrading to appear there would throw obstacles in the way of justice. He was sure the Maharajah would not wish to do so.

(ii) H.H. knew that those who applied to the Courts should be given no reason to criticize its procedures, including the examination of witnesses.

(iii) H.H. may recollect that several of his relatives and courtiers attended the Committee of Enquiry convened at Bangalore in 1833, and did not then see it as derogatory to their dignity. Moreover, they attended the Court of the Superintendent of Ashtagram as both suitors and witnesses.

(iv) therefore the objections seemed to come from H.H. himself, not from those summoned. If he so wished, H.H. could serve summonses on his near relatives, and Cubbon would request the Superintendent of Ashtagram Division to take their evidence *viva voce* in the Palace, where

---

[250] MNHL MD 436 28/2

they could also be cross-examined by the vakeels of both parties. The Superintendent of Ashtagram could also serve summonses if H.H. found it repugnant to do so himself.[251]

The solution thus offered by Cubbon seemed eminently reasonable, and there is no suggestion that the Maharajah found a way to reject it.

Mysore was but one of the Princely States with whom Governors-General communicated. As a result of experience they adopted certain conventions, one of which was explained to His Highness by Cubbon

> the Governor-General in Council does not consider it convenient that letters on important business should be addressed to him by Native Princes in any other language than their own, as it is essential that his Lordship should be satisfied that they understand the writing to which they give the sanction of their signature.[252]

Accordingly, correspondence with the Maharajah of Mysore was conducted in Kannada.

The Maharajah was exquisitely conscious of his personal dignity, and made the fact known in a letter to the 'Commissioner for the Government of my Territories' in which he referred to the 'military honours being paid to me in the persons of my Principal Officers'. He suggested that these were now inadequate because some of the posts had changed, for example Buxshey was now Principal Buxshey, 'and what was acceptable in 1833 is no longer so.'[253]

Another cause of friction should have remained privy to the Prince's household. Seemingly the Maharajah (who lacked an heir) had an illegitimate son, to whom his most respectable relatives refused to render homage. The outcome was complaints from His Highness, on which Cubbon took no action.

Thuggee in Mysore?

From about 1832 there was considerable speculation among officers in the field about the importance and extent of thuggee. Thugs were members of a sect that joined parties of travellers on the road and, having gained their confidence, strangled them, took their possessions, and buried their bodies; to this practice they gave a quasi-religious justification. There seems little doubt that thuggee was more prevalent in Central India than elsewhere. Investigations of the practice were begun about 1830 by Capt William Sleeman while in charge of Narsingpur District (Central Provinces). In 1835 he was appointed General Superintendent for the Suppression of Thuggee, and based himself at Jabalpur; thereafter the task was his principal life's work. In Mysore Dobbs, Superintendent of Chittledroog, found three bodies in a shallow grave dug in a

---

[251] MNHL MD 436 28/3
[252] MNHL MD 436 28/4 No 20
[253] MNHL MD 436 28/4 No 21

stream bed; they showed marks of strangling but no other injury. Dobbs believed thuggee to be widespread but Cubbon was doubtful. However, in 1836 Capt Elwall was appointed thuggee magistrate for the Commission and, over the years further evidence for thuggee was found. Although Cubbon would have preferred to deal with the offence in the same way as other criminal cases he coöperated fully when special courts were established to try suspected thugs and their adherents.[254] Indeed he was named as one of 'our highest diplomatic functionaries' who were appointed to preside over those courts in the main Princely States, as was his friend Maj Gen Fraser in Hyderabad.[255]

Some Personal Correspondence

A Scottish Peer, Lt Gen Lord Elphinstone, became Governor at Fort St George in 1837, and was also appointed Commander-in-Chief – in which circumstances it was, perhaps, fortunate that the Madras Army was having a quiet time. Elphinstone had stayed with Cubbon at Bangalore during his first year in office, and the warmth of their friendship was increased by the way Cubbon expressed his condolences on the tragic death of Elphinstone's cousin during Lord Auckland's ill-considered and ill-fated invasion of Afghanistan. During his final year in office Elphinstone tried to arrange a meeting in Madras, and the invitation of 11 June 1842 was written in his own hand.

> My Dear General,
> Elliott tells me that at last there is a chance of your leaving your own kingdom, and of your honouring the Company's territory with a short visit....If I were Chief Justice I am afraid that I should be tempted to have you sub-poena'd oftener, but I will only remind you of your promise, and will accept even this forced visit as an instalment, provided you take up your quarters with me during your detention in Madras.[256]

He went on to be critical of the Company's management in Afghanistan, and to remark that he had heard Lord Tweeddale had been appointed to succeed him. Elphinstone had, perhaps, been too easy-going; certainly the Duke of Wellington believed the Madras Army needed a firm hand. As predicted he was succeeded by George Hay, Marquis Tweeddale, a man with good military experience and one who had a great reputation as horseman and *sabreur*. At the outset he was somewhat prickly toward Cubbon, possibly because he did not fully understand the unusual relationship between Madras and its close neighbour. Within a couple of years, however, a warm friendship had grown up between Cubbon, Lord Tweeddale and his wife Lady Susan. For the two men matters may have been eased by their shared love of horses, and by Cubbon being able to assist the Governor obtain some fine animals. Bangalore was then

---

[254] K.N.V. Sastri, *The Administration of Mysore* 46
[255] W.H. Sleeman, *Rambles and Recollections of an Indian Official* (London 1884) 88-90
[256] MNHL MD 436 25/16

famous as a place to secure Arab horses. They were landed at Mangalore and marched across country to the east coast, but were rested for a time in the vicinity of Bangalore where the best could be bought before the remainder went on to Madras.[257] In 1847 Cubbon bought two Arabs, on behalf of Tweeddale, from 'Ally Asker, Horse Dealer.'[258] His stated profession may convey the wrong impression, for this was Mirza Ali Asker whose title shows him to have been a cultured man, and for whom a street in Bangalore was named. Visits were exchanged too. The Tweeddales spent the early months of 1847 in the Nilgiris, and stayed with Maj Gen Cubbon when passing through Mysore State. Lady Susan remained in the Hills for several months after her husband had returned to Madras and, when writing to thank Cubbon, assured him that 'both of us would be delighted to have you here, when it is convenient to you.'[259] In due course the invitation was accepted.

People of authority in India, from the Governor-General downward, became used to receiving requests for favours. Late in 1842 an unexpected request came to Cubbon from the Isle of Wight.

> My Dear Colonel Cubbon,
> I am writing to ask a favour of you for one of my sons...and perhaps for auld acquaintance sake you may be unwilling to refuse, though believe me I sometimes think it very possible I may never have crossed your thoughts from the many years that have elapsed since we were together in Bangalore. ...
> Sorrow, care and anxiety have largely fallen to my lot, and the kindness of my friends been the only props under much anxiety.

She had three sons in the Madras Army. One, Willoughby, was a lieutenant in 32 MNI and she now asked Cubbon to get him under his command in the Mysore Commission

> I ask you to remember past years and be my friend even at this distance of time and place – and gratefully shall ever remain.
> Yours most truly,
> Fanny Crewe'[260]

What did this mean? Richard Crewe had been in the Commissariat of the Madras Army, and thus a colleague of Cubbon. He had transferred out in 1829, and was eventually appointed Commandant of forces in the Nilgiris. After three years there he died in 1836 leaving Fanny with several children to bring up. And Willoughby? Born in 1820 he became a lieutenant in 32 MNI in 1840, so had only two years service when Fanny wrote. In the Commission there would, of course, be useful allowances. However, Cubbon did not get him under

---

[257] Albert Hervey, *Ten Years in India* (London 1850) vol 1 57
[258] MNHL MD 436 25/72
[259] MNHL MD 436 25/19
[260] MNHL MD 436 25/17

command, and one suspects he thought the young man would be out of place: he had married in 1841 and by 1842 was already a father.[261] Such a young and inexperienced man with a family was unlikely to be able to meet the sudden and unexpected demands that would be made upon him as an officer of the Commission.

Another letter of 1842 was more welcome. It came from his old friend William Monteith, and was sufficiently valued to be annotated 'Directions for journey home, Monteath.' Written from the Oriental Club, then in Hanover Square, 'this most comfortable Indian establishment', it gave detailed information on matters important and minor, ending with novelty 'then to Southampton and 3 hours by rail road to London 75 miles, rate of travelling 25 to 30 miles per hour.'[262] Here is evidence that Cubbon hoped and planned to take a furlough in these Islands. By way of preparation he had joined the Oriental Club in 1826.

About this time Cubbon's thoughts turned increasingly toward Nundidroog as a possible retreat from both the hottest weather and unwelcome calls on his time. There, about 48 km north of Bangalore, a great rocky mass rose more than 500 m above the plain. From some angles it resembled a huge bullock lying to chew the cud, and so got its name *Nandi* – Lord Siva's bull, and *Durga* – a hill fort. It was several degrees cooler than Bangalore, but had an unpredictable rainfall. The place had been fortified from about the end of the fifteenth century, but the work was not carried to a high state until Hyder Ali captured the place in 1762. He and Tipu then constructed an extensive fort around its summit. Mark Cubbon had known the place for many years and had visited Uncle Wilks there; but now it was within his own domain. So he built himself a house, almost on the highest point. It is a fine place, on two levels, and commands extensive views. When comparatively young he probably came here on horseback from Bangalore but later, as infirmity overtook him, he would have travelled by carriage to the foot of the hill, and thence in a dhooli to the summit. Clearly, Cubbon loved Nundidroog and, in age, stayed for extended periods.

A Welcome Change

Major J.D. Stokes of 4 MNI had succeeded Col Fraser as Resident in Mysore and Commissioner for Coorg Affairs in 1836. Stokes supported the demands of the Maharajah for restoration of his authority. He was a thorn in Cubbon's flesh, for between the two men there was a complete antagonism of opinion and feelings, and they had several official disputes. There are, however, ways around this kind of predicament if one has the patience to find them. Stokes

---

[261] Biographical card: Richard Crewe (BL (OIOC))
[262] MNHL MD 436 25/18

Commissioner's residence, Bangalore as Cubbon would have known it, before the second storey was added. (L. B. Bowring, 1860s: Courtesy of BL (OIOC))

was promoted lieutenant colonel in 1841 and, two years later, transferred to command a battalion of 15 MNI, of which Cubbon was Colonel! The post of Resident was abolished and administration of Coorg was merged with the Mysore Commission, but with another Superintendent to take care of its interests. Nevertheless, Coorg remained a Company possession and thus distinct from Mysore. Also from this time the results of Cubbon's excellent administration manifested themselves.

CHAPTER TWELVE

Commissioner for Mysore and Coorg 1843 – 1860

From 1843 Cubbon had the affairs of Mysore and Coorg firmly in his hands, subject only to scrutiny by successive Governors-General. This, therefore, is an appropriate time to name the officers of the Commission: we have met some of them already, and others will be mentioned later.

Maj Gen Mark Cubbon 15 MNI	Commissioner
Capt A. McLeod 5 MLC Mil.	Sec. to Commissioner
Lt Col A. Clarke 2 ELI	1st Assistant to Commissioner
Capt W.A. Halsted 11 MNI	2nd
Vacant	3rd
Capt W. C. Onslow 44 MNI	4th
(Three Junior Assistants)	
Major R. Budd 3 MNI	Superintendent, Bangalore Div.
Capt H. Montgomery Mad. Art.	Ashtagram Div.
Capt R.S. Dobbs 9 MNI	Chittledroog Div.
Capt C.F. LeHardy 14 MNI	Nuggar Div.
Capt Gregory Haines 18 MNI	Coorg
A.N. Magrath, Esq. Durbar	Surgeon to H.H. the Maharajah
C.I. Smith, Esq.	In Medical Charge

Cubbon was promoted Lieutenant General in November 1851. In September 1855 another Manxman, Capt Thomas Moss McHutchin of 19 MNI, joined as a Junior Assistant to the Commissioner.[263]

Relations with the Maharajah

Further insight into the character of the man with whom Cubbon had to work so closely emerges from correspondence of about this time.

His Highness resented the Government's insistence that his personal debts should be paid from his annual fifth share, which he was therefore unable to spend as he wished. He expressed this resentment to the Governor-General. In April 1844 Lord Ellenborough, then on the point of departure, returned a reply which at first had a soothing effect on the Maharajah's mind; but soon Cubbon recorded 'this has been effaced by the pernicious influence exerted by the Rajah's profligate associates – two of whom are Arrapoor Buswapajee and Vencatapajee Serbiah.' The Maharajah therefore raised the matter again with the new Governor-General, Sir Henry Hardinge. His khureeta was transmitted through the Commission, so that Cubbon was able to comment on it.

---

[263] Madras Almanac 1844, 1851, 1855.

The Government now knows the contents of the Khureeta…I shall only remark that the fourth paragraph of it affords a good specimen of the Rajah's habit of distorting expressions to serve his own purposes. I mean the interpretation which His Highness has been pleased to put on Lord Ellenborough's letter of 10 April. His Highness has, with his usual cunning, suppressed the fact that the balance of his fifth share (the withholding of which he now complains of as an infringement of the 5th Article of the treaty) was, with his concurrence, and the sanction of the Government of India, set apart and directed to be applied by the Resident to the liquidation of his debts and cannot become his own until his debts are paid.[264]

Those debts included large sums for the purchase of jewels, and Rs3 lakhs to the heirs of Nun Lal Barty, a Sowar, for goods supplied. The task of liquidating them continued. Over the years, however, relations between the two men improved, so that by 7 May 1855 Cubbon was able to write to his friend General Fraser in Hyderabad

You will be glad to hear that he [the Maharajah] is getting on quietly, and feels more at ease than the people around him would allow some years ago. Indeed, if he would only retrench his expenditure and pay off his debts, there would be nothing more to desire.[265]

Protocol in India was more precisely defined, and more rigid, than anything we know today. The Princes, for example, were graded according to the size and importance of their territories, and awarded salutes of so many guns to be fired on ceremonial occasions. At the top of the list was the Nizam of Hyderabad, the Maharajah of Mysore and three others who received a salute of twenty-one guns; at the bottom was a group of 'non-salute' States. Seating at official dinner-parties was also determined by a system of precedence. European ladies usually acquired their precedence according to the official positions of their husbands. As a group they tended to be more conscious of protocol than were their male counterparts, and sometimes questioned the precedence accorded them. About 1845 the Maharajah of Mysore held a very large European Durbar for Westerners from adjoining territories as well as his own State. Now, what was the position of the wife of a Baronet who, himself, did not hold a particularly high post in the Company's Government? Sir Henry Conyngham Montgomery had joined the Madras Civil Service in 1824 and by 1845 was Collector and Magistrate at Tanjore, a good though not exalted position. He and his wife attended the Durbar – but where should Her Ladyship be placed relative to the other guests, some of whom were senior in the service to her husband? Cubbon was to sit on the Maharajah's right hand side, and the Lady

---

[264] MNHL MD 28/5 No 88
[265] H. Fraser, *Memoirs and Correspondence of General James Stuart Fraser of the Madras Army*. (London 1885) 450

was placed on his own right. Sir Henry stood among senior officers of the Commission.[266] There seems to have been no objection on the score of precedence. However, an indifferent painting of the occasion suggests that Lady Montgomery's gown was decidedly *décolletée*, which was not in good taste for a Durbar, so perhaps His Highness objected? Incidentally, a Mrs Lewis was also present: could she have been the lady who so fascinated young Mark in 1808?

In most places where they lived in India the British built churches, and Bangalore came to be well-provided with them – ten being worthy of mention by Issar (1988).[267] The earliest of those still extant is – by a happy coincidence – St Mark's, which was raised in 1808 to provide for both military and civilian worshippers. In due course, however, a feeling grew up that the military should have its own church close to the Cantonment; and so in February 1848 the foundation stone of Trinity Church was laid by Maj Gen John Aitchison, then Commanding the Mysore Division. Consecrated during 1851 in an unfinished state, Trinity was probably the biggest 'army' church in South India, having seating for 700 people. It continued in this role until Independence, as brass plates on the two lines of pews still showed in 1992:

The Hon the Resident	General Officer Commanding
Commanding Officers	Staff
Q.A.I.M.N.S.	Chaplain
Officers	Officers

Not to be outdone, the European residents of Coorg, many of them planters, built a church for themselves within the Mercara fort at about the same time. A more modest structure than Trinity, it was usually called the 'English Church'.

Dalhousie's Regime

The Earl of Dalhousie was only thirty-five when he assumed office, and so was the youngest man ever to be Governor-General of India. Like Mornington, he possessed immense energy and an imperious temper. Already he had gained much experience of administration. As Vice-President and then President of the Board of Trade he had framed and implemented regulations for the railway system. This understanding he promptly applied for the benefit of India. In 1853 he set a plan in motion that enabled the first railway to be opened that year; at the same time a telegraph line from Agra to Calcutta was completed. By 1857 there were 320 km of railway in use, and because it proved so valuable during the Sepoy Mutiny, the Government sanctioned 8000 km of permanent way to be laid and operated by eight companies. Dalhousie's method for financing India's railways sprang from his experience in Great Britain. He

---

[266] T. P. Issar, *The Royal City* 33; also in MNHL with a key to many of the people present.
[267] T. P. Issar, *The City Beautiful* (Bangalore, 1988) 128-34

enlisted private enterprise 'directly but not vexatiously controlled by the Government' and thus committed construction of the lines to incorporated railway companies, to which he guaranteed a certain rate of interest on capital while retaining control in the hands of Government.[268]

Also like Mornington, Dalhousie was disposed to acquire territory by annexation of Princely States. Eight States were absorbed in seven years, and the annexation of Oudh in 1856 did much to bring on the mutiny of the Bengal Army in the following year. Indeed, Dalhousie seems to have regarded the Princely States as being obsolete in his 'New India' and thus anticipated the policy of another 'New India' created by Independence. During his administration, however, a number of social reforms were introduced, including trial by jury throughout British India.

For Maj Gen Cubbon the arrival of Dalhousie initiated a more cordial relationship than he had previously enjoyed with the Head of Government, or would again. It began in Madras when Dalhousie spent a few day with his father-in-law, the Marquis Tweeddale, before proceeding to Calcutta and his swearing-in on 12 January 1848. Cubbon was there in order to pay his respects to the new Governor-General; and where the Governor and Lady Tweeddale were his close friends. Unfortunately, he came down with fever, which did not prevent him from offering some sage counsel to the new arrival. An abiding friendship was forged between the two men, such that within a year the Governor-General was writing personal letters to Cubbon and even seeking out a doctor to fill a vacancy in the Commission. He also approved Cubbon's sharp action in putting down some restive polygars in northern Mysore.[269]

One comment on Dalhousie was that 'almost the only gift denied him was good health.'[270] His indifferent constitution suffered from even more blows than his constant over-work inflicted upon it. His wife's health had been delicate, so she took ship for Great Britain, but died in home waters late in 1853. This depressing event was only partly compensated by the prompt arrival of his older daughter, Lady Susan Ramsay, then a girl of seventeen.[271]

Amid his busy official life, Mark Cubbon had to deal with requests from the Island. In July 1850 Maria asked for money, to which he replied as soon as the letter arrived – in October he wrote

> The mail closes in a few minutes…I enclose an order on Messrs Coutts and Co for 500£. Love to Betsy. I am in better health than I have enjoyed for many years, and will make an effort to write her soon. God bless you both.[272]

---

[268] Dalhousie, James Andrew Broun-Ramsay, Marquis of. In *Dictionary of National Biography*.
[269] MNHL MD 25/21
[270] V. A. Smith, *Oxford History of India*. 655
[271] MNHL MD 25/17
[272] MNHL MD 25/22

He was as good as his word, for in March 1851 he wrote from Nundidroog to 'My Dearest Betsy', promising another £500 before the end of the year, and

> I was called into the country on urgent business, and afterwards laid up with a rheumatic fever which confined me to my room for six weeks, and from which I am only now beginning to recover…still so weak I can hardly guide my pen. The place from which I write is described in Wilk's Mysore…it is a mountain 1000 feet higher than the plain…the temperature is normally about 70 when it is 88 in Bangalore 30 miles off. I am occasionally subject to rheumatism in the cold season, but I hope to prevent a return of it next cold weather by taking a couple of months on the Malabar coast – the sea air agrees with me better than any other.
> I have seen a good deal of Mr McHutchin, who is now gone to the Neilghery Hills, to recover from fever…I like him much.
> I recall Lady Buchan well as a child, a beautiful child, with the promise of growing up an elegant and interesting woman.[273]

This domestic correspondence was continued when Mark wrote to Maria in May 1853 'I am now better than I have been for many a hot season; my only complaint is a tenderness of the soles of my feet which prevents me from taking as much exercise as would be good for me.'[274]

Occasionally questions arose about the behaviour of individual members of the Commission, and in 1851 Cubbon had to deal with a particularly complicated example of misdemeanor. Although Ayurveda practitioners were on hand, the Maharajah decided to appoint a Western-trained doctor for his family. Thus it came about that the Durbar Surgeon was stationed with the Court in Mysore City but was administratively part of the Commission. For several years the post was held by a Dr Lewis and then by Mr Magrath who was replaced, in 1849, by a somewhat devious character.

John Colin Campbell had served in the Army for seventeen years before becoming Durbar Surgeon, and he first became the subject of complaints in 1851-52. Several charges were made against him, charges that became intertwined in a complex way. The affair was begun by a letter of 20 August 1851 from six Hindu gentlemen of Mysore to the Medical Board, Fort St George, and a similar letter addressed to the Governor-General. These letters were referred to Cubbon for investigation and report. The essence of the original charges, and others that emerged, were: (i) Campbell was incompetent in surgery and midwifery and was subject to epileptic fits; the recent death of His Highness's favourite daughter could have been avoided by a skilful practitioner; (ii) He had been diverting funds, provided by His Highness for the 'Fever Hospital', to his own purposes so that there was a shortage of drugs; (iii) The reputation of the hospital had declined greatly since the time of Mr Magrath; (iv) Campbell had been absent from his surgery in Mysore City when

---

[273] MNHL MD 25/23
[274] MNHL MD 25/25

a Monsieur Dickman required urgent medical treatment for a serious condition; (v) Contrary to regulations (which continued until the end of the Indian and Colonial Empires) he had accepted presents from the Maharajah; (vi) A lady of Campbell's family had accepted an invitation to the *tarmasha* that ended the Dussera Festival, and this too was contrary to proper usage. The six anonymous signatories suggested that His Highness would like to replace Campbell but feared to do so lest he offend Cubbon 'with whom it appears Mr Campbell is in high favour'.

It is instructive to follow Cubbon's pragmatic approach to a tricky matter. On the one hand, he undertook a thorough investigation of the background to the complaint, and identified the complainants. His second line was to press Campbell, gently but firmly in a series of letters, to reveal the truth about the non-medical aspects of the case; these take us back a few years and emerge as the more intriguing parts.

In 1839 the Nawab of Kurnool had stock-piled large amounts of ammunition in preparation for a full-scale rebellion, but the Company had made a pre-emptive strike and he was deposed. After the place had been captured a lady from a highly respectable Pathan family (indeed, possibly a daughter of a former Ruler of Kurnool) was 'thrown upon my (Campbell's) protection' and they now had two daughters. In October 1849 the Maharajah's favourite daughter (now dead) invited 'my Beebee Sahib and the two butchahs' to attend the tarmasha arranged for ladies only on the last day of the Dussera Festival. They had gone, and had accepted the customary gifts, which amounted to Rs250 in value. Campbell strongly denied that the lady, and his jockey, had each received the gift of a house from the Maharajah; the jockey had received lesser gifts, but so had the jockeys of other people. For his own part, Campbell had at first refused an offer of gifts from His Highness but, learning that his predecessor had done so, he also accepted them for fear of giving offence to the Maharajah.

In January 1852 Lt Gen Cubbon sent his report, in nine pages, to the Officiating Secretary, Government of India. It contained a telling final paragraph in which he wished the accusers had made their charges openly for 'The names attached are fictitious and the man indicated by the first signature has been dead for the last ten years'. Two months later came a reply saying that no further investigation was required, especially in view of the pseudonymous character of the charges.

In replying to Campbell, Cubbon advised 'the lady not visiting the Palace again nor having any intercourse there' but he recognized that to have refused presents on a public occasion would have given offence to His Highness

> ...as it is the Rajah's character to be far less tenacious upon great objects than upon minor points which concern only his feelings and wishes, and his resentment might have taken a personal turn. ...It is of the greatest consequence that the Rajah should be kept in good humour, and I should much regret if any influence you may have over him should be weakened as it would at once tend

toward throwing him back into the hands of those who are looking out for an opportunity of renewing the strife by which they so long profited. [275]

While the episode of Campbell was under investigation the General had to deal with other matters concerning the Commission's personnel. Major William Anthony Halsted had been a member of the Commission for several years. He was married with three children, but turned to drink and his behaviour became such that, according to his wife, the family were known as 'the miserable Halsteds'. Matters became so serious that Cubbon had to take action, and 'Poor Halsted was sent off the day before yesterday [14 Nov., 1852] and was very violent at first.' He was invalided from the Service in 1853 but did not reform himself. Georgina Halsted, however, remembered Cubbon's handling of the case with gratitude and affection.[276]

About this time the Charter Act of 1853 was passed. It tightened further the grip of the Home Government on the affairs of India. Briefly, the Company's right to trade with China was abolished, six of its twenty-four Directors were to be nominated by the Crown, and – most important of all – patronage was abolished and replaced by open, competitive entry to the Civil Service. This last provision was seen as essential to improving the Government of India, and eventually to enabling Indians to enter the top grades of the Indian Civil Service.[277]

A potentially damaging misunderstanding arose between the Governor-General and Commissioner in July 1854. Dalhousie had been requested by a friend in Scotland, a Mr Hay, to secure an appointment in the Mysore Commission for his son, then a young officer in 50 MNI. This he had put in train but had somehow received a copy of a letter from a Col Reid to 'My Dear Alick' (Lt Alexander Charles Hay) which included

> Cunningham says that the General has every inclination to serve you, but he will not make the first move. He will be delighted to get you appointed if Lord Dalhousie (who says he leaves the appointments to Cubbon) only names you. [278]

To a man of Dalhousie's temper this was an unforgivable affront; someone had 'seemed to call in question my word.' Fortunately for Cubbon, the matter could be cleared up within two months. Friendly relations were resumed and, in due time Lt Hay joined the Commission; but a cloud remained over Reid.[279]

In an effort to recruit his health and spirits Dalhousie spent several months of 1855 in the Nilgiris with Lady Susan, now eighteen, to cheer him. Writing from Coonoor he remarked that he would be exceedingly happy to see Cubbon

---

[275] MNHL MD 25/7 (this folio has several sub-folios; first page of item 4 is missing)
[276] MNHL MD 25/15
[277] V. A. Smith, *Oxford History of India*. 722
[278] MNHL MD 25/26
[279] MNHL MD 25/27

there if it would suit him to come. In the event they met at Kotigherry (Kotagiri), a small hill-station about 25 km east of Coonoor.[280] Cubbon was so unwell that Dalhousie took a firm line when the time came to arrange his passage through Bangalore to Madras. He opposed outright Cubbon 'dragging yourself up this hill needlessly' but wished him to wait in Bangalore 'where I should be grateful for your shelter and hospitality.'[281]

Cubbon complied, but did all he could to make the three-day visit profitable for Dalhousie and enjoyable for his young daughter. For the Governor-General he prepared a General Memorandum on the administration of Mysore since the Company assumed authority. This really marked the end of the exclusively patriarchal and non-regulation system of government by Cubbon and his select body of officers. Thereafter, Annual Reports were produced.

The Governor-General was much pleased by what he saw, remarking that conditions in Mysore were better than those usually found in the territory of a Native Prince, and even in some parts of British India. Moreover, Lady Susan's letters reveal that she had been given a whale of a time. All this is clear from Dalhousie's personal letter of 2 November 1855 which also shows him to be on top form again. Cubbon, it seems, was still unwell.

> From the Duke's House in the Daulut Bagh, Seringapatam.
> My Dear General Cubbon,
> I cannot refuse myself the satisfaction of writing to you a few lines from the address I have traced at the top of the page, to tell you that my visit to Mysore [City] has in all respects been agreeable to me and highly successful. I cannot say it was perfect, for you, my dear General, were not there…and your absence was a great drawback to my pleasure, as I am sure it was a disappointment to yourself…Dr Campbell has given us a truly 'Hieland welcome' – what can I say more?[282]

The Governor-General had spent two days in Mysore where 'Susan had an opportunity of seeing a very good specimen of a Native court, and was greatly diverted with the pomp and circumstance, and not least with the mutual embraces between the Rajah and myself.' Dalhousie and his party then pushed on toward Madras, reaching Arcot in three days, and then four hours more to the railhead, whence the train carried them in less than three hours to Madras. From there he wrote another personal letter to Cubbon, on 10 November.

> In such a hurry since we crossed the Mysore border …that I have been unable to fulfil my intention of writing to you until this moment…your troopers were very attentive and I should be glad if you would put out a short order intimating my satisfaction.

---

[280] MNHL MD 25/29
[281] MNHL MD 25/30
[282] MNHL MD 25/31

[I must] express my sincere regret at leaving your bounds, and in denying myself a longer enjoyment of your friendly hospitality. You were the first acquaintance I made in India – you are one of the few with whom I shall deeply regret to part when I leave it; and even though I cling to the hope of seeing you again before I embark, it grieved me to part the other day. Susan went off with the tear in her eye.[283]

Lady Susan and Mark Cubbon enjoyed a correspondence for several years thereafter. Three days before Christmas 1855 she wrote affectionately to thank him for

…all the things you have so kindly sent me…including a drawing of Papa by Captain Martin: I am still obstinate about there being too much chin. Don't tell Captain Martin or he will hate me for ever in consequence. There was also a perfect likeness [of Cubbon by Capt Martin]… also some excellent apples…I am going to write to Grandmama by the next mail and shall tell her all about you and Bangalore.[284]

Another gift followed, something quite special. On 19 February Cubbon wrote that he had sent Lady Susan a pair of bangles which he ironically called

a specimen of the barbarous trades of this part of the world…Only one man is capable of this kind of work and since he is now very old he works slowly. Therefore I could not present them to you before you leave.

Then followed an example of Cubbon's most courtly style.

He hoped the bangles will remind you occasionally of a spot which for a few brief hours rejoiced in the light of your presence, as it once did in that of your Grand Mama, and where neither of you will be forgotten. I am so glad that in writing to Lady Tweeddale you mentioned Bangalore, where she is so well remembered.

Next came a tribute to her father, referring to his immense labour in the climate of Bengal, and how remarkable it was that any mortal man could have done to much while passing through so many trials.[285]

Lady Susan's bangles remained a source of great pleasure to her, and she shared it with Cubbon. In September 1857 she wrote from Edinburgh, enclosing a newspaper cutting that described her drawing-room dress including '*Lady S. Ramsay portait en outre des bracelets qui lui ont été offerts à son départ des Indes.*' And she added 'when I wear my bangles I enjoy the consciousness – a most

---

[283] MNHL MD 25/32
[284] MNHL MD 25/33
[285] MNHL MD 25/36

pleasing one to a female – that I am the object of envy to every member of my sex present!'[286]

Cubbon's doctors forbade him from travelling to Madras to greet the incoming Governor-General, Lord Canning, and thence on to Calcutta to take leave of Dalhousie. He assured the latter this omission was a great disappointment, particularly as Dalhousie's ship did not pass through the Madras Roads.

Dalhousie left India with his health broken, but still he exerted himself for those who had served him well. He had been trying to secure a knighthood for Cubbon, but there had been a hitch and he was put out that he had been unable to obtain the honour while still in office. To be sure, Cubbon had been gazetted CB on 4 February 1856 but Dalhousie was not satisfied. On the day after his arrival in London he took up the matter with the President of the Board of Control (Sir Charles Wood) and secured an assurance that all would be set right. A few days later he was informed that the Queen had signed the nomination. On 22 May 1856 he wrote

> It gives me sincere pleasure to be able to tell you by the first mail after our arrival in England that you are knighted, and that you either are, or in a few days will be gazetted KCB [and he rounded out the affair with] I am heartily glad that…the Queen has given to you in the end the place of honour, which all the world had already allotted to you. I am weak and can write but little now: I will write again. Susan sends her love, and I am ever, my dear friend,
> Very sincerely yours[287]

The appointment was gazetted on 2nd. June. Sir Mark's KCB was in the Civil Division, the 'star' cost twelve guineas, the Queen dispensed with the ceremony of investiture, and he returned the CB badge so recently acquired.[288]

By this time a letter took only three months between India and Great Britain, which helps us to follow some of the correspondence between Dalhousie, his daughter, and Sir Mark. In July 1856 Sir Mark tried to reassure Lady Susan about her father's eventual recovery, even invoking the opinion of that 'sound and thinking man, Dr Campbell.' It was, however, Lady Susan who made the running. In September she wrote

> I must write again to ask you to accept the picture of myself which I send you with this note. It is very conceited of me to think so; but I do think that I could not send you anything that would please you better – and if I am conceited you can't complain for I am sure you did your best to make me so with your kindness to me.

---

[286] MNHL MD 25/51
[287] MNHL MD 25/40
[288] MNHL MD 27/4

Her father was stronger than when she had written in May. They had been staying with the Tweeddales where 'you were inquired about over and over again.'[289] All of which could only have been pleasing to a seventy-year old! By October she was begging him to write again.

Dalhousie's letter of 25 November was superscribed with obvious relish 'Lt Gen Sir Mark Cubbon KCB.' He acknowledged Cubbon's letter of August, asked for news of India from time to time, and requested Cubbon to drop the 'My Lord' in favour of something less formal, saying 'I am only an exploded Lord Sahib as you know.' He believed he was mending slowly, though still on crutches. Then he relayed a message from Susan 'Give him my love and tell him he is a duck, adding I was to translate this into what she called proper language, but I prefer sending the message to you in the vernacular.'[290]

At this time Dalhousie was seriously ill and forced into inactivity, seen as yesterday's man, and ignored by many of those who had formerly sought his presence; but, as he wrote 'One person treats me with honour and consideration, now as ever – the Sovereign I serve.'

More the pity, therefore, that Sir Mark's wrote infrequently. Then, in June 1858, Dalhousie received a letter from the Captain of the *Trafalgar* stating that he had brought a grey Arab from Cubbon for Lady Susan Ramsay. There had been no prior warning! Of course, Dalhousie wrote a warm letter of thanks, but chided Sir Mark for not having written for some time 'but if you will be a Trappist we can't make you speak; …Now farewell for the present, my dear old friend – Susan will write for herself.'[291]

Sir Mark had been long from these Islands, and perhaps attitudes had changed – as they have changed again. He must have been surprised, therefore, when Dalhousie stated that no one could assent to his daughter riding a stallion in this country. Seemingly there was now a widespread opinion that 'riding of an entire horse [is] neither decent nor safe for anybody, much less a lady. Consequently, and despite the animal's good temper, Dalhousie had him castrated.[292] But as Susan wrote, the horse was called 'General' and 'adored for your sake'[293]

Thereafter the correspondence lagged again on Cubbon's side. Dalhousie died in 1860, and in due time Lady Susan married the Hon Robert Burke, brother of the 6th Earl of Mayo.

A New Governor-General

Charles John Canning took up office on 29 February 1856 and, despite the many demands on his time, wrote to Cubbon on 26 March to regret that they

---

[289] MD) MNHL 25/43
[290] MNHL MD 25/45
[291] MNHL MD 25/57
[292] MNHL MD 25/58
[293] MNHL MD 25/60

had been unable to meet in Madras so that he had been deprived of the pleasure of a personal acquaintance. He went on

> I desire to assure you of the confidence and satisfaction with which I look forward to receiving your assistance in the conduct of all affairs connected with the charge which you have so honorably administered…and of my wish to give you, when necessary, effective support.
> I would, at the same time beg of you, whenever there be convenience in so doing, to write me freely and unreservedly in private letters. Many matters may arise which may be more satisfactorily treated in such a correspondence than officially.[294]

This was a promising beginning. Unfortunately, Canning could not refrain from involving himself in detail. On 11 August, his Private Secretary wrote that the Governor-General had observed the post of Superintendent of the Nuggur Division was vacant because Major Porter was on leave, and that his Lordship 'wished to know who was to fill it.'[295] Cubbon did not improve matters by not replying to the letter before October, when the Secretary wrote again to remind him. The matter was then resolved.

Canning was the unluckiest man to hold the post of Governor-General of India. Fifteen months after he assumed office the Sepoy Mutiny erupted, and for the remainder of his tenure he had to deal with it and its aftermath. Moreover, he did not bear principal responsibility for that terrible event. To be sure, Oudh was annexed in 1856, but that was essentially a 'last straw' to Dalhousie's annexations. Indeed, a variety of reasons underlay the revolt. They ranged from a legend that the Company's Sirkar would last only a hundred years from the Battle of Plassey (23 June 1757) to an undoubted affront to the sensitivities of both Hindus and Muslims by the introduction of new cartridges said to be greased with a mixture of beef and pork fat, an affair that was mishandled by Canning's military colleagues.

On Sunday 10 May 1857 the Sepoy Mutiny – a full-scale revolt by the Bengal Army – began at Meerut. Mutineers carried the news post-haste to Delhi 65 km away. There they induced the Sepoy garrison to join them, and thereafter the old capital was the main focus for operations. Other cities in Hindustan also became involved: Lucknow, Jhansi and Kanpur were among them. Eventually forty-seven battalions of the Bengal Army mutinied, only seven refrained. The Company's resources were stretched to the limit, so that it called up forces from Punjab, Madras, China and Great Britain. Delhi finally fell to the Company in September 1858.

Both beginning and end of the affair were attended by cruelty and viciousness: initially by the mutineers scenting victory, finally by the Company made fearful by the closeness of the call. The best among Indians and British

---

[294] MNHL MD 25/39
[295] MNHL MD 28/8

remained above such excesses. Among these was the Governor-General who thereby earned himself the title 'Clemency Canning' – which initially conveyed the destructive ridicule of *The Times* and other journals, but later became a tribute to his statesmanship and moderation.

In July 1857 Dr Campbell passed to Cubbon intelligence of 'thousands of Muslims who had passed [through Coorg] on the road to Mysore, nearly all armed and without women or children.'[296] Nothing serious followed and Mysore remained largely untouched by the unrest that racked northern India, though there is a story that Cubbon stationed Coorg soldiers in several parts of the State as a precautionary measure. Certainly he was able to convey to the Governor-General some unfavourable remarks made by the Madras Sepoys on those from Bengal. On 30 May he wrote

> It will be satisfactory to Lord Canning to know that everything is tranquil in these parts, in spite of the seditious agency of the Press for years past in stirring up the Native Troops and Inhabitants to mutiny and revolt; not that there are no elements of discord here, but the most desperate will not dare to shew their teeth unless some great calamity should befall General Anson's force.[297]

The Maharajah himself was able to sum up the position in February 1858 'My own country, I am happy to say, has continued free from contamination, and I am quite certain that this happy circumstance is owing to the wise and judicious measures adopted by Sir Mark Cubbon.'[298]

In Durbar at Allahabad, Canning read Queen Victoria's Proclamation of 1 November 1858 which transferred the Government of India from the East India Company to the Crown. In addition to being Governor-General he became the first Viceroy – the Queen's personal representative, though she was not proclaimed Empress of India until 1876. In Great Britain, Indian affairs came under control of a Secretary of State – the first being Sir Charles Wood. He had recently completed six years as President of the Board of Control, and obviously felt himself secure in the saddle. In India itself new measures included strengthening central government, making a start in associating Indians with the Supreme Government, recognizing the loyalty of the Princes by guaranteeing their territories, and comprehensively restructuring the army.

The increased sensitivity toward local feelings soon showed itself in Mysore, and even affected the military. For example, the Commander-in Chief, Mysore Division wanted to acquire land in order to create a 'compact and well-regulated cantonment in Bangalore.' The Governor-General, however, supported Gen Cubbon's opinion that land and buildings in the town were held by private persons under grants made by the Rajah. It was therefore essential to give the occupiers 'an assurance that no man's just title will be infringed and

---

[296] MNHL MD 25/49
[297] MNHL MD 28/10
[298] H. Fraser, *Memoirs and Correspondence of General James Stuart Fraser.*

Lady Canning

A year earlier, in November 1857, Canning wrote Cubbon a cordial business-cum-personal letter. It told of preparations to move against the besieged Lucknow, and of complications due to the importance Muslims attached to the place. However, his main purpose was to tell Cubbon that Lady Canning would be visiting the Neilgherries, probably in April or May of 1858, she would 'pass through your dominions', and asked him to speed her on her way. Canning felt some reassurance to be necessary: 'I believe there never was a better traveller than Lady Canning, or one better disposed to make the best of whatever difficulties may lie in the road.' She was to be accompanied by Major Bowen (who was known to Cubbon) and the Hon Mrs Stuart, wife of Canning's Military Secretary, and to this lady we are indebted for a valuable account of the journey.[300]

Lady Charlotte Canning was, by all accounts, a charming person, and unusually accomplished. More than competent with her pencil, compiler of an informative journal, and for nearly twenty years a valued correspondent of the Queen. Her route took her to Madras and thence to the Nilgiris by way of Bangalore where, on 20 March, she

> ...arrived at 7 am in our transit carriage with a layer of red dust all over us. The party drove through the lines of the 60th Rifles to General Cubbon's charming bungalow. This was lovely in the early light – the deep verandah enclosed by a trellis covered with creepers in full bloom, one bright scarlet, the other blue. We found the whole house prepared for us, the chivalrous old man of seventy-four having put himself into a tent. He is a very handsome, keen-eyed intelligent man, and the quantity of anecdote of the deepest interest that he told us has been more entertaining than I can describe.[301]

Sir Mark had indeed vacated his house completely in favour of a tent in his garden. Lady Charlotte was at once charmed and embarrassed. The first emotion is clear from her description (from Nundydroog) to her sister

> I am visiting a charming old general, Sir Mark Cubbon, fifteen hundred feet above the table-land and with a view of about a hundred and fifty miles of country on all sides...and the old gentleman himself is very delightful. He has been all this century in India, but seems to know all that has gone on all over the world, and is the most *grand seigneur* old man I almost ever saw.[302]

---

[299] MNHL MD 28/12
[300] MNHL MD 25/62
[301] A. J. C. Hare, *The Story of two Noble Lives*. (London 1893) Vol 2 426
[302] A. J. C. Hare, *Two Noble Lives* vol 2 427

A view of Lady Charlotte herself is given by Mrs Stuart 'It is very nice to see her with all her old generals – they are so courteous, and evidently so delighted with her; and she united the *grande dame* and the pleasing companion to perfection.'[303]

After two days in Bangalore the party had moved on to Nundidroog. It left Bangalore at 4 am, drove for three hours to the foot of the hill, and thence its members were carried up a zigzag path in tonjons by a swarm of bearers. They reached the summit about 9 am and were delighted by the freshness of the air and vast views over a grand, rugged countryside, as Lady Canning described. From Nundidroog she travelled overnight to Mysore, where she was received by the Maharajah, and then moved on to Coonoor. By mid-June she was preparing for her return journey, and her embarrassment evinced itself when she wrote to Cubbon

> The time of my return to Calcutta draws so near that I must write you a word to tell you of my journey, and to ask you once more for your very kind hospitality (for the night of 25 June). I hope you will lodge us in a very much smaller compass than before and not turn yourself out of your own house. We have been living in such small rooms that we are accustomed to quarters very different from those you so kindly prepared and I shall be quite in despair if I thought you were living in a tent in this damp weather….I shall look forward with great pleasure to my little visit to you and long to have your opinion on many subjects in the last eventful weeks.[304]

Sir Mark at Seventy-five

Now, near the end of his life, one may ask what kind of man young Mark had become. The answer is to see him as described by his contemporaries.[305]

Physically, he was six feet tall or thereabouts. His eyes and hair were brown, and he sported side-whiskers that turned greyish before his hair. He had a fresh complexion. For most of his life he was energetic and had a great delight in climbing hills. When he toured as Commissioner the camp was wakened by a bugle at 2.30 in the morning and a start was made directly. He and his colleagues walked for the first hour or so before mounting and riding to the next camp-site, which was reached about day-break. Then he and the more active members of his party climbed a nearby hill before returning to camp for breakfast and the business of the day.

In the fashion of his times, shooting would have been a frequent activity, and often a source of fresh meat. When visiting the Nilgiris he could have

---

[303] A. J. C. Hare, *Two Noble Lives.* vol 2 405
[304] MNHL MD 25/63
[305] Based on R. S. Dobbs, (1882) 112-22 and a letter of 7 June 1882 from Dobbs to Rev. S. N. Harrison quoted in K. N. V. Sastri (1932) 313-4. Physical aspects from notes to a portrait by Maj G. M. Martin in Nat. Portrait Gallery, London

Sir Mark Cubbon about 1855, drawn by Capt. G.M. Martin of the Mysore Commission. (Courtesy of National Portrait Gallery, London).

ridden to hounds in pursuit of jackal in lieu of the fox. Indeed, horses were his principal passion. As Commissioner he kept a stable of fifty animals and, in his latter years, enjoyed having them paraded in review before him. The best were trained for racing and entered at the meetings that the Maharajah, and many Indians and Europeans alike, found such a pleasant diversion. There is a story, however, that his entrants never won a race, and his explanation that he felt it would be improper for people to gain or lose by gambling on his activities.

At home in Bangalore or Nundidroog his social life was very much that of the old Indian: his breakfast was always open to all-comers. His intimate friends and assistants were particularly welcome at his dinner-table, and with them he felt free to joke or exchange light banter. He did not enjoy large parties, and had such a dislike of balls that he never allowed a dance in his house.

Sir Mark's conduct toward ladies was characterized by a degree of consideration that verged upon deference. Nor was this confined to women of influence like Lady Canning or Lady Susan Ramsay. For example, he gave up his own bedroom to seventeen-year-old Miss Dobbs, daughter of one of his Superintendents – whose thoughts on an elderly bachelor's bedroom are a matter for speculation. Moreover, he insisted that even a young girl who shared his carriage should occupy the forward-facing seat. He had a special pleasure in giving a horse as a wedding present to his lady friends. When that same Miss Dobbs was about to be married he rejected all the animals in his own stables, and purchased a splendid Arab that turned out to be an excellent mount.

Apart from the reference to 'Mrs Lewis' there is no indication of an attachment to any European lady, nor of a wish to marry. Anglo-Indians of his generation not infrequently married, or formed less formal associations with, Indian ladies: Major James Archilles Kirkpatrick (in Hyderabad) and Dr Campbell were but two such. However, there is no evidence that Cubbon did so – even before he became a public figure.

As we shall see, winding up of his estate included the sale of houses. I have not attempted to trace them, but his retreat at Nundidroog would have been one. He owned other properties at various times. For example, in January 1847 he purchased a fine bungalow which is now the premises of the Bangalore Club (originally the Banglore United Services Club). Another bungalow in the same neo-classical style is Balabrooie – which suggests a link with Sir Mark, especially as some of his Officers (including Dobbs) lived there.[306]

While he husbanded the State's funds with great care, he was indifferent about his own money. A legacy from Uncle Wilks was left untouched, seemingly forgotten, but he spent or sent to his family most of his salary of £6000 a year. Equally contrary was his attitude toward his own reputation. On the one hand he had a positive dislike of popularity and dreaded that his improvements in Mysore should be become widely known; on the other, he wished to be well thought of by successive Governors-General. He was similarly ambivalence about his correspondence: for most of his life, business letters usually received prompt attention, but personal letters often remained unanswered. This extended even to those he loved, liked or respected, such as his parents and sisters, Dalhousie and Lady Susan. Perhaps the demands of official correspondence, much of which he drafted himself, overcame any inclination toward personal communication.

Sir Mark's colleagues could not understand his silence about his own family and, indeed, about Manx affairs. Even when other Manxmen in the Commission, McHutchin for example, mentioned the Rev Thomas Cubbon with admiration he refused to be drawn.

Some insight into his style of life is given by his purchases. His tailor's bill with W. Buckmaster & Co, of 3 New Burlington Street, London show that in 1853 his purchases included

2 x superfine Blue Cloth Braided Frocks, silk fairings	@ £12. 12. 0 each
12 yds Oxford Buckskins	@ 13. 6

and he paid £110 on account.[307]

---

[306] T. P. Issar, *The City Beautiful* 76-7, 92-3
[307] MNHL MD 27/9

By this time he had been forbidden to take alcohol, but in March 1857 he purchased for his guests, from Carbonell & Co., Wine Merchant, on a/c Messrs Arbuthnot

2 doz Pale Brandy	60/-	£ 6. 0. 0
12 fine Champagne	84/-	50. 8. 0
6 Old Port	56/-	6. 16. 0
24 Superior Sherry	60/-	72. 0. 0
4 fine Claret	84/-	16. 16. 0
Freight & Bills of Lading		4. 10. 0
Insurance on £170		2. 13. 0
		169. 3. 0
Discount on Wine & Brandy @ 10%		16. 4. 0
		£ 152. 19. 0 [308]

In 1858 some of the books purchased from John Gladding of London were

Fielding's Works 10 vols	£ 3. 3. 0
Byron's Works 6 vols	1. 17. 6
Napier's Peninsular War 6 vols	2. 10. 0
Saturday Review vols 1-10 variously priced[309]	

    Cubbon's closest associate was probably Maj Gen Dobbs, who had served in the Commission for a few months under Morison, continued with Cubbon, and then worked with his successor. He had, therefore, an unequalled opportunity to observe Cubbon's methods and to compare them with those of other Commissioners. He considered that Sir Mark was pre-eminently a statesman of the Munro type: one who met the folk under his care on their own ground, believing this to be the very core of good government in India. He was especially in his element when disentangling webs of local intrigue. He fought the Maharajah's Court with its own weapons, but with one exception – he abhorred and never used spies. Indeed, he was wont to relate with relish how a former Resident, Arthur Cole, surrounded the Maharajah with well-paid spies, but was baffled by the Maharajah giving them twice the sum to tell Cole only what the Maharajah wanted him to hear!

    He was intensively conservative by disposition, but this was counter-acted by two attributes. One was his wide reading of contemporary journals, both English and Indian, which opened his mind to reforms when convinced they were required by public opinion. The second was his readiness to give his deputies great freedom to exercise their own judgement on matters in which he believed they possessed practical knowledge, and to back them unreservedly.

    Serious reading of all kinds seems to have been his principal intellectual pursuit, and this included a study of the Sub-continent's languages and

---

[308] MNHL MD 27/10
[309] MNHL MD 27/12

literature. Indeed. there were few alternatives. Performances of Western classical music were rare events, and those mainly private concerts by practiced amateurs; to assist these people Williamson provided detailed information about the spare strings that should be taken to India, and how ladies should pack their pianos.[310] For Cubbon, amateur theatricals could have had little appeal.

In his religious beliefs Cubbon was certainly an individualist, and here the contrary element of his nature again showed itself. He always expressed a strong disgust for the priestly pretensions of the Clergy, and believed Popery and the liberty of the human mind to be irreconcilable; but he insisted on a strict observance of the Sabbath, required the Courts to remain closed, and refused to receive visitors. Like many another he had cast about for what he could believe and, near the end of his life, wrote 'I know it is supposed by many that I have either never given any attention to the subject or am a deliberate unbeliever....but this is a mistake.' Indeed, some years earlier he had settled down in Arianism. This free-thinking attitude might have been expected from one who had immersed himself in the literature of the European Enlightenment, the age of reason.

There is a story that he used his 'non-religious' reputation to the advantage of his subordinates. A Governor of Madras was strongly hostile toward public officers who held evangelical views, and attributed any disaffection among Indian to their activities. Cubbon rebutted these charges, remarking humorously to his assistants that it was as well they had a chief to protect them, who was himself beyond suspicion of religious fanaticism.

Many observers, Macaulay and Lady Canning to name but two, were astonished that he was so well informed about the world even though he had spent his entire adult life in one part of India. In fact, their view is itself surprising because India has a diversity that can open and broaden the mind of a discerning observer; while a lifetime of analytical reading may build up an immense store of information and understanding that requires only opportunity to display itself.

Throughout his life Cubbon's attention seems to have been focussed upon the tasks allotted to him, both as a young officer or Commissioner. His early experiences, together with the advice of Uncle Wilks and Col Agnew, led him to conceal his opinions on sensitive matters. In his prime, his free time was occupied by a combination of enthusiastic physical activity – riding, walking, hunting, studying the countryside – and the intense enjoyment of serious reading. In such a full life there was no time for trivial pursuits, and he did not miss them.

---

[310] T. Williamson, *The East India Vade-mecum*. (London 1810) vol 1 1-50 (alphabetical listing)

CHAPTER THIRTEEN

Cubbon's Administration 1834 – 1860

Sankar has characterized the destruction of the old order in India under Warren Hastings and Cornwallis as a necessary preliminary to the birth of New India under Bentinck and Hardinge. In support of his contention he evoked the words of Charles Edward Trevelyan 'The system established by Lord Cornwallis was based on the principle of doing everything by European agency. …The plan which Lord William Bentinck substituted for this was to transact the public business by Native agency under European superintendence.'[311] We have already noticed how Lord Bentinck and the Directors in London stated that the Commission should maintain, and work through, indigenous structures for the government of Mysore. Bentinck himself had a clear view of what had gone wrong and how the Commission should operate, and recorded it in a series of Minutes

> Our departure from the spirit and intentions of the original treaty [of 1799], and not wholly the personal defects of the Rajah himself, are responsible for the vices prevailing in Mysore. [27 Sep. 1831]
> The only object of the Commission is to promote the welfare and prosperity of the state of Mysore …to establish a better system of government therein and to put an effectual stop to the anarchy and disturbance that have latterly pervaded it. [10 Feb. 1832]
> During the suspension of the Rajah's rule (the Commission) should perform all functions and perform all duties of a Regency. [27 Apr.1832][312]

and he enjoined the Commission to study Mark Wilks's Report of 1805.

When Lt Col Cubbon took charge Mysore had an area of about 76,340 sq km with an estimated population of 3 millions. So Macaulay's comparison of Mysore being 'probably as large and as populous as Scotland' was reasonably accurate for population in 1834, but wildly astray for area.

A proper Civil Service was instituted in August 1834 with, as its key officers, the Commissioner, four Superintendents, and a number of Amildars. Sastri has recorded that Bentinck made all initial appointments at the same time, including the Amildars. He specified the maximum number of Europeans, but set no limit on the number of Indians.[313]

By November 1834 Cubbon was pointing out that it would not do to re-appoint men who had held office at the time of the insurrection because the

---

[311] Jadunath Sankar, *India through the Ages*. 67
[312] K. N. V. Sastri, *The Administration of Mysore under Sir Mark Cubbon* 21-2
[313] K. N. V. Sastri, *The Administration of Mysore* 154

ryots simply did not trust them. In 1841 he wrote with regret that the local public servants were combining 'to depress the rising spirits of independence among the people.'[314]

The administrative structure remained unchanged from what it had long been. The basic unit was the taluk, each under an Amildar who combined the functions of Collector and Magistrate and was assisted by a small staff. Every taluk comprised several sub-divisions, each with its Sheikdar who had the duties of collecting the revenue and policing his region. At the grass-roots was the village, each with its Patel (headman) and Shanbhogue (clerk); a few or many villages reported to the Sheikdar of their region. Superimposed upon this traditional structure were the four Superintendents of Divisions and the Commissioner himself. Every Amildar was responsible to the Superintendent of his Division. The European officers maintained contact with their subordinates, and with the people themselves, by frequent and extensive touring: the Superintendents within their Divisions and the Commissioner throughout the State. This had been done by the best Indian officials for centuries, and Cubbon encapsulated its value in 1841

> In no country, perhaps, has more been effected by the personal character of the public officers that in India, and nowhere, therefore does the success of public measures more depend upon the degree of mutual confidence subsisting between those officers and the inhabitants.[315]

This personal contact was supplemented by giving information through notices (written in Kannada) posted in public places, and in newspapers. An effort was made to avoid corruption. Regulations were drawn up for the guidance of Superintendents and Amildars, with the intention of protecting the public against officials attempting to secure private gain. Salaries of the Indian officials were increased above what they had been under the Maharajah – though probably insufficiently. Travel allowances were paid to all civil servants, even to peons – something that had not been done before. All allowances, no matter how small, were paid promptly. As an ultimate sanction, many officials who had not followed the Regulations were dismissed over the years, two Europeans being among them.

There was also a move toward rationalizing procedures, for example in the Amildars' offices. For years, records in every taluk had been kept in both Marathi and Kannada – the so-called 'double daftar' system. However, it was decided that from June 1835 only one language was to be used for official purposes in any individual taluk; and gradually only Kannada was employed. This was to have an unforeseen result after Independence.

The central headquarters had nine departments (katcheris) to coördinate action in the divisions and taluks; they were Revenue, Posts, Police, Military,

---

[314] K.N.V. Sastri 157
[315] K.N.V. Sastri 150

Public Cattle (Amrit Mahal), Public Works, Judiciary, Medical, and Public Instruction. Only the last two departments were creations of the Commission. The whole was overseen by a small Secretariat with the Secretary to the Commissioner at its head.[316]

Even when dealing with apparently routine matters of government, the Commission had to take some special factors into account. Of fundamental importance was its perceived position as a Christian group in control of a predominantly Hindu population and a substantial Muslim minority. This affected the development of both judicial and educational systems. Cubbon's general policy was to continue supporting religious institutions in a similar manner to the Maharajah, and he appointed his Head Sheristadar (a Hindu) as virtual controller of religious affairs. Indeed, Cubbon was fortunate in inheriting an excellent man from Morison. This was R. Vencata Row, whose qualities were recognised by conferment of a title and a special retirement pension, and who was succeeded in 1838 by a man of equal ability and probity, Krishnamma Naidu.

Broadly, three kinds of Hindu religious institutions had to be considered: (i) Temples, for which the main expenses were repairs and ceremonies. Cubbon expected wealthy temples to finance these from their own resources, but made grants to the smaller or poorer ones. (ii) Maths, which continued to receive the support given formerly by the Maharajah, but not his lavish concessions. (iii) Free-feeding houses were given support at the same level as by the Maharajah, namely about Rs50,000 a year. Moreover, all public servants received a bonus for the annual Ganapati festival, officials going on pilgrimage were helped, and appropriate prayers arranged and paid for during droughts and other times of distress.[317]

Another complication for the Commission was the matter of arrears. It inherited debts of two kinds: those owed by Mysore State to bankers, the troops, public servants and to the Madras Presidency; and those owed to the State by its subjects. Policy on the first category was set out at the time of assumption

> The British Government will guarantee to the Rajah's troops the payment of all arrears to which they may be justly entitled, and to those who have claims upon the Mysore Government an investigation with a view to a settlement of such as may be found just and reasonable.[318]

The troops were paid without delay because they had been making up for their lack of wages by exacting free board and lodging from the ryots and thus adding to their distress. Although the records of the Maharajah's government were confused and fragmentary, between October 1831 and July 1834 Rs14

---

[316] K.N.V. Sastri 73
[317] K.N.V. Sastri 127
[318] K.N.V. Sastri 25

lakhs of debts were paid off. Thereafter, Cubbon was extremely patient. He rejected no claim because of a delay in making it, so that a further Rs22 lakhs were paid by 1858.[319]

Debts owed to the Government were handled differently. Two categories were recognise: those arising between accession of the Maharajah and assumption by the Company, and those arising since that assumption of authority. The first category was much the larger and was of various kinds, ranging from unpaid land revenue to 'sums fraudulently received by public servants but not recovered' – and again the records were fragmentary or non-existent. In 1838 Cubbon proposed that the entire sum, amounting to some Rs44 lakhs, should be remitted in the belief that much of it had, in fact, been paid to public servants who had kept the money for themselves. Moreover, he considered that any attempt to secure these arrears would be generally perceived as unjust and vexatious. The Directors in London had reached the same conclusion and endorsed Cubbon's proposal as 'a most proper and necessary measure' – and one which was received with immense satisfaction throughout Mysore.[320]

Consonant with this expression of his wish to give just treatment to the ryots was Cubbon's insistence that the Company's military forces should treat the people decently – paying them immediately for goods and services, and not damaging crops or property when moving through the State. During Cubbon's tenure the judicial system was transformed. Initially a case-by-case system seems to have been followed, so that a body of case-law was formulated. These laws were applied to all classes of the people, except where custom dictated otherwise; and so a sense of equality before the law was engendered. Moreover, there was a general prohibition of corporal punishment or humiliating practices such as torture and mutilation, and the Courts therefore came to be seen as comparatively beneficent institutions.[321]

So much for the general structures and functions of Government under the Commission. Some specific aspects may now be considered.

Finances and Revenue

In 1834-35 the total income of the State was Rs68 lakhs, and in 1860-61 Rs97 lakhs; the maximum was Rs99 lakhs in 1859-60. The main contributions came from land revenue, which amounted to Rs36.5 lakhs and Rs61.5 lakhs in the first and last years of Cubbon's administration. There was a surplus of receipts over expenditure in nineteen of the twenty-seven years that he managed the affairs of Mysore, and the total surplus amounted to Rs9,227,400.[322] His reason for building up such a considerable surplus was to finance construction of a

---

[319] K.N.V. Sastri 72-3
[320] K.N.V. Sastri 182-3
[321] K.N.V. Sastri 61
[322] K.N.V. Sastri 200

large water reservoir – the Mari Kanave Reservoir which he proposed in 1854, but was not realized for fifty years.[323]

No fewer than 769 petty taxes were swept away: on marriage, on incontinence, on a child being born or given a name or having his head shaved. This relieved the people from a tax burden of Rs10.75 lakhs a year, and from much irritation.[324] In doing so, he pointed the way for Mr Manmohan Singh, Finance Minister in the government of Prime Minister Narasimha Rao (1991-96), who has been given credit for dismantling the 'licence-permit Raj' and unravelling much of the red tape that had stultified the Indian economy since 1947.[325] Indeed, Cubbon introduced only one new tax, on coffee production, and even that reduced the burden on cultivators.

Agriculture

Then, as now, agriculture was the backbone of the Indian economy, and land rents provided 50-63% of Mysore's revenue in Cubbon's time.[326]

Topography determined the agriculture of a region. Broadly speaking, the State was either malnad (hills, mainly the Western Ghats and their inland extensions), or maidan (plains) which was watered by the four main rivers, their tributaries, and the irrigation canals dug from them. Three kinds of cultivation were recognized: dry (for ragi or finger millet, *Eleusine coracana*), wet (for rice), and garden (for coconuts and vegetables). The area under dry cultivation was about four times that of the other two combined. Ragi was the staple grain of the ordinary people, but other grains, pulses and oil seeds were grown on dry land. Coomry was a particular form of dry cultivation employed by the hill people for growing ragi. Essentially a slash-and-burn system, it had all the defects inherent in that practice.

In Mysore, as over much of India, rain at the right time was the key to both a good harvest and sufficient grazing for cattle. Unfortunately, rainfall was unreliable: for example, at Nundidroog the average annual rainfall over a period of seven years was 2710 mm, but the range was 1730 to 4426 mm. When Cubbon became Commissioner there had been a drought for three years. A few good years followed, but 1838-39 was disastrous so that only half the normal crop of ragi was produced and, although there was little loss of human life, cattle died in shocking numbers.

Leases were usually for one year at a time, but might be for as many as five years. Assessment for payments on the Government's land was ryotwari – under which every individual dealt directly with the Government, and not through a middle-man. Moreover, a ryot was allowed to pay his rent in five or

---

[323] Imperial Gazeteer of India vol 18 – Mysore Section (Oxford 1908)
[324] W. G. L. Rice, *Mysore and Coorg – a Gazeteer.* vol 1 304
[325] Mark Tulley, 'The Cassandras are prophesying again' *The World Today* vol 52 No.3 (1996) 64-6
[326] K.N.V. Sastri 179

six instalments, beginning at any time between October and December according to the harvest-time in his region. He could therefore sell his produce when it suited him and then settle with the Government, so he had no need to borrow in order to pay his rent.

Taxes were also used in a constructive way. For example, in order to bring waste ground into cultivation a lower tax was charged on the first two to four years of cultivation; and to encourage the planting of two crops per year, the tax-rate on the second crop was set at 60% of that on the first. Among the taxes affecting farmers that Cubbon abolished were those on ploughs, mills and shops. He was liberal in remitting the land revenue when the ryots were affected by drought, flood or fire.

Early in his tenure Cubbon adopted measures to ensure that grain was neither wasted nor hoarded. The Company's troops were forbidden to damage crops along their line of march. Duties on grain were abolished in order to reduce the market price. A network of roads and tracks was built so that supplies could be moved quickly to districts in need: between 1831-32 and 1851 some 2580 km of cart road were built and bridged.

Coffee had long been a cash-crop in South India. According to tradition, a Muslim Saint had brought a few seeds of *Coffea arabica* from Arabia and planted them on the Baba Budran Hills of western Mysore, and certainly it was growing there by the late 17th century. *C. arabica* is the coffee of the uplands (1525 to 1850 m) and from its beans (seeds) is brewed a beverage of superior flavour and aroma, which is still widely available in South India. Cubbon exerted himself to encourage the cultivation of coffee, which can be a suitable crop for small-holders. His new coffee tax, introduced during 1838-39, was a flat rate of Rs1 per maund (approx 3 kg). The price then obtained by growers was Rs4 per maund so that the tax was effectively 25%; but it replaced the former váram, or government's 50% share, so that the actual amount of tax was halved.[327]

Land for coffee cultivation was made easily available to both Indians and Europeans, but this had not always been the case. Bevan has described the situation existing about 1838.

> The rent paid for coffee-grounds [sic] is half the produce. Until recently this was farmed by a speculator who had purchased the monopoly from the Rajah's Government. He exercised a most oppressive and arbitrary sway over the cultivator, by compelling him not only to give half [the crop] as rent, but also to sell the remainder at a price much below its marketable value. Colonel Cubbon, the present Commissioner, has very properly refused to renew the lease of this monopolist, but has thrown the sale of the article open to public competition, and has thus conferred great benefits on the cultivators.[328]

---

[327] W.G.L.Rice, vol 1. 304
[328] H. Bevan, *Thirty Years in India, 1808-38*. (London 1839) vol. 2 198.

Toward the end of his tenure Cubbon noticed that a few Europeans had accumulated large holdings without planting them. In 1860 he varied their leases so as to force them to plant 1240 coffee bushes per hectare within five years or forfeit their estates partly or completely.[329]

There was a long tradition in India of producing **sugar** from the sap of the toddy palm (*Caryota urens*) by boiling it to evaporate the water. Consequently, when the thick-stemmed 'noble' sugar cane (*Saccharum officinarum*) came to India from the Pacific region, the villagers applied the same technique to the juice squeezed from it. The product, however, was impure, dark in colour, hygroscopic, and deteriorated quickly. Commercial exploitation required a factory to extract and refine the juice on a large scale. Cubbon therefore gave all possible help and encouragement to Messrs Groves and Company when, in 1847, they established the Ashtagram Sugar Works – a modern, steam-powered plant. Their product was excellent. It won the prize and medal for the best crystallized sugar at the Great Exhibitions of 1851 and 1861 in London, and secured an honorable mention at the Universal Exhibition of 1867 in Paris.[330]

During Cubbon's time the story of **silk** production in Mysore was a sad one. He tried to improve the product by introducing new cultivars of the mulberry, and by providing training for selected staff. Moreover, the Chief Engineer (Mr Green) invented an excellent machine for reeling silk off the pupating silk-moths. When properly prepared, Mysore silk was of excellent quality and would have found a ready market in London. Unfortunately, the producers took a short-term view and preferred to turn out larger quantities of inferior silk and sell it locally.[331]

Cubbon was keen to establish a station where experimental work could be carried out on plants. Eventually this was done at the Lal Bagh, one of the chief ornaments of Bangalore. These splendid gardens had been founded by Hyder Ali in the 1760s and continued by his son. After 1799 they became the property of a Major Waugh, and this continued until 1819 when they became a branch of the Bengal Botanic Gardens. Until 1831 the gardens were under the general supervision of the Resident, but then became a responsibility of the Commissioner. In 1839 Cubbon founded an Agri-Horticultural Society and transferred Lal Bagh to its care. Despite the encouragement he gave it, the Society ceased to exist in 1842. In 1856 Dr Cleghorn, Chief Conservator of Forests for South India, recommended that a botanic garden be established. In August of that year Lal Bagh became the Government Botanic Gardens intended 'to carry out horticultural pursuits, designed for the improvement of indigenous plants, and for the introduction of exotic plants of economic importance and for the supply of those to the hills and plains when acclimatized.'[332]

---

[329] K.N.V. Sastri 112
[330] W.G.L. Rice, vol 1. 449
[331] K.N.V. Sastri 111
[332] M. H. Mari Gowda, *History of Lal Bagh*, in T. P. Issar (1988) 256-9

Even today the **trotting bullocks** of Mysore attract attention, and formerly they were deservedly famous. The original Hindu dynasty developed this breed of cattle by crossing Trichinopoly Brahmini bulls, which are still renowned for their speed and endurance, with the local Mysorean animals; the result was the Halikar breed. The cows are white, but the bulls usually have a bluish tinge over fore and hind quarters. Hyder Ali saw the value of these cattle as draught animals and especially for moving his artillery. Consequently, he set up a breeding establishment, the Amrit Mahal, to maintain and improve the breed. Indeed, Cubbon himself wrote 'It was this establishment that enabled Hyder Ali to march 100 miles in two days and a half to the relief of Chidambaram.' In 1800 the Amrit Mahal was made over to the restored Hindu Government, but it then deteriorated so far as to be resumed by the Company – an operation with which young Mark Cubbon and his friend Henry Harvey were involved. By 1823 the number of cattle under care of the Amrit Mahal had doubled to about 22,000, grouped into thirty herds.[333] After becoming Commissioner, Cubbon retained an interest in his early charges and encouraged the work of the Amrit Mahal. As late as 1975 the establishment continued with its headquarters at Hunsur. A pleasing sight in modern Karnataka is that of a farmer washing his bullock after a day's work – with particular attention to its legs and feet.

Three breeds of **sheep** were local to Mysore, each one being maintained by a different sub-caste of shepherds. These breeds were never crossed, partly because of physiological or behavioural differences among them, and partly through antagonism between their shepherds. They were shorn twice a year, and their mutton was eaten, especially by the Muslim population. Moreover, rams of one breed were selected for fighting: the animals butted, kicked with their fore-feet, and even bit their opponents. Large bets were placed on these contests. Cubbon established a sheep-breeding station, under the supervision of a European officer, at Heraganhalli. Each year, Merino rams were imported from Australia, crossed with local ewes, and the progeny distributed throughout the State. By this means the size of the local animals was increased, and the quality of their mutton and wool improved. The wool was sent to England for sale. However, in 1863 the breeding station was given up because it did not meet its running costs.[334]

Public Works[335]

The two principal needs for engineering works were encapsulated in an aphorism of Cubbon's successor, L. B. Bowring 'What the roads are to the malnad (hills), irrigation is to the maidan' (plains). In dealing with road-building

---

[333] W.G.L. Rice vol 1. 166
[334] W.G.L. Rice vol 1. 171-3
[335] K.N.V. Sastri 98-101

and irrigation Cubbon was fortunate to have a first-rate Chief Engineer in Frederick Green.

Four categories of road were recognized of which the two most important, trunk roads and provincial roads, were metalled. Four main bridges had been in place in 1834, and six more were built. The network of inter-village paths was improved. Four passes were cleared through the Western Ghats. Other forms of communication were introduced as they became available. When the telegraph line from Ootacamund to Madras was being constructed in 1855-56, Cubbon made sure that it ran by way of Bangalore and Mysore. Later, when the Madras Railway Company refused to run a branch-line to Bangalore from the main southern line, he persuaded the Government of India to order that the work be started in 1859.

Cubbon's interest in water conservation amounted almost to an obsession, and his desire to fund construction of the Mari Kanave Reservoir has already been noted. That interest extended to small and local means of conserving water. For centuries Bangalore had possessed numerous tanks for holding water – really small reservoirs. The largest of these, Halsur Tank, covered about 50 ha and had been constructed by Kempe Gowda II during the latter part of the 16th century. The Commission spared no effort in keeping Halsur and a dozen more tanks in good condition. Elsewhere the ryots were encouraged to maintain their village tanks by giving them a remission on their land-rents for so doing.[336]

Public Health[337]

Initially the Maharajah led the way in introducing Western medicine to his State. Indeed, whereas Cubbon's policy was to utilize practitioners in the indigenous Hindu system of medicine or Ayurveda while building up a pool of competence in Western medicine, the Maharajah took up the new system with enthusiasm. Under the Maharajah's Government a Durbar Surgeon was attached to the Court, and also superintended His Highness's Hospital in Mysore City. The first holder of the post was a Dr Lewis.

In 1833 the Commission set up a dispensary in Bangalore fort and next year one in the cantonment, both under the charge of Dr C.I.Smith, an Assistant Surgeon in the Madras Service. Cubbon recognized his worth by transferring responsibility for all medical matters to him in 1834-36. A small hospital and dispensary was built in the pettah in 1839, and this proved so popular that a new hospital with fifty beds was opened there in 1847. In 1852 the pettah hospital was enlarged, and one for seventy in-patients built in the cantonment bazaar. Four years later the pettah hospital was enlarged yet again. The staff was increased proportionately: more surgeons and apothecaries were taken on, and

---

[336] Z. Futehally and K. Chandy, *The Water Tanks of Bangalore*, in T. P. Issar (1988) 252-5
[337] K.N.V. Sastri 88

a team of seventy-five vaccinators was built up. Indeed, vaccination became very popular.[338]

These developments reflected an increasing acceptance of Western medicine in Mysore.

Education[339]

Cubbon summed up his policies as (i) to establish schools that would teach in the vernacular languages; (ii) to provide translations into those languages of standard Western books; (iii) to enable those who wished to learn English to do so.

In pursuit of his first policy a Government Press was opened during 1841-42 in order to provide cheap text-books in Kannada. English-language education began at the same time as in Madras when, in October 1840, the Maharajah opened a free English school at Mysore under the supervision of a Methodist missionary. In the same year the wife of Rev J. Sewell of the London Missionary Society opened two schools for girls in Bangalore. As elsewhere, there was considerable prejudice against the education of women. Dobbs recorded a conversation in 1835 with a Brahmin gentleman, Sreenavassa Rao, who remarked 'I assure you, Sir, that we have the greatest difficulty in keeping our women in order, and if they were educated they would turn us out of the house.'

In 1842 Rev J. Garrett, a Methodist minister, started an English-language school at Bangalore, assisted by a monthly subvention of Rs50 from the Commission. Named the Native Educational Institution it became the bell-wether of schooling in the State. In 1851 it was made into a High School with a subvention of Rs800 a month. Garrett remained in charge, and it is obvious that Cubbon recognized his abilities. Other High Schools were founded with it as a model. The Bible was taught in all these schools, but attendance was optional.

In 1854 Sir Charles Wood issued his celebrated Despatch on Education, which had as one of its purposes 'extending far more widely the means of acquiring general European knowledge.' Dalhousie welcomed whole-heartedly the new impetus it gave to education, and ensured it was felt in all parts of India. Its effect ran from bottom to top of the educational system: emphasis was to be placed on primary education, grants-in-aid were to be made to encourage private bodies to found high schools, and a university was to be established in the capital cities of the three Presidencies.

The new system came to Mysore in 1856, when the Commission took direct control of education. A Department of Public Instruction was formed with Capt Stephens as Director and Frederick Green, the engineer, as Inspector of Schools. Much was achieved under their guidance (i) eighty vernacular schools

---

[338] W.G.L. Rice vol 1 648
[339] K.N.V. Sastri 82-8

were set up, one in each taluk; the people were encouraged to propose where a school should be sited but, if they did not do so the Government took the initiative; (ii) four Anglo-Vernacular schools were established, one per District; (iii) a Central College was founded, together with two teacher-training institutions; (iv) a proper Inspectorate was instituted, with three additional members of staff; (v) the Government Press was enlarged to provide English-language text books.

Next year the system was extended to Coorg with the establishment of six Vernacular schools, one per taluk.

In 1857 the educational budget was Rs125,000, but only Rs42,000 was actually spent. One reason for the under-spend seems to have been a distrust of schools by parents who feared their children might be converted to Christianity. Perhaps for this reason, teaching of the Bible in High Schools was abandoned. Nevertheless, a missionary, the Rev Garrett, succeeded Stephens as Director of Education in 1859; and he remained Principal of the Bangalore High School, which became affiliated to the University of Madras.

Some insight into the operation of the system is given by a letter of 21 January 1859 from Garrett to Sir Mark. 'A new school will probably be completed within 18 months of this time...and I recommend ordering from England a supply of Philosophical Apparatus sufficient for a good course of scientific instruction...which is very attractive to the Natives.'[340] He enclosed a list of such apparatus as would be required to illustrate the leading principles of Natural Philosophy (Physics) and perform a series of scientific experiments. Garrett hinted at the difficulty of operating far from the source of supply when he mentioned the non-arrival of modern text books – like those used in Madras Government Schools as distinct from Mission Schools.

His Reward?

The foregoing gives an indication of the range of Sir Mark's responsibilities. How much was he paid for shouldering them?

The salary of the Commissioner was fixed in 1831 (when there were two) at Rs4083 per month or Rs48,996 per annum, plus a tent allowance of Rs5 ½ per day while on tour. This continued for the twenty-seven years of his tenure. Elsewhere the total annual salary has been quoted at £6000; which would have had a purchasing power of at least ten to fifteen times that amount by 1995.

In 1858 a Mr H. Ricketts reported on Indian salaries – possibly as part of an 'economy drive' after the Mutiny. He recommended that the Commissioner should receive the same salary as a Judge of the Sudder Court of Madras, or Rs42,000 per annum, and invoked the pleasant climate of Bangalore as partial justification for his conclusion! Here, indeed, is an example of a bureaucrat acting alone and thus being able to 'take a view' of a subject. Ricketts's

---

[340] MNHL MD 436 28/13

recommendation was 'Whenever a vacancy may occur, I would reduce it to that sum.'

In response Sir Mark pointed to 'a high salary, that leading test of dignity and confidence among the Natives,' and went on to propose that if the salary were to be reduced it should be done immediately, saying

> It would do less harm to cut down the pay at once than to do it when the place comes to be held by one whose authority would not have the advantage of the prestige attending a quarter of a century of tenure.

To give him credit, Ricketts responded handsomely

> ...such an offer from anyone else would suffice to stamp his character as one of rare disinterestedness; coming from General Cubbon it seems almost impertinent to notice it with admiration, for it is only in unison with the whole tenor of his life, which has been one long act of devotion to the public service.[341]

And thus he virtually acquiesced in abandoning the measure.

When Dalhousie visited Mysore in 1855 Cubbon prepared a General Memorandum for him. This is seen as marking the end of the Non-Regulation System of government followed hitherto by the Commission – a system under which the ordinary laws or 'regulations' were either not in force or came into force only through a declaration of the Government of India. Annual Reports were produced thereafter and, as a further consequence, the next Commissioner was a civilian.

---

[341] K.N.V. Sastri 161

CHAPTER FOURTEEN

Charles Trevelyan and the Transfer of Mysore 1860

Charles Trevelyan

In 1860 Sir Mark faced the greatest single challenge of his career, and its outcome virtually settled the position of Mysore until Independence. It sprang from the appointment of Sir Charles Edward Trevelyan as Governor of Madras in 1859. Born in 1807 as the fourth son of Rev George Trevelyan, he passed with distinction through Charterhouse and the EIC's College at Haileybury where he established a reputation for academic brilliance. He entered the Company's service as a Writer in 1826, and passed out in second place from its College at Calcutta before being posted to Delhi in the following year.

An indication of Trevelyan's metal may be gained from his career in Delhi. He had been posted as Assistant to the Resident, Sir Charles Metcalfe, one of the greatest men of British India. Their time together was brief because Metcalfe was called to Calcutta as a member of the Supreme Council under Lord Bentinck. In June 1827 he was replaced in Delhi by Sir Edward Colebrook, a man who had spent forty-nine years in the Company's employ and obviously possessed great influence. A member of an older generations of Anglo-Indians, he had slipped into the habit of corruption – or perhaps it is more correct to say that Lady Colebrook had slipped and drawn her husband after her.

The Colebrooks' corrupt activities were several, but one example will suffice – that of *nazar,* the offering of presents to a ruler or other superior as a token of allegiance or respect. The practice dated at least from Mughal times and, in States such as Hyderabad, it continued until the 1930s when *nazar* to the Nizam consisted of gold or silver coins. Like some other Mughal institutions, *nazar* had become attached to the Company's Sirkar. Clearly, it offered an opportunity to buy favours. As early as 1765 Lord Clive had implemented an order that the Company's servants were not to accept presents for personal gain. This was reinforced by instructions from the Company's Select Committee of 1781 to Lord Cornwallis: there was to be a reform of abuses by the Company's servants, the methods by which they grew rich must be scrutinized, they must not accept presents. By 1827 employees of the Company were already forbidden to keep *nazar.*

A convention was adopted to cover gifts (except flowers and fruit) that were presented on ceremonial occasions. They must not be retained by the recipient but placed in the Government's *toshakhana* or treasure chamber. If the recipient wanted to buy the gift he could do so at its market value, but usually the gifts were sold at periodic auctions. This practice was followed until the very end of

British rule in Asia, as I have observed. However, the Colebrooks either kept their gifts or arranged for their value to be marked down at the auctions.

As Assistant to the Resident and a member of his official 'family' Trevelyan soon became aware of this and other irregularities. He expressed his concern to the Resident but was ignored. At this, Trevelyan's quality became apparent. Stage by stage he took what he considered to be appropriate measures: first he withdrew from the Resident's 'family'; then he laid charges against Colebrook's private agent; and, when Colebrook informed him that he would be prosecuted for conspiracy, Trevelyan formally charged the Resident with corruption. This was done on 30 June 1829, and shows the determination and courage of one who was just twenty-two years of age. There followed a series of manoeuvres by Colebrook, his friends and associates that would have deterred an older and more experienced man than Trevelyan. But the Governor-General appointed two Commissioners to examine the charge and receive evidence; and on 29 December 1829 Colebrook was found guilty of accepting and misappropriating *nazar* and of countenancing the same by his family. He was removed from the post of Resident, suspended from the Company's service, and finally dismissed by the Directors.[342]

Trevelyan himself was transferred to Calcutta in 1831 as Secretary to the Political Department and, from 1836, as Secretary to the Sudder Board of Revenue. To Calcutta in 1834 came Miss Hannah Macaulay, sister to Thomas Babington Macaulay. Her brother had disembarked at Madras and gone to meet Bentinck in the Nilgiris. Charles therefore had several months to make his number with Hannah before Macaulay appeared. In December 1834 they were married in St John's Cathedral, Calcutta – and Trevelyan then set out a plan to study Greek history and literature with Macaulay!

Macaulay and Lord Bentinck both thought well of Trevelyan, but were not blind to his weaknesses. As Bentinck remarked to Macaulay

> That man is almost always on the right side of every question: and it is as well that he is so; for he gives a most confounded deal of trouble when he happens to take the wrong one.[343]

Macaulay's own assessment was

> He is rash and uncompromising in public matters. ...But he has so strong an understanding that, though he often goes too fast, he scarcely ever goes in the wrong direction...He is a man of genius, a man of honour, a man of rigid integrity, and of a very kind heart.[343]

In January 1838 Charles and Hannah returned to England. Two years later he became Assistant Secretary to the Treasury in London, and held the post for

---

[342] Percival Spear, *Twilight of the Moghuls* (Karachi 1973) 168-74
[343] Thomas Pinney, *Selected Letters of Thomas Babington Macaulay* 139

nineteen years. It gave him scope for his administrative energies, which ranged widely. From 1845-47 he was responsible for relief works in Ireland, where he arranged assistance for nearly three-quarters of a million men and women, and for which he was appointed KCB. He became known to Anthony Trollope, himself a Civil Servant, and appeared in his novel 'The Three Clerks' as Sir Gregory Hardlines. Trollope's sketch is revealing of Trevelyan's character

> To be widely different from others was Mr Hardlines' glory. He thanked God that he was not as those publicans at Somerset House, and took glory to himself in paying tithes of official cumin...he was appointed Commissioner of the Board of Civil Service Examination, with a salary of £2000 a year...[and] was made a KCB.[344]

This account of Charles Trevelyan may allow the reader to appreciate the kind of man to whom Cubbon found himself opposed, in his seventy-fifth year. Sir Mark knew of Trevelyan's early work in India, and had been much impressed by it. For example, Macaulay described how, when he visited Bangalore in September 1834, a copy of Trevelyan's report on internal transit-duties (advocating tax-free movement of goods among the States and Provinces of India) 'was on Colonel Cubbon's table at Bangalore; and Cubbon, one of the ablest and most enlightened men in the Service, praised it in terms so high that, till I read it, I thought them hyperbolical.'[345]

Sir Charles was offered the post of Governor of Madras on 6 January 1859 with a salary of £12,800 a year. Never one to procrastinate when an enterprise was begun, he left England on 18 February and travelled to Madras by the overland route which began by sailing through the Mediterranean to Alexandria and ended by taking ship from Suez to Indian ports. He assumed office in Madras on 28 March and immediately set about the tasks he had identified for himself. Hannah, who had remained in Britain, was distressed to read of the extent of his activities. He had decided that the matters requiring most urgent attention were sanitation, sewage, and water supplies. The Peoples' Park and the storage reservoir called Trevelyan Basin were but two of his creations. Nor did he forget to show himself to the community – and to all sections of it. Between 29 March and 31 July 1859 he entertained 1955 people to breakfast, 836 to tiffin, 2090 to dinner, 1793 to 'at homes', and had 550 children to tea; and he removed the exclusion of Indians from public balls given to celebrate special occasions.[346]

---

[344] Anthony Trollope, *The Three Clerks* (London 1855 repr 1959) 58-60, and *An Autobiography* (London 1883 repr 1980) 111-2
[345] Thomas Pinney, *Selected Letters* 140
[346] Raleigh Trevelyan, *The Golden Oriole* (London 1987) 333

The Proposed Transfer

At this point another participant must be noticed again. In June 1859 Sir Charles Wood became Secretary of State for India, having already served for several years as President of the Board of Control. He and Trevelyan were acquainted and now began a frequent and detailed correspondence. From the beginning, Wood's letters make clear his concern about the financial situation which the Mutiny had created: the Indian public debt had almost doubled to £98 million, and the projected deficit for 1859-60 exceeded £7 million. In a letter of 26 June 1859 Wood told Trevelyan 'according to the financial accounts from Calcutta, there will be a deficit of 7 millions in the year commencing April 1860 – civil expenditure I see no prospect of reducing: so it turns on military reduction and possible increase of income.'[347]

Despite their friendship, Wood seems to have been uneasy about Trevelyan. His letter of 26 July 1859 includes

> You must forgive me if I repeat my warning to you to be cautious in your mode of proceeding ...you will damage your own powers of usefulness if you set against you those powers that be with whom you must act for the good of India, and the development of your own views.[348]

Wood's letter of 10 October conveyed some bad news for Trevelyan, 'Wilson is going to Calcutta and will I hope get the finance into better order.'[349] James Wilson had founded the 'Economist' newspaper, where he had been succeeded as editor by his son-in-law, Walter Bagehot. An authority on the currency, he had been Financial Secretary to the Treasury and had crossed swords with Trevelyan. Now he was to be the fifth member of the Supreme Council and one of the most influential men in India. Trevelyan had cause for concern.

Wilson arrived in Calcutta at the end of 1859. His ship had called at Madras, where he had gone ashore and taken breakfast with Trevelyan, and doubtless been favoured with firm opinions about what should be done.

Despite this development, however, Trevelyan's tidy mind was busy with ideas for bringing order to the Indian scene. He raised with Wood 'the question of effecting an exchange with the Nizam of Hyderabad for that portion of his Territories which lies to the north of the Godavery, so as to make the frontier line coincident with the left bank of the river.'[350]

He had ideas, too, about the position of Mysore. Reduced to its essentials, his reasoning ran as follows. Mysore State had a long common frontier with Madras Presidency, had formerly been administered from Fort St George, and

---

[347] Letters from Sir Charles Wood to C. E. Trevelyan Jun 26 1859 – May 20 1860 (UNL) letter 1, 26 Jun 1859
[348] Letters from Sir Charles Wood (UNL) unnumbered letter, 26 Jul 1859
[349] Letters from Sir Charles Wood (UNL) letter 13, 10 Oct. 1859
[350] Letters from Sir Charles Wood (UNL) letter 13, 10 Oct. 1859 referring to a memorandum by Capt. F. Haig.

Madras was its nearest neighbour – much nearer than Calcutta. The Maharajah was an elderly man who had no heir, nor was he disposed to adopt one – yet. If Fort St George were again responsible for Mysore, permission to adopt (should His Highness change his mind) could be refused, he would die without an heir, whereupon the State could be annexed and amalgamated into Madras Presidency – and an untidy situation would be made good!

The propriety of this course was highly questionable, and ran contrary to the most authoritative British opinion, for Sir Charles Metcalfe's celebrated Minute on adoption states

> Those who are sovereign Princes in their own right and of the Hindu religion, have, by Hindu law, a right to adopt, to the exclusion of collateral heirs, or, of the supposed revisionary right of the Paramount Power [Government of India] …the British Government is bound to acknowledge the adoption, provided that it be regular and not in violation of Hindu law.[351]

The Hindu law to which Metcalfe referred is presumably the Code of Manu (AD 100-300) which specified the rules of domestic conduct and ceremony. The relevant passage runs

> He whom his father and mother give to another as his son, provided the donee have no issue, if the boy be of the same Gotra [Clan], and affectionately disposed, is considered as a son given; the gift being confirmed by the pouring of water.[352]

Trevelyan and Wood were willing to ignore all this, arguably in the interest of administrative convenience. Moreover, at first certain circumstances contrived to aid their scheme.

The Hon H.B. Devereaux, of the Bengal Civil Service, had been appointed Judicial Commissioner following Dalhousie's acceptance of Cubbon's strong case that the post be created. Late in 1859 two serious matters of discipline became known, which had apparently escaped his notice – and Sir Mark's! Capt W.F. Stephens had served the Commission for eleven years when Sir Mark suddenly recommended his removal on account of conduct incompatible with the public interest; Canning had concurred in this. Major Miller (Superintendent of Cantonment Police, Bangalore) had also been removed from office for 'highly illegal and oppressive conduct' that had been reported through the ordinary judicial process, but not by Sir Mark. Canning found the explanations of Cubbon and Devereaux to be wholly unsatisfactory, saying he had 'never yet seen a case of greater or more inexcusable neglect of duty' and he reported the affair to the Secretary of State.[353]

---

[351] V. N. Mandlik, *Annexation versus Adoption* (1866) 12 (Manu), 39 (Metcalfe) (BL (OIOC) Pamphlet PT 1034)
[352] *ibid*
[353] MNHL MD 436 28/15 (this folio contains several items)

No doubt this case influenced Sir Charles Wood who, on 10 January 1860, wrote to Trevelyan 'I am also going, I think, to give you Mysore. I am disgusted with Cubbon's negligence and Devereaux's misconduct as to the offices there. They have got into "scrapes" of gravest standing and been permitted to go on, uncorrected.' This was also an implied criticism of Canning.[354]

Two days later (12 January) Wood wrote to the Governor-General in Council (copying his letter to Cubbon)

> I have read with great regret the letters of your Lordship's Government… respecting removal from Political employment of two officers connected with the Mysore Commission…two such cases could not have occurred without considerable remissness on the part of the Chief Officers of the Commission.[355]

Having rehearsed his appreciation of the whole affair Wood found that Devereaux had 'signally failed in his duty'. He was to be removed from his post and another appointed to it. Sir Mark was in effect 'excused' on account of his high character and the administrative ability he had displayed over twenty-five years, which 'makes me regret the more this remissness.'[355]

On 26 January Wood informed Trevelyan that

> a despatch also goes out by this mail directing the transfer of Mysore to you. This will accomplish three or four desirable things; placing it under you, enabling you to appoint a local Commissioner, and you can do what you think right in a quiet way to prevent adoption. We have allowed it to the Chiefs who have behaved. But you are right in saying that the pendulum seldom swings steady.[356]

Wood's despatch to the Governor-General directed him, at his earliest convenience, to make arrangements to place the Mysore Commission under the immediate superintendence of the Governor of Madras in Council.

From this point onward the correspondence becomes more difficult to place in correct sequence because of the period of six weeks in transit: what had Wood received from Trevelyan or Wilson when he wrote a particular letter? Moreover, Wood wrote an execrable hand, which became more difficult to decipher as events unfolded and stress increased.

By some means Cubbon learnt of the intended transfer (in the despatch dated 26 January), to which he was wholly opposed. Since 1834 he had followed Lord Bentinck's instructions to the letter in the belief that the Maharajah or an heir would again rule Mysore. So he took action, and wrote from Nundidroog on 6 March 1860.

> To: The Officiating Secretary to the Government of India, Foreign Department.

---

[354] Letters from Sir Charles Wood (UNL) letter 12, 10 Jan 1860
[355] MNHL MD 436 28/15
[356] Letters from Sir Charles Wood (UNL) letter 13, 26 Jan 1860

> Having received private but authentic information that orders have issued from the office of the Secretary of State for India that the control of Mysore shall be withdrawn from the Government of India, notwithstanding the Despatch from the Honorable the Court of Directors dated the 31st of May 1838 No 34, I have the honor to request that you will be so good as to tender to the Honorable the President in Council the resignation of my appointment as Commissioner, and to add my respectful solicitations to be relieved as soon as his Honor may find convenient. [He went on to point to the] apparent tranquillity of the State and the fact that the current revenue exceeds that of any former year in Mysore, that is not less than 93 lakhs of Rupees.[357]

Cubbon must have received his copy of Wood's critical assessment of 12 January before 8 March, for on that date he acknowledged it by letter to the Secretary to the Government of India. He reported further that the Hon Mr Devereaux had left for England on 14 February. For his own part, he had already tendered his resignation as Commissioner for Mysore and Coorg on 6 March and

> had I not done so, it must be obvious to His Excellency the Right Honorable the Viceroy and Governor-General that the letter under acknowledgement would render it impossible for me, with satisfaction to myself or advantage to the State any longer to retain the position I have so long held…it is my intention shortly to address the Government to point out some important facts, which I cannot but believe must have escaped observation.[358]

The Maharajah heard of what was afoot and was dismayed. On 15 March he wrote to Sir Mark.

> I was much distressed to hear that my country, which has been under the control of the Bengal Presidency from the year 1832, has now been transferred to that of Madras, and that in consequence of this change, you have resigned from your office of Commissioner. Having experienced the benefit of your wise Councils on all occasions, coupled with your wise and just administration of my Country for upward of 25 years, I cannot but regret the change that has taken place both to yourself and my Country.[359]

He enclosed an unsolicited khureeta which Sir Mark despatched to the Governor-General on 17 March

> My Lord,
> …The transfer of the management of my Country from the Supreme to a subordinate Government without any reference to me, as though I had no

---

[357] MNHL MD 436 28/15, letter 1.
[358] MNHL MD 436 28/15, letter 3
[359] MNHL MD 436 28/15, letter 5

longer any interest in the matter, or any rights to uphold, fills my mind with apprehension and alarm.

He went on to invoke the terms of the treaty with the Earl of Mornington (1799) and to point out

1. the degradation in the eyes of all Natives and especially his own subjects which would follow a transfer;
2. the aid he had provided during the Mutiny, including 2000 of his own Silladar Horse;
3. that transfer would not improve the condition of his country, but would interfere with a restoration of the Government to himself or his heirs;
4. that the present Government of Mysore was operating well and cost-effectively, revenues were good and the Panchayat was operating with the utmost success;
5. that the proposed changes would require very strong reasons and 'I most emphatically deny that any such reasons exist.'

He ended with

And now my Lord I have stated my case, and fully relying on your Lordship's well known service of justice I confidentially leave the issue in your Lordship's hands. I am an old man and have suffered much, and you my Lord will I feel assuredly save me from this crowning indignity.[360]

Word of what was in prospect spread through the bazaars of the South, and brought consternation in its wake. On 16 March three Sowars in Mysore sent Canning a letter covering a petition signed by many thousands. It referred to Cubbon's resignation 'on account of certain approaching changes and to beg that the resignation may not be permitted to take place.'[361] So much for Wood's notion of making changes 'in a quiet way' – but Wood knew India only on paper.

As promised, Sir Mark addressed the Government of India about those important facts that believed must have escaped notice. His letter of 29 March pointed out that the Hon Mr Devereaux was probably in London and thus able to explain his conduct; he would therefore confine himself to 'censures that have been passed on myself.' This was followed by a detailed explanation of what he had done, and why. For example, Wood had taken exception to the way Sir Mark had asked his senior British and Indian officers for their opinions of Capt Stephens. This had been done because Stephens had claimed he was well-regarded by 'all respectable persons' – and Cubbon saw the action he had taken as the most convincing means of disabusing him. Maj Miller was a field

---

[360] MNHL MD 436 28/15, letter 6
[361] MNHL MD 436 29/17

officer of thirty years standing who had rendered good service during the Mutiny, but Cubbon recalled that he had personally expressed concern about defects in the Bangalore Police in his Annual Reports of 1857 and 1858.

In his last paragraph Sir Mark reminded the Governor-General of the tranquillity that had been maintained in Mysore during the Mutiny while elsewhere the situation was different, including Madras itself where

> the very grounds of Government House were occupied by guns and troops, thereby disseminating feelings of insecurity and alarm throughout the Presidency. [He had hoped that] some oversights in minor matters...would have been leniently viewed and dealt with, yet I am told...that the Governor-General has never yet seen a case of greater or more inexcusable neglect of duty.[362]

Here is a spasm of pain similar to that felt by young Mark during the Officers' Revolt fifty years before.

Now the game took a turn that favoured Cubbon and the Maharajah. Through carelessness, over-confidence, or arrogance Wood had not consulted Canning about the transfer of Mysore from his jurisdiction to Madras. His despatch of 26 January arrived on the Viceroy's desk without warning. This was not the way to treat the Sovereign's personal representative; and the Viceroy was not pleased.

Canning was in camp when the despatch arrived. He telegraphed to Calcutta for the relevant papers, and considered his response carefully. His reply of 30 March to Wood, three weeks after receiving the despatch, was both comprehensive – it ran to thirty-one paragraphs – and masterly. There were sarcastic passages too

> if the opportunity had been allowed me of being the channel of communication to His Highness... although it has not been deemed necessary to require the opinion of the Governor-General in Council regarding it [the transfer] I cannot but think that it has not received all the consideration that it deserves.

Canning conceded the administrative convenience of the transfer, but then marshalled one practical or emotional argument after another against it. He pointed out that the Secretary of State's action had already offended and somewhat alienated the Maharajah; and its hint of annexation could alienate his fellow-Princes. He told Wood bluntly that a reconsideration was essential in respect of 'so venerable and loyal a Prince'; he had told the Maharajah that there would be no change in the position of Mysore pending a reply from London, and he had asked Cubbon to remain in post for the time being.

Sir Mark was delighted by this, and annotated his copy in red 'Lord Canning to Sir C. Wood against the transfer.'[363]

---

[362] MNHL MD 436 28/15
[363] MNHL MD 436 30/25

On 3 April a letter went to Cubbon from the Viceroy's office. Having noted his letters of 6, 8 and 29 March it went on

> In reply I am directed to acquaint you that a reference has been made to Her Majesty's Secretary of State in Council on the subject of transfer of Mysore to the Government of Madras and that pending the answer that may be received to that communication, His Excellency requests that you will retain the Office of Commissioner.[364]

Sir Charles Trevelyan knew nothing of these developments. Always self-confident, he had no doubt that what he wanted would happen, and wrote in his own hand on 13 March to

> My Dear Sir Mark Cubbon,
> I should not do justice to my feelings if I remained silent on the occasion of your resignation of Chief Commissioner of Mysore. It does not belong to me to bear testimony to your long, honorable and highly useful public career – but I may allude with satisfaction to many friends whom we have had in common – and I dwell with emotion on the warm interest which Lord Macaulay felt in you and the high appreciation he entertained of your character. The intercourse with you, although short, made a great impression upon him; and you were a frequent theme of his conversation.
> We have been informed by a despatch from the Secretary of State that Mysore is to be retransferred to the superintendence of the Madras Government. It would have been an advantage for me if you could have retained office for a time – but as this cannot be, I hope you will give me the full benefit of your counsel and such suggestions in reference to the future administration of the Province and the comfort of the Raja, as your <u>experience may dictate</u>. My object…will be to respect existing interests and to keep things, as much as possible, in their present course until we perfectly understand the subject, and clearly see our way to any improvement.[365]

Whether Trevelyan would have got away with his scheme for Mysore is debatable. In any event, another factor intervened in the shape of his injudicious, not to say headstrong, reaction to Wilson's proposals for getting India's finances into better order.

James Wilson had addressed himself to the financial problems of the sub-continent with energy matching that of Trevelyan himself, though arguable directed more prudently. His arrival in Calcutta and his premature death on 11 August 1860 were separated by only nine months. During that time he remodelled the processes of administration, introduced annual budgets and statements of account, identified important economies, imposed an income tax for five years on non-agricultural incomes – and enraged Trevelyan who was

---

[364] MNHL MD 436 28/15, letter 8
[365] MNHL MD 436 29/15 (In the original of this letter, held in MNHL, the three words have been underlined in red pencil, presumably by Sir Mark himself).

bitterly opposed to direct taxation of any kind. Amid all this, Wilson took the precaution of sending Bagehot copies of all his letters to Wood, so that any necessary supporting action could be taken in London.

When Wilson's budget was introduced at Calcutta on 18 February 1860, Trevelyan was in Ootacamund but news of its contents made him hasten back to Madras to consult his Council. On 4 March he telegraphed his reactions to Wilson's proposals, implying an adverse opinion on the part of the Council as well as himself. Moreover, he demanded that the customary three months be allowed between proposal of the measures and their implementation, so as to permit a thorough public discussion. His message was sent without using cypher. He received a reprimand from Calcutta for sending an 'open' telegram on such an important matter, and the original consultation period of one month was retained. Undeterred, he took the desperate measure of sending his Council's Minutes on Wilson's proposals to the Governor-General in Calcutta – and to the press in Madras, presumable in the hope of mobilizing public opinion on his side.

This indiscretion apart, Wilson had identified some extravagances in Madras, and had notified them to both Canning and Wood – to the dismay of the latter, who had already found it necessary to remonstrate with Trevelyan on the same subject.[366] By this time Canning had lost the last shreds of confidence in Trevelyan's judgement and reliability, and demanded that he be recalled.

On 10 May Wood wrote two letters that close this story. One informed Sir Charles Trevelyan that the Cabinet had decided unanimously to recall him. He left for Britain in June, after fourteen months in office, and was replaced by Sir Henry Ward, the Governor of Ceylon.

Wood's second letter was addressed to the Governor-General. No reasonable man could have rejected the case that Canning had assembled, and Wood was sufficiently reasonable to accept it. His letter was almost conciliatory, and ended 'You will, therefore, inform the Rajah…that Her Majesty's Government resolved to cancel the former instructions and direct that no immediate change in the system of administering Mysore will take place.'[367]

Once again the bazaar telegraph outpaced other means of communication. It was not until 28 June that an official letter went to Cubbon, yet on 4 May he replied to an invitation

> Lt Genl Cubbon begs to acknowledge the receipt of a most warmly expressed friendly letter of the 3rd instant from the inhabitants of Bangalore Cantonment, inviting him to an entertainment, to be given as an expression of pleasure on their part, consequent upon the prospect of his continued residence among them…but it is out of his power to be present.[368]

---

[366] Letters from Sir Charles Wood (UNL) letters 18 (10 Mar) and 19 (26 Mar 1860)
[367] MNHL MD 436 30/26
[368] MNHL MD 436 29/18

The Governor-General's letter of 28 June to Cubbon confirmed that the earlier instruction to transfer superintendence of the Mysore Commission to Madras had been cancelled; and it went on, not quite accurately 'as it was primarily on account of the transfer that you tendered the resignation of your office it is the wish and hope of His Excellency in Council that you may now be induced to retain it.'[369]

A Khureeta went to the Maharajah to convey the good news, and to acknowledge both the justice of His Highness's case against transfer, and the extent of his services to the Government especially during the Mutiny. It concluded

> It is satisfactory to me to know that throughout the time of which I have spoken your Highness has had the advantage of the support and council of so tried and devoted an officer of the Crown, and one so devoted to the welfare of your Highness's State as Sir Mark Cubbon.'[370]

As well as his own letter, Sir Mark received a copy of the Khureeta so he was on top form when he replied on 23 July

> [The Khureeta] contains the most satisfactory news the Maharajah ever received and I have taken care that it shall be delivered with every accompaniment of pomp and circumstance that could enhance its importance, and add to his gratification. [He referred next to] the alarm which for some time prevailed that Mysore would immediately become subject to the wildest experiments; and that all offices worth holding would be filled by hangers-on from Madras, to the exclusion of the Natives of the country.
> [And finally] I cannot find words to express my deep sense of the honor conferred on my by His Excellency in Council's expression of a wish that I should retain my office. I shall ever consider it an honor and a duty cheerfully to meet His Excellency's wishes and only hope that I shall not disappoint the expectations which I fear have been too generously formed – at the same time I must be prepared for greater difficulties than I have yet encountered, in consequence of the feverish excitement, if not the spirit of opposition, encouraged by the proceedings of the late Ruler of Madras.[371]

Sir Mark was a good as his word about 'pomp and circumstance' in arranging for delivery of the Khureeta. Since he was unable to travel, it was carried from Bangalore to Mysore City on 24th July by Lt Col Macqueen, Officiating Secretary to the Commissioner, in readiness for delivery on 26th as specified by the Maharajah. A large crowd had gathered in the vicinity of the Palace, where a wing of 6 MNI and a band were drawn up together with all available State Forces. Macqueen was carried to the Palace on His Highness's state elephant.

---

[369] MNHL MD 436 28/15, letter 10
[370] MNHL MD 436 28/15
[371] MNHL MD 436 28/15

There he was met by the Maharajah, who took him by the hand and led him to the Hall of Audience. The Khureeta presented, the Maharajah placed it upon his throne and strewed it with flowers. There was a Royal Salute, a discharge of muskets, and His Highness scattered Rs1500 among the assembled crowd.[372]

Some insights into this event are provided by correspondence between James Wilson and his wife. Mrs Wilson – Eliza – became unwell in Calcutta and was advised to recuperate at Ootacamund. She and her daughter took ship to Madras, where they were received hospitably by Trevelyan, and then travelled on by way of Bangalore and Mysore to Ooty. While staying with Sir Mark at Nundidroog, Eliza wrote on 8 June 1860

> My Dear James
> …Since 23 April we have been on the move. As it happens we are better placed than we should be anywhere else on the road, the climate is delightful, standing at 74, and the General appears to be very well pleased to have us, and the ladies are very nice. The house is Liberty Hall, but still the party at table is too much for me and I am glad to stay away from dinner. You should see Sir T. Munro's Minutes on the liberty of the press in India, in his life by the Rev G.B. Gleig. Both Lord Canning and the General (the latter being quite an oracle on Indian affairs and his administration has been most successful) agree with him.
> The General says that the Government presses improvements too quickly on he people who are so slow and suspicious of innovations. They are not sufficiently advanced for a free Press, and certainly the Press in Madras has acted like wildfire among the natives; on income tax the natives from time immemorial have had two sets of accounts. The General expects by this mail a decision on the annexation of Mysore to Madras Presidency. He would not serve under Sir Ch. Trevelyan under any circumstances and only awaits a successor…He has been sixty years in India without going home.
> The Gen. [General Sir Mark Cubbon] received the news by telegram of the Governor's recall, and drank a glass of champagne, which he is not allowed to do, to the good news, and he read part of the letter to me this morning saying that if Sir Charles was not recalled both you and Lord Canning would resign. He did not give the authority, but I see by the Home News that mischief is doing. The tobacco tax has been in operation here from time immemorial, and the revenue of Mysore has increased under the General's administration from four hundred thousand to a million yearly.[373]

On 13 June she wrote

> The Rajah of Mysore fired 40 rounds on the news of the Governor's recall, 21 being a royal salute. We shall return with the General to Bangalore and remain with him until it is time to move on to Dr Campbell's, where we shall rest a few days, getting to the hills at the end of the month.[374]

---

[372] MNHL MD 436 28/15
[373] E. I. Barrington, *The Servant of All* vol 2 (London 1927) 292
[374] E. I. Barrington, *The Servant of All* vol 2 292

A letter from James Wilson, which must have crossed with some of his wife's, ran

> My dear Eliza,
> It has been a source of great pleasure to us to receive such cheerful accounts from you. With regard to Mysore, the Home government have cancelled their former orders, and it has to remain under the Supreme Government as heretofore. The despatch came by the last mail...Lord Canning and all of us are extremely anxious that General Cubbon should remain. We feel that his presence is a great source of strength to us, especially after what has happened at Madras. It will really be a national calamity if he were to insist upon resigning now. Lord Canning writes to him by this mail. The recall of Sir Charles Trevelyan so promptly – even before they had our reply to his Minute – has produced a great effect here: and it has modified, if not put an end to the opposition to my taxes as they are called. The appointment of Sir Hy. Ward has given great satisfaction.[375]

A similar reaction came from Lt Gen Sir Patrick Grant, Commander-in-Chief at Fort St George

> My Dear Sir Mark,
> Will you permit me to offer you my sincere congratulations on the gratifying termination of the long-pending Mysore question. I heartily rejoice that it has been brought to a close with increase of honor and satisfaction to you and in a way that enables you to meet the wishes of the Governor-General and forego your determination to forego your high office.[376]

During this time the routine business of administering Mysore had gone on. For example, Sir Charles Wood wrote to the Governor-General to regret that Sir Mark had not yet submitted a list of the Natives of Mysore who had aided the British Government during the Mutiny. Cubbon replied on 2 June 1860 to praise the way that

> Malcontents were effectually deterred from breaking into open violence by the sleepless vigilance and fearless attitude of the Superintendents of Divisions... But to no one was the Government more indebted for the preservation of tranquillity than His Highness the Maharajah.

The most revealing part of his letter, however, followed an assurance that the Commission was at all times kept informed of developments. He said

> There is nothing that the Natives of these parts more earnestly deprecate than having their names brought to public notice as giving information of an

---

[375] E. I. Barrington, *The Servant of All* vol 2 294
[376] MNHL MD 436 25/74

intended political outbreak...those who helped the Commission wished to remain anonymous; they have already been rewarded in a way that could not possibly expose them to resentment. [377]

Canning concurred, and with that Wood had to be satisfied. One group, however, could be publicly acknowledged: the people of Coorg, who had stood out against the Mutiny. As one of his last acts in office, Cubbon issued a proclamation. At its head was a medallion representing a Coorg warrior.

Notification
26 February 1861

In consideration of the exalted honour, loyalty and intrepidity characteristic of this little nation of warriors, and in recognition of its conspicuous services in aid of the British Government, it is my pleasing duty to notify hereby for general information, by virtue of the power vested in me by the Government of India, that the provisions of the Act commonly called the Disarming Act are not applicable to the people of Coorg.[378]

---

[377] MNHL MD 436 28/15, letter 13
[378] W.G.L. Rice, *Mysore and Coorg* vol 3

CHAPTER FIFTEEN

The Journey Home 1861

Lt Gen Sir Mark Cubbon KCB was forced to resign by ill-health. For several years he had suffered the agonies of gout, without any sign of ill-temper. Recently, however, a more general malaise was overcoming him. On 22 December 1860 he wrote from Nundidroog to the Governor-General, tendering his resignation 'from 1 March 1861 if convenient to his Lordship … on the urgent advice of my medical attendants'.[379]

A letter of acceptance was sent without delay

> …will arrange relief by 1 March…notification of your successful appointment will be made in the gazette…His Excellency The Governor-General cannot delay till then the expression of thanks and respect which he feels due to you for your long and eminently successful conduct of an administration which has repeatedly been marked by the Commendation of the Home Government and of the Government of India, and for worthily sustaining the credit of the British rule and securing to it the attachment of every class of the Indian people with whom you have been in contact.[380]

Just before his departure Sir Mark was described as 'very well and in good spirits' but 'as a skeleton…his face so very thin and narrow'.[381] He left Bangalore in mid-March with the intention of sailing to Suez and taking the overland route to the Mediterranean. He planned to spend some time in Malta – certainly until the weather in the British Isles would be tolerable. At Southampton he was to be met by his old colleague, Mr Chalmers, and they would take the railway directly to the home of Col and Mrs Haines, near Shrewsbury. There he would remain for a time, with other Indian friends about him, until he felt able make the journey to the Isle of Man. He would be accompanied by Dr Campbell throughout his journey.

Many tributes were paid to Sir Mark. One of the most telling of these was in a speech from a young man connected with the Government High School

> Within the last few years Rs83,000 have been laid out in founding English and Vernacular Schools in all the Divisions, beside a monthly grant of Rs2900. More than a thousand of the Hindu and Musselmen youths received their educations almost wholly at the Government's cost. It shall not be long before the Government High School of Mysore shall vie with the Madras University.[382]

---

[379] MNHL MD 436 28/14 letter 1
[380] MNHL MD 436 28/14 letter 2
[381] MNHL MD 436 29/7
[382] MNHL MD 436 29/16

Sir Mark Cubbon, aged about 73 years and obviously
physically infirm. (Courtesy of Director MNH)

More personal expressions of affection are contained in letters from the portraitist Major Martin and his Wife who were also going home with their three children – but travelling by separate routes because cholera was rife in the State and they wanted to ensure that some among them survived. So Martin travelled with the two older children, and his wife and baby by another way. Martin wrote to Sir Mark

> I thought you looked well when you started from Bangalore...I could not bear to say goodbye to you so I stepped to one side till you were gone, and saw the last of you from behind a tree on the road.[383]

Cecilia Martin was still in Bangalore on 22 March when she wrote to Sir Mark, who had already arrived in Madras

---

[383] MNHL MD 436 25/78

I am so very glad that you reached Madras without feeling as much fatigued as really the state of the road would have led one to expect… it is strange to be staying in any other house in Bangalore but yours, which now looks so deserted. …I would not mind waking up to find the earth had swallowed up all the buildings – even the big flagstaff. …best love…[384]

Sir Mark's last letter was written from Madras on 21 March 1861.

My Dearest Sister Elizabeth,
I am thus far on my way home, and expect to sail on the 28th, but shall be obliged to stop at Malta (so the medical men tell me), and not to land in England until the month of May is pretty well advanced. I should like to hear from you at Malta, just to say how poor Maria is, and beg you to keep in mind that if the doctors recommend the change to any particular place, you will be certain to meet me there, be it ever so far on the Continent or elsewhere. I have nothing to care for now but you two; and I pray we may be all spared to give me time to make some little atonement for past neglect.
I am leaving India with more numerous and weighty marks of public respect than I can recollect any other official receiving on quitting office. Having little vanity in my composition, I never imagined I possessed the respect of 10 millions of people, or that anything could stir up a Native Community to make such manifestations in favour of a European. The addresses are too bulky to send you, but I enclose an article I have cut out of this day's Madras newspaper. Now God bless you both. With affectionate regards to poor Maria.[385]

Although there seems to be something amiss with dates given in the records, the main facts are clear. At Suez Sir Mark collapsed and died of 'liver or an abscess in the lungs'. This was almost certainly due to *Entamoeba histolytica*, which causes amoebic dysentery – and he had experienced bouts of dysentery since 1805. From the gut, the organism can get into the portal vein and thus move to the liver, where abscesses may be formed years after the initial attack of dysentery. Rarely the lungs may also become involved. Just before he died Sir Mark turned to Campbell and said 'What heavenly weather!'

After the event Campbell rose to the occasion, and there was much to be done: a lead-lined coffin had to be secured, onward travel arranged, a message sent ahead – and this was made the more difficult by Sir Mark's silence about his family in the Isle of Man. So he telegraphed Lt Col Macqueen, now Judge Advocate-General of the Madras Army, who was on furlough in Britain

I grieve to inform you that our dear General breathed his last at Suez on the afternoon of 23 April. I am coming home with his remains. I hope to reach Southampton on 9 May.
J. Campbell
Malta 1 May[386]

---

[384] MNHL MD 436 25/79
[385] K.N.V. Sastri, *The Administration of Mysore* 312

Macqueen did the best he could, and telegraphed Lady Buchan. She, in turn, sent a cable to the most capable member of the family, Mark Wilks Collet of Liverpool. This was the grandson of Anne Wilks, sister to Mark who had married John Corlett of Douglas and, in the United States, seen that name become Collet. Cousin Mark broke the news to Elizabeth by letter on 3 May and followed it with another next day, when he had more information from Lady Buchan and a request that he receive the remains at Southampton. His letter ran

> ...if such be your wish, I will gladly undertake any duties you wish me to perform & have only to beg that you will kindly give me your wishes as promptly as may be, as there is not much time left for correspondence.[387]

Cousin Mark applied himself to his task. He agreed to meet Col Haines in Southampton, and tried to both ease Elizabeth's mind and bring her to decisions about the funeral. She had written on the 5th and he replied next day: no, it would not be possible to reopen the coffin; should he open Sir Mark's papers? Was the funeral to be at Maughold? If so, when? He reckoned that, if no delay occurred, he should be able to bring the remains to Douglas on 16th at latest. Should he employ an undertaker in England or in the Isle of Man? Finally, he asked Elizabeth to telegraph her preferences, and drafted a telegram for her

> Funeral Wednesday fifteenth
> (or Thursday seventeenth according as you decide)
> Employ Liverpool undertaker
> OR
> Employ (the name, address of the party in the Island)[388]

On 7 May he wrote again.

> My Dearest Betsy,
> I have just discovered that I have made a mistake in my last letter to you speaking of 17th as Thursday. It is Friday the 17th – we should cross on Thursday and the funeral would be on Friday the 17th if you decide on that day. I am sorry if I have confused you by this mistake.
> In haste[389]

But it all turned out well. Several of Sir Mark's old friends were in Britain at the time: Macqueen, Haines, Chalmers and, of course, Campbell. Macqueen met Campbell at Southampton, and these two with Haines accompanied the coffin

---

[386] MNHL MD 436 27/20 (this folio contains several letters)
[387] MNHL MD 436 27/20
[388] MNHL MD 436 27/20
[389] MNHL MD 436 27/20

to Liverpool and on to Douglas – not Ramsey as Elizabeth had wanted. On their arrival, as Macqueen recorded in a letter to Dobbs[390]

> ...a gun was fired, colours were hoisted half-mast high at the Government House, in the Harbour and at the Custom House. After nightfall the body was moved from the vessel to a church near at hand [the former St Matthew's] and at ten next morning [17th] we went to the church, found all the Volunteer Artillery out and the clergy and town authorities in their official dresses. Every shop was shut and the whole population crowded the way we were to pass by. The Volunteers accompanied us through the town, from which the burying place was fully distant seventeen miles, by a hilly, narrow road.
> The shipping in Douglas and all along the coast had their colours half-mast high. Every church, Catholic and Protestant, tolled their bells and at intervals along the way were groups of well-dressed and also of the poorer class of people. When we came within three miles or so of the old burying-ground we were met by an immense concourse of people, and perhaps 300 ladies, or such as appeared to us to be so. The Rifles were out and a society of something like Freemasonry, Oddfellows, picturesquely attired, joined the procession, and the crowd and all followed till we arrived at the General's last resting place. When the coffin was taken out of the hearse, a gentleman came up and said it was the wish of everyone that Haines, Campbell and myself [Officers of the Commission] should with one of the countrymen [Mr Collet] form the pall-bearers, and this was done. The service was read, and the old man was the first to be laid in the tomb intended to contain the remains of his brother and surviving sisters. A clergyman present stated that he had always received £150 a year from the General, but had to say nothing about it. Haines, Campbell and myself entered the tomb and being affected at taking our last sight of what contained all that remained of what we thought the best and greatest of men, the crowd surrounding us testified the most sincere sympathy and respect.
> We did not get back to Douglas, the post-town, until past eleven at night, but I am sure no three men would have been more satisfied than we were, with all the honours paid to the old man's memory. The Archdeacon [Joseph Christian Moore] said 'In that vault lies the greatest man this Island has produced for centuries back.'

Lady Susan Ramsay remembered her old friend. On 2 June 1861 she wrote to M.W. Collet Esq., Rosemount, Liverpool

> I have received the letter from the Rajah of Mysore which you transmitted to me...please convey my condolences to Sir Mark's sister. It was impossible to know Sir Mark without loving him and admiring him, and none could feel more warmly toward him than both my Father and myself. He was a very dear friend of mine and I have mourned him truly.[391]

---

[390] Account is based on R. S. Dobbs, *Reminiscences of Mysore* 120-22, amplified from 'Mona's Herald' of 15 May 1861
[391] MNHL MD 436 27/22

Epilogue

Miss Elizabeth Cubbon's tasks did not end with the funeral. She and Maria were living at 5 Albany Terrace, Lezayre Road, Ramsey; Maria was a permanent semi-invalid, and their older brother William was clearly failing. Everything rested on Elizabeth's shoulders.

Sir Mark's boxes of effects had to be unpacked and sorted. Some unexpected things emerged, such as a loaded revolver. She was much agitated because there was no sign of the gold mourning ring her mother had sent to India, the one containing locks of their parents' hair. Had Mark lost it; didn't he care for it? It might be in the coffin, but Dr Campbell was too far away to be asked about it.

Worst of all, casual to the end about his own affairs, neglectful of Uncle Wilks's advice 'you will of course always have a will by you' Sir Mark had died intestate. William and Maria gave power of attorney to Elizabeth, who then set about the process of securing guarantors and petitioning the Church Authorities for release of Mark's estate.[392] Some real Manx worthies rallied around to help. Then, in December, to round out a terrible year, William died.

Sir Mark's Indian estate was being handled by John Vans Agnew. His statement of account at 14 August 1862 showed that Cubbon's holding in Government Securities exceeded Rs3.5 lakhs; payments for houses and discharge of debts were still coming in, and £5874 had been transferred to Mark Wilks Collet who was looking after financial matters for the family in Britain.[393]

Legacies from their parents and brother Mark had made the two sisters quite well-to-do. Moreover, they were agreed that a memorial to their brother was called for in Ramsey, but were perplexed about what it should be. Eventually they hit upon the idea of retirement cottages for widows and unmarried daughters of the clergy – places where they would be secure for the rest of their lives. Their decision was reached about the same time that plans for building a new Grammar School (the second such) were coming to fruition. The Grammar School that Mark had attended had been declared 'ruinous and dilapidated' a dozen years before but was still in use. By 1862 the Trustees of the School had funds enough to buy a parcel of land fronting on Waterloo Road. Elizabeth and Maria were able, in turn, to purchase part of this land, on which they built a terrace of houses in a style that matched the new Grammar

---

[392] Archidiaconal Wills: Cubbon, Mark (Sir), 1861 (MNHL Admin. 1st book, No 47; and MF/ GL771)
[393] MNHL MD 436 27/19

school.[394] The two end gables carry plaques to record the facts: that on the south end 'Mysore Cottages', and on the north gable 'Elizabeth Cubbon 1865'.

Maria did not live to see their project completed, for she died in February 1862. Elizabeth soldiered on until 1869, and died just before her eighty-first birthday. Their considerate cousin Mark Wilks Collet went on to become a Director of the Bank of England, eventually its Governor, and a Baronet.

In Mysore the new Judicial Commissioner, Mr C.B.Saunders, served as Acting Commissioner for a few months. In 1862 Mr Lewin Bentham Bowring, of the Bengal Civil Service, was appointed to the post. He had been Private Secretary to Lord Canning, and had won the approval of Field Marshal Lord Roberts VC for his presence of mind in an emergency.[395]

Elliott records that when Sir Mark left office he handed over a treasury containing a large accumulated surplus, of which £300,000 was invested in Government bonds. His intention was to execute two large irrigation works that would have brought great benefit to the State, one of which was the Mari Kanave scheme. Sir Mark recognised that the safety and prosperity

> of the people, and thus the success of the administration (in a region with an unreliable rainfall) lay in water, water, and yet more water. Those who came after thought that the secret of government lay in departments, departments, and yet more departments... Mr Bowring was merely a minister,...was told to introduce a system, and he did introduce a system.[396]

It is not surprising, therefore, that the old make-shift offices within the Bangalore fort soon became too small. Indeed, Bowring thought them inadequate from the outset, so he prepared plans for a rather grand secretariat building, officially the Attara Kacheri, ie the 'eighteen offices or departments.' Appropriately, it was also called 'Bowring's Attara Kacheri'. Bowring must have been persuasive, for construction began in 1864 and the building was finished within four years at a cost of Rs450,000. Behind it, an extensive garden was laid out; named Cubbon Park it survives as one of the city's 'lungs'. Before the main entrance of the Attara Kacheri was placed an equestrian statue of Sir Mark, executed by Baron Carlo Marochetti. It was unveiled by Mr Bowring before an immense crowd, in a ceremony that began at 5.30 pm on 21 March 1868 and was concluded with a march-past of the Mysore Division together with the Maharajah's Silladar Horse.[397]

The statue had been paid for by public contributions from all levels of the community led by the Maharajah. Dobbs recorded that the likeness of the late General was remarkably good and the success achieved by Baron Marochetti

---

[394] Constance Radcliffe, *Shining by the Sea: a history of Ramsey 1800-1914*. (Douglas 1989) 158-9
[395] F. S. Roberts, *Forty-one Years in India* (London 1897) 263
[396] R. H. Elliott, *Experiences of a Planter in India* (London 1871) 208, Appendix A2
[397] T. P. Issar, *The City Beautiful* 48

was mainly due to the assistance he received from Major Martin, a gifted artist, and formerly an officer in the Mysore Commission.

No doubt Sir Mark would have approved of Bangalore's park as something of benefit to all the people. The statue, however, may not have pleased him. Shortly before he left Bangalore he was approached with a proposal of having his statue erected in some conspicuous part of the Cantonment. His response was predictable

> If I might venture to offer a suggestion, I would propose with great respect, that instead of erecting a statue, you would find some charitable institution which would answer the purpose in view equally well, be far more gratifying to me, be useful to society, and ultimately, I think, be regarded by yourselves with greater satisfaction.[398]

But a statue it was! Elizabeth Cubbon was kept informed of what was happening in Mysore. A progress report came to her in the form of a slim volume entitled 'Proceedings of a Public Meeting of Subscribers to the Cubbon Memorial held in the High School – Bangalore, 16th August 1862' and inscribed by the Secretary of the Fund, Major C.P. Taylor

> For Miss Cubbon with Major Taylor's respects
> In memory of a great and good Man
> Bangalore 24th August 1862 [399]

The Proceedings run to fourteen pages and, inter alia, make clear that 'the wish of the Natives themselves is to perpetuate Sir Mark Cubbon in Mysore in the same way as Sir Thomas Munro has been perpetuated in Madras'. The Maharajah himself was unequivocal 'I beg distinctly to state that the amount subscribed by me is intended for a statue, and a statue alone.'

In Coorg the memorial was more utilitarian and in keeping with Sir Mark's preference. There, the leading Headmen passed a valedictory notice and resolved to build a memorial school for one hundred boys. It was completed about 1865, and seems to survive as part of the Junior College in Mercara (now Medikeri), a conclusion which is supported alike by local informants and architectural style.

The Maharajah continued to hope, and plan, for a restoration of Mysore to his authority. Bowring has a story that involved that intriguing character Dr Campbell. In 1862 the Maharajah formulated a scheme to send Campbell to London with a proposal to the British Government that, if sovereignty were restored to him he would, in his will, bestow Mysore on the Prince of Wales. Seemingly, Campbell carried out this task, arguing that the agreement would be

---

[398] MNHL MD 436 13/25
[399] Many years ago the late Mrs. R. J. Quirk, of Ballaquaggan (Malew), purchased this volume from a second-hand bookseller. It is now in the MNH Library.

worth 30,000 bayonets to the British Government because of the satisfaction it would give the other Princes. Sir Charles Wood was minded to agree, but the Cabinet overruled him partly because such an action, taken in secrecy, would undermine the Governor-General's authority.[400]

Thereafter His Highness followed a more conventional tack. Thanks to the intervention of Canning and Cubbon, and a measure of good luck, he could adopt an heir if he were so minded. This he did in June 1865: an infant of two and a half years from a family into which he had twice married. Soon afterward John Stuart Mill introduced into the House of Commons a petition calling for Re-establishment of Native Government in the Tributary State of Mysore. On 16 April 1867 Disraeli's Government agreed, and the Viceroy was advised to 'maintain the Maharaja's family on the throne in the person of his adopted son.'[401] Perhaps having in mind his own lack of preparation for government the Maharajah selected Col Gregory Haines (formerly of the Commission) as the child's guardian and to superintend his education. In March 1868 the Maharajah died, and six months later his heir was placed on the gaddi. On 25 March 1881 the eighteen-year-old Maharajah was invested with full powers to rule his State – the so-called Rendition. Thereafter it remained in direct political relations with the Government of India, in common with another six of the greatest States. The Commission was disbanded, and the Governor-General was again represented by a Resident. The Cantonment was made over to the Government of India and a division of British troops continued to be quartered there.[402]

Such faults as Krishnaraja Wadiyar III may have possessed were not shown by his successors. His heir by adoption, His Highness Sir Chamarajendra Wadiyar, earned a high reputation despite surviving only until 1894. His reign was followed by a Regency of seven years during which a truly remarkable Lady, the Maharani Regent, held sway. There were two further Maharajahs, the second of whom ruled 1940-47. Both give the impression of being upright gentlemen with enlightened views. Beneficial public works were carried out on a considerable scale.[403]

During the months preceding Independence in August 1947 the Princely States were persuaded or cajoled into acceding to either India or Pakistan, and Mysore was the last to do so when it joined the Indian Union in November 1947. For some time thereafter it retained its identity, albeit with the last Maharajah being transformed into an agent of Central Government, with the title of Rajapramukh, as part of an evolving system of government for the States that aimed at eventual removal of the ruling Princes.

Another factor then emerged to bring about change. As a reaction to the northern protagonists of Hindi for the national language, pressure mounted in

---

[400] L. B. Bowring, *A Memoir of Service in India* 201-2 (BL (OIOC) Ms Eur G91)
[401] T. L. Kantam, *Tourist Guide to Mysore* (1932) (MNHL G88 C12/2.) 12-13; and *Encyclopaedia Britannica* 11th Ed. (1910-11).
[402] L. B. Bowring. *A Memoir of Service in India* 241
[403] T. P. Issar, *The Royal City* 10, 16

South India for a redefinition of the States using the main languages as criteria. In 1953 Andhra Pradesh was formed from the Telegu-speaking parts of Madras. Later a States Reorganization Commission (1956) recommended a thoroughgoing realignment, as a result of which Hyderabad joined Andhra Pradesh, and Mysore formed the nucleus of a Kannada-language State called Karnataka after 1973. Coorg became a district of the new State with the name of Kodagu.

In December 1971 rule by the Wadiyar dynasty was finally abolished, together with the rest of the Princely Order. But that family, and Sir Mark Cubbon himself, are still remembered as any visitor may see.

Cubbon remembered: Mysore Cottages, Ramsey, built by his sisters Elizabeth and Maria (SLT, 1995).

Appendix 1: Biographical Names

Agnew, Patrick Alexander (? –1813). Commissioned 2nd Lt in 4 MNI 1774. Lt 1780, Capt 1785, Major 1796, Lt Col 1798, Col 1804, Maj Gen 1811. Adj-Gen Madras Army 1799-1807; suspended after Vellore mutiny. On furlough 1808-10. Returned to India 1811 as Col 21 MNI. Served as Adj-Gen to force that captured Java (1811-12), and was sent back to Britain to report on the campaign. Died at Bath 1813.

Arbuthnot & Co., Bankers. A business founded about 1800 when George Arbuthnot, from Aberdeen, went to Madras as an independent merchant and joined the company of Francis Latour, which had been started in 1777. It underwent several name changes before becoming Arbuthnot & Co. Sponsored a number of the earliest industrial projects in India. Bank crashed in 1906, and Sir George Gough Arbuthnot was convicted of misappropriation.

Auchmuty, Samuel (1758-1822). Born in New York. Joined the British Army 1777 and served in 3 campaigns against the Americans. Later served in India including 3rd Mysore War (1790-92), Egypt and South America. C-in-C Madras 1810-12 and commanded expedition to Java (1811-12). Knighted. C-in-C Ireland 1821-22.

Bertram, Archibald Nathaniel (?- 1816). Commissioned 17 MNI 1801. Lt 1809. Capt 1810. Sent to 1st Bn Pioneers, which he eventually commanded.

Bowring, Lewin Bentham (1824 -1910). Educated Haileybury and Fort William College, Calcutta (2 medals & Degree of Honour). Bengal Civil Service 1843-70. Assistant Resident, Lahore. PS to Lord Canning 1858-62. Chief Commissioner for Mysore and Coorg 1862-70.CSI 1867.

Briggs, John (1785-1875). Joined 15 MNI 1801. Took part in both Mahratta wars of 19th century. Political Officer under Malcolm, whom he accompanied to Persia 1810. Lt Col 32 MNI 1825. Resident at Sattara, from whence he was posted to Mysore as Senior Commissioner 1831. To Nagpur as Resident 1833, and retired from there 1835. Maj Gen 1838. Elected FRS for his contribution to study of Indian languages.

Burgoyne, John (1713-85). 7th Baronet. Entered Army at an early age. Commissioned to raise a regiment (later name 19th Dragoons) for service in India. Embarked for India early 1782. Promoted Maj Gen on Madras Staff 1783. Suffered much ill-health and died at Madras. Not the Burgoyne of Saratoga.

Campbell, John Colin (? –after 1867). Practiced medicine in India 1834-49. Durbar Surgeon to Maharajah of Mysore 1849-65. His residence was Chamundi Vihar (not the extant building) about 1 km from Palace. Married an Indian lady, whose memorial is the Dargah Tomb in Nazarbad Road, Mysore. Travelled to Britain with Cubbon 1861. Returned to Mysore, but eventually retired to Britain, with his younger daughter & a niece 1865; was active in public life there 1865-67.

Casamaijor, James Archibald (? –1866). Member of famous Anglo-Indian family. Writer 1802. Asst to Resident in Mysore 1812-25. Acting Resident 1825-27. Resident 1827-34. Resident in Travancore-Cochin 1834-36.

Close, Barry (1756-1813). Appointed Cadet 1771 and Ensign 1773. Served throughout siege of Tellicherry by Hyder Ali's forces 1780-82 and distinguished himself in action. Capt 1783. In 1784 & 1787 conducted negotiations about disputed boundaries with ruler of Mysore. Deputy Adj-Gen 1790-93 & served with Cornwallis during first siege of Seringapatam. Adj-Gen & virtual Chief of Staff during 2nd siege 1799. Member of Commission that arranged future government of Mysore. Resident at Mysore 1799-1801 and Hon ADC to Governor-General. Transferred to Poona, and retired from there 1810. Gen & Baronet 1810. An outstanding scholar of Persian, Arabic and Hindustani.

Appendix 1: Biographical Names

Cole, the Hon Arthur Henry (1780-1834). 4th son of Earl of Enniskillen. Writer at Madras 1801. Secretary to Resident in Mysore 1806-09. Acting Resident 1809-11. Resident 1811-25. Retired 1827 after long leave.

Collet, Mark Wilks (1816-1905). Born London as 2nd son James & Anne Collet, and thus a grandson of John and Anne Corlett/ Collet (née Wilks). Married twice: 1 daughter, 1 son. Director, Bank of England from 1867; Governor 1887-96. Baronet 1888. .

Cosnahan Family. For two centuries this was one of the most prominent Manx families, particularly in the Clergy. The young man mentioned in the text, James Mark Cosnahan, died 1812 in India during his 19th year. His father. Deemster John Cosnahan, & Catherine Cosnahan (later Wilks) were siblings. See also Moore. Sir George.

Cunningham (sic) **Family**. There is a linkage here with the Capt (later Major) John Taubman who was Wilks's fellow-officer in the Manx Fencibles of 1779. In 1791 his sister Christian (1773-1852)married Lt Col William Cuninghame (1754-1825) 'an Irish officer of the garrison' who had served with the 58th Foot. They lived at Ballanorris in the Parish of Arbory. Cuninghame was with John Taubman in the Royal Manx Fencibles of 1793, and was a MHK 1806-24. Other prominent members of the family were Robert (1793-1832), presumably a son, who owned Ballanorris and was a MHK; and Patrick Taubman Cuninghame, who held both Ballanorris and Lorne House, Castletown and was a MHK for 14 years. See also Taubman. (Spelling and dates as on monuments in St Columba's Church, Arbory).

Devereaux, the Hon Humphrey Bohun (1812- ?). Son of Viscount Hereford. Educ. Haileybury. Joined Bengal Civil Service. Judicial Commissioner, Mysore & Coorg 1859-60. Retired 1867.

Dobbs, Richard Stewart (1808-88). Born Co. Antrim. Cadet 1827 posted to 9 MNI. Lt 1833. Joined Mysore Commission 1834. Superintendent Chittledroog Div 1854 & Nundidroog Div 1863. Retired as Maj Gen.

Durand, Horace (? – 1834). Son (?) of Col John J. Durand who had commanded Madras European Regt early in 19th century. Lt in European Regt 1797. Capt 1804 and served in 5 MNI about that time. Col 1834 & commanded European Regt..

Fraser, James Stuart (1783-1869). At school showed a predilection for languages and astronomical calculations. Lt 18 MNI 1799. ADC to Sir George Barlow during 'officers' revolt.' Present at several actions during conquest of Coorg 1834. Appointed Resident in Mysore and Commissioner for Coorg 6 Jun 1834; assumed post in Mysore City 10 Oct 1834. Resident Travancore-Cochin Jan 1836. Officiating Resident Hyderabad Sep 1838; Resident Dec 1839. Due to strained relationship with Governor-General resigned post 1852 and retired to Britain. Lt Col 1824; Col 1829; Maj Gen 1838; Lt Gen 1851; Gen 1862.

Fletcher, Henry (1727-1807). Long in the service of EIC, commanding two of its ships & rendering conspicuous service. Chosen Director of EIC 1769-87, being always re-elected when he retired by rotation; Chairman 1782-83. Had high reputation for generosity and integrity. MP for Cumberland 1768. Baronet 1782.

Grant, Patrick (1804-95). Son of an officer in Bengal Army. Ensign 11 Bengal Cavalry 1820. Saw extensive service in N. India, including with Sir Charles James Napier. Maj Gen 1854. C-in-C Madras Army 1856. KCB Jan 1857. When Gen George Anson (C-in-C India) died suddenly in Jun 1857 Grant was called to Calcutta as temporary C-in-C; later resumed Madras appointment, until Jan 1861 when he returned to Britain. GCB 1861. Lt Gen 1862. Later Field Marshal and Governor of Chelsea Hospital.

Appendix 1: Biographical Names

Haines, Gregory (1809-74). Ensign 18 MNI 1827. Lt 1835. Joined Commission, Superintendent of Coorg 1844. Capt 1845; Major & Superintendent Bangalore Div 1856. Officiating Judicial Commissioner 1857. Retired 1859. Selected by Maharajah as first tutor & guardian of his adopted son Chamarajendra Wadiyar.

Harris, George (1746-1829). One of several children of Rev George Harris, Curate of Brasted. Entered RMA Woolwich as Cadet 1759. Saw much action in India & West Indies, & showed himself to be a courageous man. Served as Secretary & ADC to Gen Medows when Governor & C-in-C Bombay (Sep 1788- Jan 1790) & Madras (Jan 1790 – Aug 1792). Served in campaign of 1791-92, & went back to Britain with Medows 1792. Returned to India as C-in-C Fort William, then C-in-C Madras 1796-1800 and local Lt Gen; also administered Govt 1797 to Feb 1798. Selected by Mornington to command campaign against Tipu 1799. Returned to Britain 1800. Lt Gen in Army 1801, Gen 1812. Created Baron Harris of Mysore and Seringapatam 1815, GCB 1820. His grandson, the 3rd Baron was Governor of Madras 1854-59, and a life-long friend of Viscount Canning.

Hildesley, Mark (1698-1772). Born at Marsden, Kent where his father was Rector. Vicar of Hitchin, Herts. Awarded DD. Lord Bishop of Sodor and Man (1755-72). A story about him is recorded by the perpetual Curate of Maidstone, John Denne. One Sunday in 1770 a servant in livery came to Denne saying his master would give him a sermon if he chose to accept it. Denne accepting, a grave gentleman went into the vestry, soon emerging to mount the pulpit in Lawn Sleeves – the distinctive mark of a Bishop. Denne was taken aback because he thought he knew all English Bishops by sight, but after the service found him to be the Bishop of Sodor and Man (Ditchfield, G.M. & Keith-Lucas, B: A Kentish Parson).

Kirkpatrick, James Archilles (1764-1805). Served in Madras Army. EIC's Resident in Hyderbad 1798-1805 as Maj and Lt Col. Played major part in persuading Nizam to ally himself with British. Suspected of divided loyalty by Mornington, who instigated an enquiry by Lord Edward Clive and his secretary, Mark Wilks.

Kirkpatrick, William (1756-1812). Half-brother to James Archilles Kirkpatrick. As officer EIC's Army served as Resident at Court of the Maharajah Scindia of Gwalior, and in Hyderabad (1794-98) as Lt Col.. Secretary to Mornington. Member of Commission for the Settlement of Mysore (1800).

McHutchin, Thomas Moss (1825-73). Born in the Isle of Man, son of Deemster John McHutchin (appointed 1820, died 1847). Entered Madras Army as Ensign in 19 MNI 1843. Capt 1848. Joined Mysore Commission Sep 1855. Brevet Major 1860; Major 1865; Lt Col 1870. In bad health during last 3 years of life. Married 1851 and had 9 children, fifth being named Mark Cubbon McHutchin.

Mackenzie, Colin (1753-1821). Born Stornaway, Isle of Lewis. Largely self-taught in mathematics. Ensign in Engineers, Madras Army 1783. Capt 1793; Major 1806; Lt Col 1809; Col 1819. Began his first survey 1784. Served 3rd Mysore War (1790-92) & was ordered to survey Baramahal. After Seringapatam (1799) began survey of Mysore which lasted until 1810. Surveyor-Gen Madras 1807. Served with expedition to Java 1811-13. CB 1815. Surveyor-Gen of India 1815-21. A pioneering student & collector of Indian antiquities.

Mackenzie, Colin (1806-81). Joined 48 MNI 1825. Lt 1827. Met Cubbon 1833 near Gersoppa Falls (Chap 10). Served in Coorg campaign (1834). Later served in Afghanistan and N. India. Eventually Lt Gen and CB. Left India 1873.

Mackintosh, James (1765-1832). Qualified in Medicine at Edinburgh University, but turned to law & political philosophy. Practiced as barrister in England. Politically a

Appendix 1: Biographical Names

Whig, he was determined to (i)refute Hume's Tory interpretation of history of England, (ii) write an appropriate interpretation of differences between 'Glorious Revolution' (1688) and French Revolution (1789). To secure financial independence he spent 1804-11 as Recorder of Bombay (ie Judge having criminal and civil jurisdiction). MP for Nairn 1813; member of Board of Control for India in Whig Govt of 1830. FRS; Knighted. Collected much material for his history, but wrote only section for Feb 1685 to Feb 1689. Published 1834 and reviewed by Macaulay in 'Edinburgh Review' 1835.

Macleod, John McPherson (1792-1881). Writer (Madras) 1811. Sec to Govt in Financial & General Depts 1824. Tamil translator to Govt 1825. Persian translator to Govt 1826. Member, Board of Revenues 1829. Commissioner for Govt of Mysore 1832-3. Sent to Hyderabad on special duties 1834. Member, Indian Law Commission (with Macaulay) 1835. Returned to UK 1838. Retired 1841. KCSI 1866. PC 1871.

McQueen, Lachlan (? - ?). Posted 3 Lt Cavalry 1828. Lt 1832. Capt & Deputy Judge Advocate-Gen 1841. Lt Col and Judge Advocate-Gen 1859. Also served in Commission. Retired Mar 1861.

Maddrell, Henry (1765-1842). Second son of Robert & Ellinor Maddrell of Ballamaddrell, Arbory. As Chaplain of Ramsey he was Master of Ramsey Grammar School (1790-1803) when Mark Cubbon studied there. Became Vicar of Kirk Christ, Lezayre where he remained until his death. Archdeacon's Registrar. Buried in churchyard of St Columba's, Arbory, about 1 km from Ballamaddrell. (Information kindly provided by Dr S.H.P Maddrell).

Malcolm, John (1769-1833). Born Westerkirk, Dumfries. When father was ruined by speculation, he left village school, aged 12, and was taken by an uncle who was a merchant in London. Entered Madras Army 1783. At first a harum-scarum laddie, he came to grips with career during a visit to Hyderabad 1791, when he began to master Persian. At Seringapatam 1792. Jan 1799 joined Nizam's contingent and worked with Arthur Wellesley. A Secretary to Mysore Settlement Commission. Joined Wellesley 1803 for Maratha War, but became ill and so missed Assaye and Argaum. Appointed Resident in Mysore 1804 but was engaged on other tasks for several years. At first got on famously with Mornington & undertook various missions for him, but later relations cooled. Maj Gen and GCB 1820. On leave in Great Britain 1822-27, where wrote 15 chapters of 'Life of Clive' (completed by another). Variously employed, Central India, but left country 1830. MP for a time.

Marriot, Charles (? - ?). Served in 5 MNI with Cubbon. Lt 1797. Adjutant 2/5 MNI 1801-4. Capt 1804. Retired as Major 1822.

Martin, George Matthew (1820-1900). Lt 42 MNI 1839. Capt & Officiating Superintendent Coorg Div 1856. Superintendent Bangalore Div. 1860. Retired as Major 1861. Married 1851 Cecilia Cockburn Campbell (1833-77). A talented artist, he drew Dalhousie, Lady Susan Ramsey and Cubbon. Sketches of Cubbon were used by Baron Marochetti in making his statue.

Medows, William (1738-1813). 2nd son Sir Philip Medows. Ensign 50th Foot 1756: served in Germany 1760-64, N. America, St Lucia, Cape of Good Hope. On own initiative sailed with large body of troops to Madras to assist against Hyder Ali 1783. Governor and C-in-C Bombay 1788-90. Jan 1790. Held same posts Madras but was no match for Hyder Ali. Subordinate to Cornwallis 1791-92. Led storming party that captured Nundidroog 19 Oct 1791 and commanded right column in night attack on Seringapatam 16 Feb 1792. After the peace he resigned his share of the prize money (£15,000) in favour of the troops. Returned Britain Aug 1792. Gen and Governor Isle of Wight. Knighted.

Appendix 1: Biographical Names

Meuron, de. Family of soldiers from Neuchatel, not then part of Swiss Confederation. Charles Daniel (1738-1806) began his career at 17 and served in Swiss Guards. In 1781, as Colonel Proprietaire, raised the Neuchatel Regiment de Meuron (1 020 strong) for Dutch VOC. It reached Ceylon 1782 & served at various places in S. India, Ceylon & the Cape. About 1785 he left the Regiment, when brother Pierre Fredrich became commander. In 1795, after prolonged negotiations, he ceded the Regiment to EIC. In 1797 went to England to finalize matters; these completed 1798 and he was appointed Maj Gen in British Army. Died Neuchatel. Pierre Fredrich (1743-1813) opposed the British invasion of Ceylon more successfully than other forces. When Regiment was ceded to EIC he was made Military Governor of Ceylon and Commander of troops at Tuticorin until 1799. Regiment took part in campaign against Tipu, and he commanded troops at Vellore & Arni. Retired 1807. When Regiment was ceded to EIC two other members of family were serving as Lt Cols. Regiment disbanded 1816.

Monteith, William (1790-1864). Appointed Chief Engineer in Madras Army 1832, and held that post intermittently until 1842. Retired 1847 as Lt Gen.

Moore, George (1709-87) of Ballamoar, Peel. MHK for many years and SHK 1763-80. Knighted 1781. Indirectly linked to Mark Wilks: Sir George's son, James, married Catherine Cosnahan (1759-1837) and they had one son, named George (1780-1800). James died soon after the boy was born, and Catherine then married James Wilks, elder brother of Mark. The couple had at least 3 children but no grandchildren. Sir George secured letter(s) of introduction for Mark Wilks when first he went to India.

Morison, William (?- 1851). Infantry Cadet 1799 but transferred to Madras Artillery 1800. Brevet Major and CB 1821. Lt Col 1827. Commissary-General, Madras Army. Resident in Travancore and Cochin 1828-32. Member of Commission on Insurrection in Mysore 1831; Senior Commissioner for Mysore 1832. Extraordinary Member of Supreme Council of India. May 1834; 3rd Member of Council 1835. Maj Gen & on furlough 1841. KCB 1848.

Munro, Thomas (1761-1827). Born Glasgow. Infantry Cadet 1779; arrived Madras 1780. Served with Cornwallis at siege of Bangalore. Administrator in Baramahal 1792. Rejoined Army 1799, served Seringapatam, and was a Secretary to the Mysore Settlement Commission. Administrator of the 'Ceded Districts' (1800-07) where he established the ryotwari system of land tenure. Maj Gen and KCB 1819 while on furlough in Great Britain. Baronet. Governor of Madras 1819; died in office, of cholera.

Rama Sawmy, (? - ?). Mark Wilks's spelling of the name of his friend & factotum. Correctly Ramaswami – Lord Rama – a common Hindu proper name in the South.

Rumbolt, Thomas (1736-91). Educated for EIC service, and entered as a Writer 1852. Transferred to military service soon after arrival Fort St George; served with Clive at Plassey where his bravery was noted. Member of Bengal Council 1766-69. Retired to Britain 1769 and became MP for New Shoreham. Governor of Madras 1780-82; retired due to ill-health, & faced claims of oppression & corruption. MP for Weymouth 1781-90. Baronet.

Saunders, Charles Burslem (1821 - ?). Educated Haileybury. Bengal Civil Service. Judicial Commissioner for Mysore & Coorg 1860. Acting Commissioner for various periods after Cubbon's retirement.

Sleeman, William Henry (1788-1856). Member of long-established Cornish family. Cadet, Bengal Army 1809. Ensign 1810; Lt 1814. Served in war with Nepal 1814-16. Capt 1826; Major 1837; Lt Col. 1843; Maj Gen. Appointed KCB 4 Feb 1856 and died at

Appendix 1: Biographical Names

sea 6 days later on way home. Most of his career was spent in investigating thuggee, and attempting to remove it.

Smith, Charles Irvine (1809- ?). Born Trichinopoly, son of Lt Michael Smith 1/3 MNI. Assistant Surgeon Madras 1831. Joined Commission as Surgeon.

Stokes, John Day (1802-62). Cadet and posted 4 MNI 1817. Capt 1827, Major 1836. Resident in Mysore 1836-43. Lt. Col 1841. Transferred to 15 MNI 1843. Col 47 MNI 1851. Maj Gen 1854. On furlcugh 1861.

Stowell, Rev Joseph (1772-1801). Educated Douglas Grammar School & Academic School, Castletown. Tutor to family of Governor Shaw 1792. Ordained 1794. Next year left Shaw to found the seminary that attracted Wilks's favourable assessment. Moved to Peel 1799 & died of typhus soon afterwards. Clearly a scholar of considerable force.

Stuart, James (? –1793). Appointed Capt 56th Foot 1755,and saw much service in N. America, Martinique & Havana. Transferred to EIC as Col and 2nd in Command at Madras. There he found serious dissention between the Governor (Lord Pigot) and his Council. On orders from a majority of Council he arrested Pigot Aug 1776. Succeeded as C-in-C on death of Sir Robert Fletcher Dec 1776. When news of Pigot's arrest reached London, Stuart was suspended by Directors. Court-martialled Dec 1780. Restored to post Jan 1781. Maj Gen 1781. While besieging Cuddalore was suspended by Madras Govt and sent home. Fought duel with Lord Macartney, a former Governor. Often confused with the following.

Stuart, James (1741-1815). Entered HM Army. Went to India 1781 as Brevet Lt Col 78th Foot. Served under Medows (1790) and Cornwallis (1791-92) in war with Tipu. As Maj Gen led expedition against Dutch in Ceylon. Commanded Bombay's contingent at Seringapatam 1799. C-in-C Madras 1801. Lt Gen 1802. Served in Maratha War 1803. Retired 1805. Gen 1812.

Taubman, John (1746-1822). Son of John, the 'Great Taubman' (1720-99), and Esther Christian of Ballastowell, Maughold. Held a commission in 6th Dragoon Guards. Joined Manx Fencibles as Capt; promoted Major. MHK 1777-1821 and Speaker 1799-1821 in succession to his father (Speaker from 1780).

Vira Raja of Coorg (? –1863). Succeeded 1820. Deposed 1834. Lived in London for several years (where he met Macaulay again), and died there. Queen Victoria stood Godmother to his daughter.

Webbe, Josiah (1768-1804). Writer Ft St George 1783. Sec to Board of Revenue 1790, and to Govt of Ft St George 1797. Became its first Chief Secretary 1800. Resident in Mysore 1804, but was shortly transferred as Resident in Gwalior; died on way to take up the post.

Wilson, James (1805-60). In business in London & became an authority on the currency. Founded 'Economist' newspaper. Liberal MP 1847 & served as Financial Sec to Treasury & Vice-President of the Board of Trade. Finance member of Supreme Council of India 1860, and died in office.

Wood, Charles (1800-85). MP for Halifax Dec 1832 & held seat for 32 years. President of Board of Control Dec 1852 until 1858; passed an 'excellent India Act' in 1853. Sec of State for India Jun 1859 to Feb 1866. Knighted, and created 1st Viscount Halifax.

Appendix 2: Geographical Names

Ceded Districts: Former districts of Hyderabad: Bellary (gained by the Nizam from Tipu's Mysore after Seringapatam 1799), Cuddapah and Kurnool. The Nizam fell into debt over his Subsidiary Treaty and ceded the three districts to the Company in 1800 in lieu of his arrears. They were incorporated into Madras Presidency with Major Thomas Munro in charge.

Chenerogapatam (Chennaroyapatam): Town 95 km NNW of Mysore City.

Chilambram (now Chidambaram): Town on east coast 209 km S of Madras and 10 km from Porto Novo.

Chittledroog (Chitaldrug, now Chitradurga): Town about 200 km NW of Bangalore and 100 km S of Bellary. Stands at foot of a cluster of hills that were fortified by local poligars in 17th century and captured by Hyder Ali in 1779.

Cuddalore: Coastal town about 205 km S of Madras and less than 32 km S of Pondicherry. Purchased by EIC from a son of Sivaji; remained in their hands until 1758 when it was taken by Lally. Restored to EIC under preliminary arrangements to Treaty of Paris (Sep 1783).

Gersoppa Falls (Jog Falls): On Shiravati river in NW Mysore, 260 km from Bangalore. There are 4 separate falls, of which the uppermost is the Raja or Horseshoe – where the water descends sheer for 253 m into a pool 40 m deep.

Goomnaigpolliam: Town in Mysore 200 km NE of Mysore City.

Hooly Onoore (also Hoolionaar, Holehonoruru): Town in Mysore about 200 km NW from Mysore City; situated on right bank of Bhadra river and a few km above its junction with the Tunga (where the Tungabhadra river is formed). The fort is large and square, with two towers on each face and a tower at each angle; despite these it is not a strong place. During the rains its W wall is washed by the Bhadra. At one time was centre of a populous district. In 1792 was taken by a British detachment, then plundered and destroyed by the Marathas.

Kurnool (Karnul): Town and district in N of Madras Presidency., close to border with Hyderabad. Town is at junction of Hindri and Tungabhadra rivers. Aurangzeb made over the district to a Pathan family, as Nawabs; they built a fort and palace. In 1838 the Nawab began accumulating munitions with the intention of revolt, but the Company took the fort and deposed him.

Nemawar: Town on the Narbada river, about 595 km ENE of Bombay and similar distance NNW of Hyderabad City.

Newtown in Ashold (I. o. M.): Kneen (1925) states that Ashole or Asholt was the name given to a large intack also known as Hamilton's Croft and Mount Murray (Santon); it was probably the old name of the Mount. Newton or Newtown was a house and estate on this site. According to Mr Peter Kelly (pers. comm.) the architectural style of the house in J Warwick Smith's watercolour of 1795 (IOMMM 7215) suggests it could have been that occupied by John and Margaret Wilks in 1717. Seemingly the Wilks's house was replaced by what became the 'old' Mount Murray Hotel, and no trace of it remains.

Nilgiris, Neilghirries: A mountainous and beautiful region of S India where several hill-stations have been established. Most notable are Ootacamund (Ooty, 2267 m) about 160 km from Mysore City. Settled by Europeans from 1821, and formerly site of the summer residence of the Governor of Madras. The military station at Wellington is 14.5 km away; Coonoor (1860 m) 25 km from Ooty; Kotagiri (1985 m) 29 km from Oooty and 21 km from Coonoor, the first hill-station in the Nilgiris (1819 m).

Appendix 2: Geographical Names

Nuggar, properly Nagar (also Bednur): Nagar means 'the city'. A town near the W border of Mysore State, about 203 km NW of Bangalore. Capital of Division having the same name.

Panjalamcoorchy (now Panchalamkurichi): Town with old fort in Tinnevelly District, about 80 km N of Kanya Kumari.

Rayakotta, Rayakottai: A hill-fort about 64 km SE of Bangalore. Commands S end of Palakad Pass. Captured by the Company 1791 and used as the main supply route by Cornwallis.

Sankery Droog, Sankaridrug: A spectacular fortified hill 40 km SW of Salem in the Baramahal.

Secunderabad: Former cantonment situated 8 km N of centre of Hyderabad City. Named for Nizam Sikandar Jah (reigned 1803-29).

Sera: Town in Mysore, 135 km N from Seringapatam on a tributary of Vedavati river. Before it and the surrounding district were captured by EIC (1791) all villages were fortified, seemingly because of the inter-village strife that went on during periods of famine due to unreliable rainfall. Villagers, both men and women, threw stones with great force and accuracy to repulse attackers. Under Dilawar Khan there were 50,000 houses in district, but after being taken by Hyder, Tipu and the Marathas the number was reduced to 3000.

Tinnevelly: Town about 80 km due N of Kanya Kumari, and situated about 2.5 km from left bank of Tambrapurni river.

Trichinopoly, now Tiruchirapalli: Town 275 km SE of Mysore City and 320 km SSW of Madras, near S bank of Cauvery river.

Appendix 3: Glossary

Adawlut Court: term of Mughal origin. A Court of Justice before introduction of the Indian Penal Code in 1863.

Amildar: 'one bearing office'; in Mysore a collector of revenue.

Arianism: a variation of the Christian faith. Founded by Arius (ca 250-336), a Libyan theologian who was trained in Antioch and became a presbyter in Alexandria. About 317 he proposed, in opposition to his Bishop, that the Son is not co-equal or co-eternal with the Father, but is only the first and highest of finite beings. Among others, Milton held Arian or semi-Arian beliefs.

Anglo-Indian: in Wilks's and Cubbon's time, one of British birth who was living, or had lived for a long time, in India.

Ayurveda: the Hindu system of medicine.

Bahadur: literally 'hero' or 'champion'. Initially a title of honour conferred by the Mughal Emperor. Thus 'Company Bahadur' meant 'brave or valiant Company.'

Bazaar: a permanent market or street of shops.

Beebee, Bibi: originally the title 'Lady'.

Butchahs: an anglicized plural form of the Hindustani 'bachchaa' – a male child. Campbell's usage [Chap 12] seems odd because both were girls; the feminine form is bachchii and the plural [children] is bachche.

Buxshey, Buxee: title of Mughal origin. Strictly a military paymaster, but the office developed into something akin to Adjutant-General.

Cantonment: a permanent military station.

Catamaran: a raft made of 3 - 5 logs lashed together [from Tamil: kattu = binding, maram = wood].

Chauth: a lien on 25 percent of the revenue of a place.

Chin-cough: whooping-cough.

Chamunda: a manifestation of Durga [see Dussera].

Chunam: strictly, lime prepared to be used as plaster. Also means fine-quality polished plaster.

Commissioner: as used about Coorg and Mysore, an official appointed to act on behalf of the Governor-General in Council.

Coomry: from Marathi 'kumbari' – a hill-slope of poor soil. Also system of agriculture followed by hill people in which a section of forest is felled and burnt, and the ground then planted with crops for one or two years, after which the cultivators repeat the procedure elsewhere.

Daftar: essentially a register or public record.

Dak: 'post' in the sense of mail, thus the transport of letters etc. by relays of men and horses; also any arrangement for travelling by relays. Dak-bungalows are rest-houses, maintained by the Government and spaced at distances hat approximate to a stage of a journey.

Diwan: the Prime Minister of an Indian State, or a chief finance minister under the Mughal dynasty, whether of the central government or of a province.

Diwani, diwanni: the office of Diwan. Also, and especially, the right as Diwan of receiving revenues of Bengal, Bihar & Orissa conferred on the EIC by Shah Alam in 1765. Sometimes used for the territory so granted.

Durbar: a court or levée.

Dussera, dasara: an important Hindu festival which is the culmination of the Navaratra festivities. Navaratra [lit 'nine nights'] begins on the 1st night of the month of Asvina (Sep-Oct). Both festivals are dedicated to Durga, consort of Siva and the most popular Hindu goddess. Dussera was especially celebrated in Mysore where, during the 18th to 20th centuries, there was a great procession led by the Maharajah with the State Forces.

Farman: a royal grant or order.

Gaddi: throne of a Hindu Prince.

Ganapati: Hindu festival to mark the birthday of Ganesh; celebrated on 4th day of month of Bhadrapada (Aug-Sep).

Gopuram: high pyramidal gateway-tower of a Dravidian temple.

Intack: in the Isle of Man, rough land outside the boundary of arable land, used for grazing.

Jagir: a hereditary assignment of land and the entailed rents.

Jemadar: an Indian officer equivalent to 2nd lieutenant.

Keys, House of: the lower House of the Manx Parliament (cf Legislative Council). Self-nominating until 1866, but thereafter popularly elected. MHK – Member of the House of Keys. SHK – Speaker of the House of Keys.

Khureeta, kharita: official letter between the Governor-General and an Indian Prince. It was contained in a sealed silk bag.

Maratha Confederation: a regional grouping that secured special influence in western India and the Deccan. After the death of Sivaji in 1680 influence passed to a line of astute Brahmin Chief Ministers, the Peshwas, around whom the other Maratha Princes combined to form a confederation to oppose common enemies. The members were: Peshwa at Poona, Holkar of Indore, Gaekwar of Baroda, Sindia at Gwalior, Bhonsla Raja of Nagpur.

Masnad, masnud: a cushion; throne of a Muslim Ruler.

Massula-boat, mussula-boat: the surf-boat used on the Coromandel Coast where they can still be seen. The planks are sewn together with coir twine & the joints between planks filled with a caulking of twisted coir.

Mate, matey: this term had various meanings but, as used by Agnew [Chap 9 – matey boy] it meant an assistant having some authority, eg a chief clerk.

Math: a sort of monastery where a celibate priest lives with his disciples, one of whom succeeds him.

Measures & Weights: large quantities [money, people] are usually stated in **lakhs** [100 thousand] or **crores** [10 millions or 100 lakhs]. Common units of weight included **seer** – about 0.91 kg or 2 lbs, & **maund** – about 37 kg or 82 lbs

Mirza: (lit 'prince born') a title of honour prefixed to the name of a learned man or official.

Munshi: a name commonly applied by Europeans to an Indian teacher of Hindustani, Arabic or Persian. Extended to mean a well-educated Indian gentleman.

Nawab: Governor of a town under Mughal rule; later the title of a Muslim ruler.

Nevayet: corruption of Marathi for 'new comer'. The descendants of people who were driven from Arabia during the first century of the Muslim era and landed on the west coast of India. At least until the time of Wilks they had avoided marriage with other groups, considering themselves as an extended family.

Non-Regulation: the situation in various Provinces of British India whereby the laws [formerly called Regulations] were either not in force or came into force through a specific declaration of the Government of India. Such Provinces were usually under the direct authority of the Government. In these Provinces soldiers were still eligible to hold office in the civil administration.

Pagoda: the name for coins that were currency in S. India for a long period. The word may be derived 'Bhagavati' [goddess] because an image of the Goddess Durga

Appendix 3: Glossary

appeared on most of the gold coins. There were two variants: the star pagoda was reckoned at Rs3.5 & the canteroy pagoda at Rs3.0. [See Rupee].

Panchayat: a council (properly of five persons) set up to decide on important matters for a village etc.; it served also as a jury or arbitration court.

Pandal: a lightly constructed shelter or shed.

Pathan: a common name for people of Afghan descent in India; probably derived from 'Pushtun' – the name the Afghans give their own people.

Pettah, pete: the town adjacent to a fortress. Often separately fortified so that the fortress functions as the citadel of an extensively fortified town.

Polygar, poligar: originally subordinate feudal chiefs. Many aspired to make themselves independent, often by force. A term restricted to Madras Presidency.

Q.A.I.M.N.S.: Queen Alexandra's Indian Military Nursing Service.

Ragi: *Eleusine coracana*, a reddish-coloured grain that is an important staple, especially in Mysore. Possesses the great merit that it can be stored for ten or more years & so is a valuable famine-food.

Regulation: see Non-Regulation.

Resident: representative of the Governor-General at an important Indian Court.

Rupee: standard coin under both Mughal and British rule. Extended to the whole country in 1818. The sub-units were 16 annas per rupee and 4 pice per anna. Between the World Wars the rate was about Rs13.3 per £1.

Ryot: in the Anglo-Indian sense 'a tenant of the soil'; one who occupies land as a cultivator or farmer.

Ryotwari: a system under which settlement for land revenue was made directly between the Government agency and every individual cultivator or Ryot – not with the village community or with a landlord or middleman. It was established in Madras Presidency by Sir Thomas Munro.

Sardeshmuki: lien on 10% of the revenue of a place.

Sepoy: from the Hindustani 'sipahi' – a soldier. A Private soldier in a British Indian Army.

Sheristadar: (lit 'register keeper'). The chief administrative officer of a court.

Silladar, sillidar: (lit 'arms-bearer') from silah – arms/weapons. A cavalry soldier who provided and maintained his own horse, clothing and equipment (but not his rifle) and who received a higher rate of pay than one whose needs were met wholly by the Government. Sometimes sponsored by a well-to-do relative. Hence a regiment composed of such men was 'a corps of Silladar Horse.'

Sirkar, sircar: from Persian sah = 'head', kar ='work', thus 'head of affairs'. Term came to mean the State or Government; the Company Sirkar is the 'Company's Government.'

Sowar: an Indian cavalry trooper.

Stadhouder: chief executive of the Dutch Republic; appointed by the provincial assemblies, but himself having the right to appoint officials – including members of the assemblies.

Subsidiary Treaty: one that provided for the Ruler of an Indian State to pay for the upkeep of a military unit controlled by the Company (the Subsidiary Force). It has been described as obtaining security at the price of dependence on the Company.

Sudder: 'chief', eg the Sudder Board of Revenue was the one in Calcutta as distinct from those in Madras or Bombay.

Taluk: a division of a District under an Amildar or Native Collector.

Tappal: the equivalent of **dak** in S. India.

Tarmasha: a popular entertainment.

Thug, thuggee: from the Hindustani & Marathi words for 'cheat' or 'swindler'. One European definition was 'a robber and assassin of a particular kind, who sallying forth in a gang…and in the character of wayfarers, fall in with other travellers on the road, gain their confidence, and take an opportunity to strangle them by throwing handkerchiefs around their necks; and then plundering them and burying their bodies.'

Tonjon: a vehicle for carrying people. It had the body of a bath-chair slung upon a palanquin pole.

Vakeel, vakil: an attorney; an authorized representative.

Writer etc.: originally Writers were clerks in the factories (trading establishments) of the EIC. There were four grades of the EIC's civil staff: Senior Merchant, Merchant, Factor (executive head of a factory), Writer. As the Company's Sirkar developed the Writer became the junior grade of covenanted civil servants.

Maps

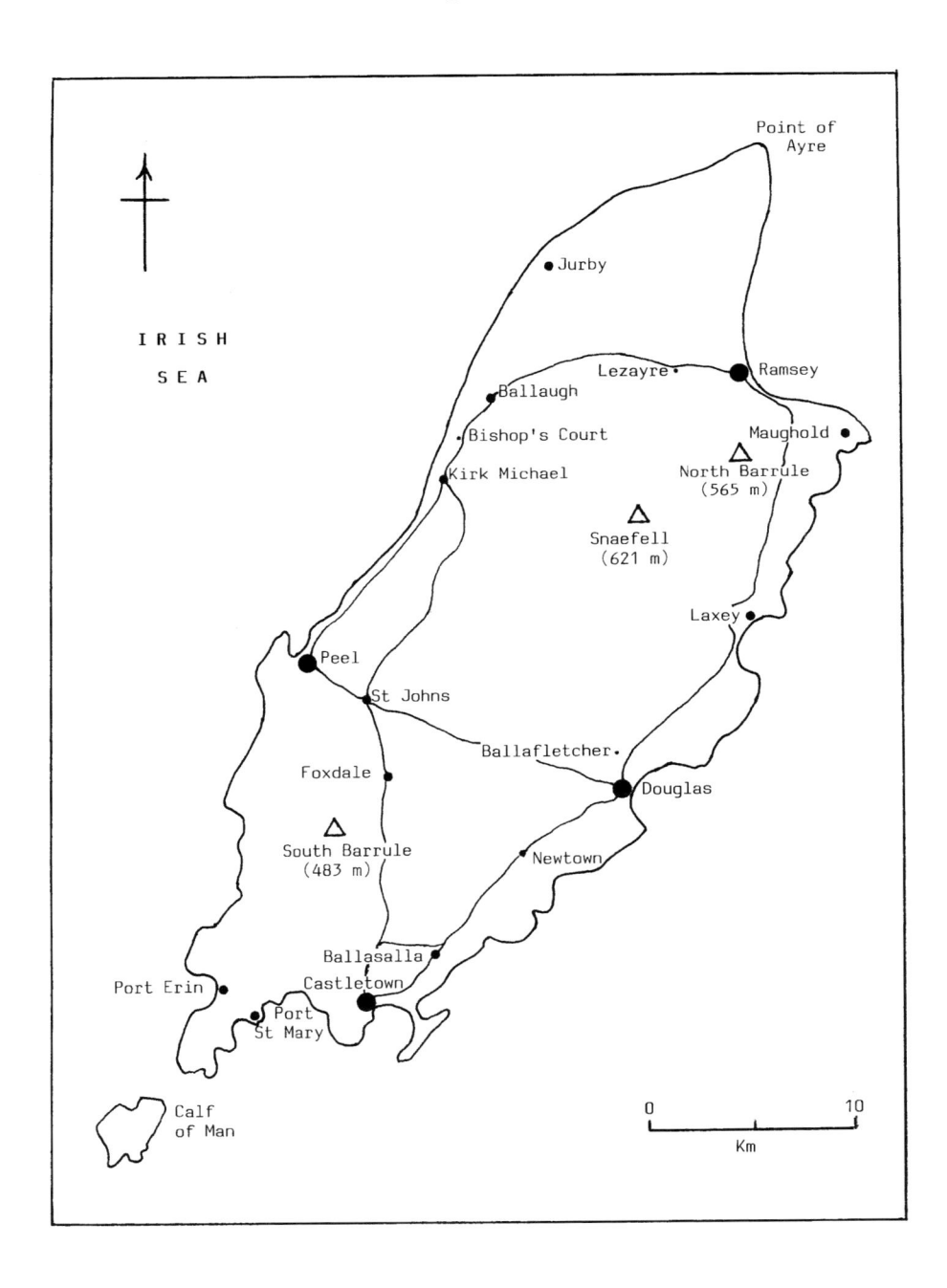

Map 1: The Isle of Man with main places and the road system of 1789

Map 2: Indian Sub-continent. The boundaries are those in force just before Independence and the Partition into India and Pakistan.

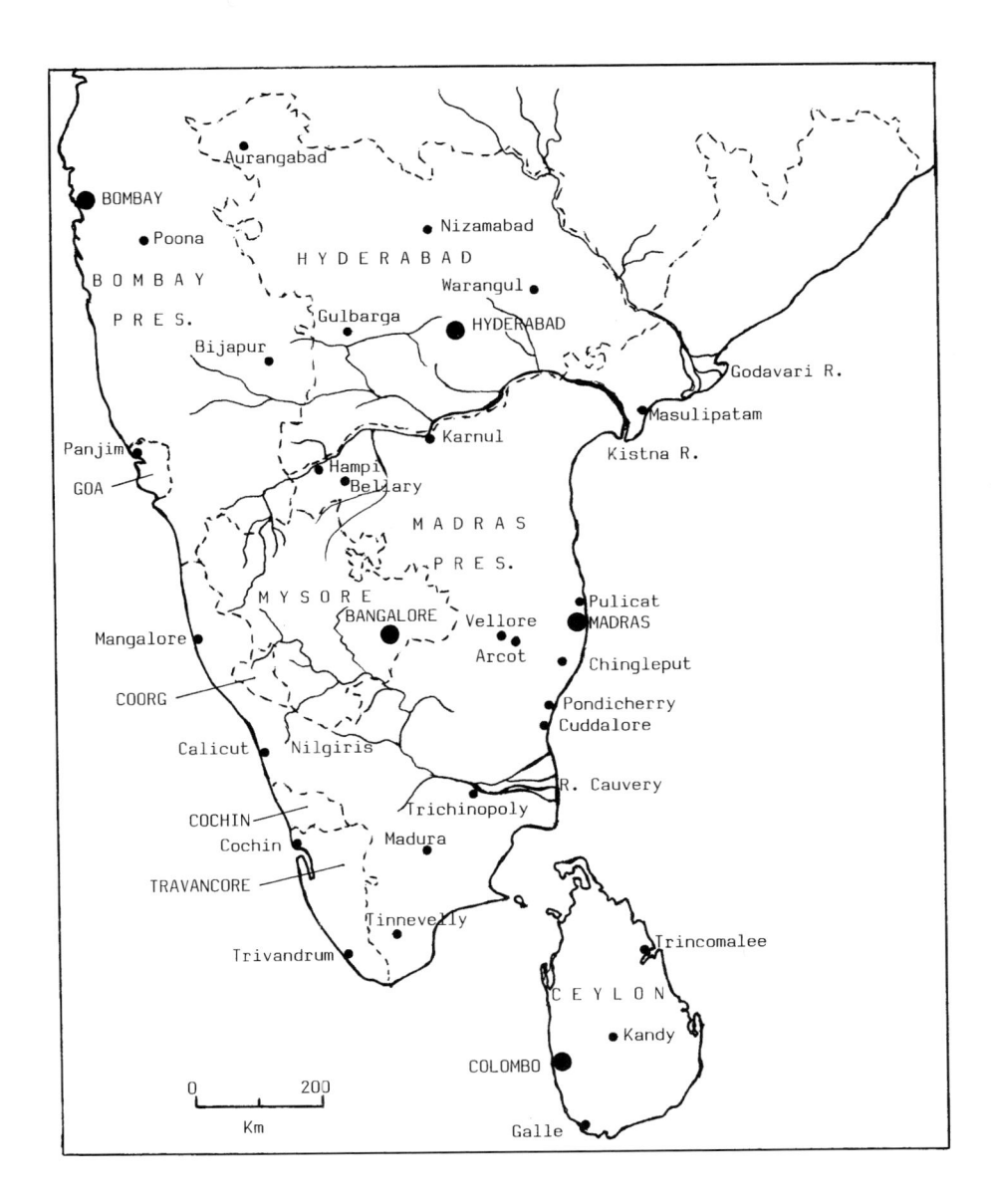

Map 3: South India showing main places mentioned in the text. Boundaries of the three Presidencies, and Princely States, are those existing just before Independence.

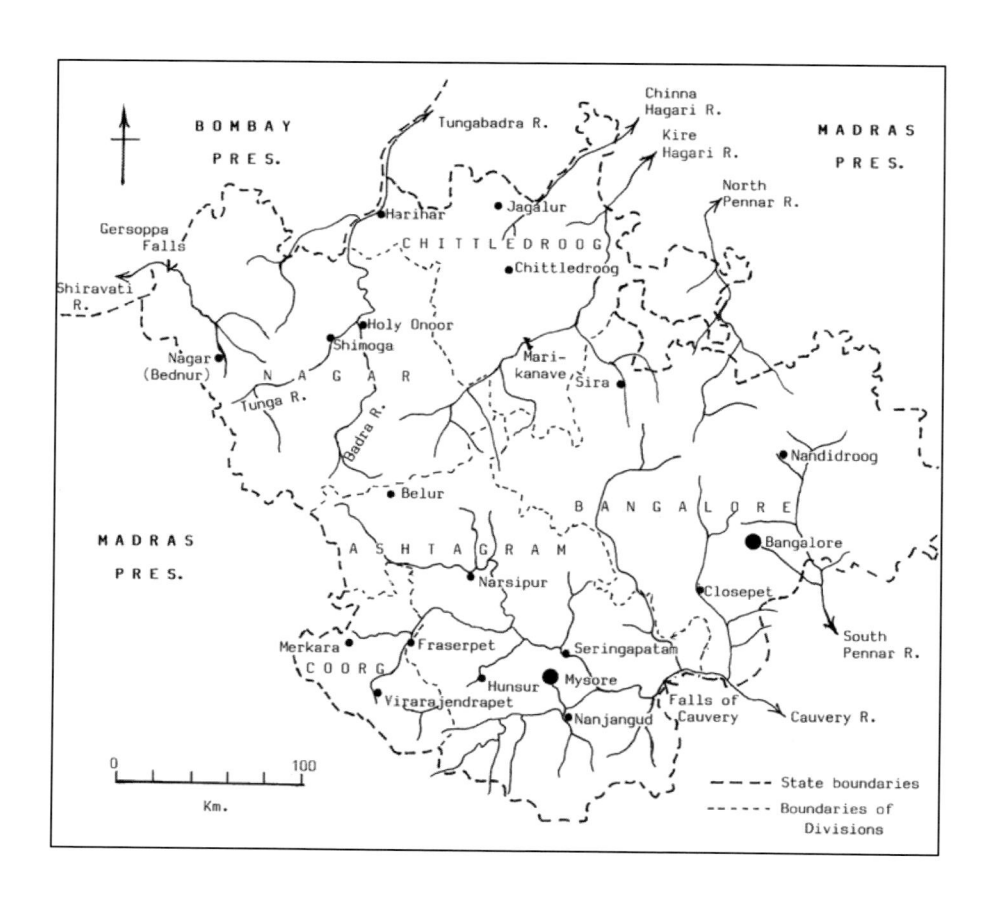

Map 4: Mysore and Coorg as in Cubbon's time

INDEX

Agnew, Col. Patrick A., 51, 67, 68, 76, 78, 87, 88, 91-3, 96, 100-5, 150, 189, 198
Aurangzeb, Emperor, 24-8, 34, 195
Baird, Gen Sir David, 40, 41, 63
Ballafletcher – see Kirby
Bangalore, 5, 25-7, 46, 48, 49, 76, 88, 89, 93, 105, 114, 116, 117, 120-4, 126, 128-32, 134, 136, 139, 140, 144-48, 157, 159-61, 165, 167, 171, 178-80, 184-5, 191-3, 195, 196
Barlow, Sir George, 84, 92, 95, 99-101, 105, 190
Bellary, 25, 65, 78, 80, 84, 85, 89, 92, 94-5, 195
Bentinck, Lord William Cavendish, 71, 88, 91, 92, 99, 113, 116-19, 121, 151, 163, 164, 168
Bombay, 30, 33, 37, 40, 41, 63, 85, 108, 123, 191, 192, 194, 195, 200
Bowring, Lewin B., 113, 122, 131, 158, 184-, 189
Briggs, Col John, 2, 3, 117, 189
Buchan,
   Sir John, 98-110
   Lady Laura, 54, 56-7, 72, 85, 91, 96-7, 98, 101-3, 136, 181
Calcutta, 1, 33, 44, 45, 61, 62, 75, 122, 134, 135, 141, 146, 163, 164, 166, 167, 171-3, 175, 189, 190, 200
Campbell, Dr John Colin, 136-9, 141, 144, 148, 175, 178, 180-3, 185, 189, 192, 197
Canning
   Lady Charlotte, 145, 146, 147, 150
   Viscount Charles John (Earl 1859), 1, 141-5, 167, 168, 170, 171, 173, 175-7, 184, 186, 189, 191
Castletown (IOM), 9, 10, 12, 15, 19-21, 55-6, 190, 194
   Grammar/ Academic Schools, 20
Ceylon, 30-31, 39-40, 59-60, 100, 104, 173, 193-94

Charter Acts
   (1833), 111
   (1853), 138
Clive, Lord Edward, 61-67, 70-2
Close, Barry, 5, 44-5, 49, 54, 63-4, 68, 75, 100, 113
Collet
   Mrs Anne (née Wilks), 19, 37, 43, 57, 88, 190
   Mark Wilks, 19, 181-4, 190, 191, 193
Compagnie des Indes Orientales, 31
Coorg, 49, 75, 113, 114, 116-20, 123, 125, 130, 131, 132, 134, 144, 155, 161, 169, 177, 185, 187, 189-94, 197, 204
Cornwallis, Earl Charles (later Marquess), 4, 45, 46, 48, 49, 61, 80, 84, 99, 119, 121, 151, 163, 189, 192, 193, 194, 196
Cosnahan, James Mark, 3, 54, 103, 106, 190, 193
Cradock, Gen Sir John, 81, 88-9, 91, 92, 94, 99
Cubbon
   Elizabeth, 135, 181-6
   Lt Gen Sir Mark, 1, 2, 4-5, 68-70, 73-81, 89, 116-7, 148, 178
      Commissioner for Mysore and Coorg, 118, 121-7, 130-2, 138, 146, 147, 150-63, 165, 167-9, 171-2, 174-6, 184, 189-93, 197
   early life, 52-4, 56-8
   funeral, 181, 183
   Mrs. Margaret (née Wilks), 16, 20, 109, 110
   Rev Thomas, 13, 16, 20, 21, 79-80, 109, 110, 148
Dalhousie, Earl James Andrew Broun, 134, 135, 138, 139, 141-3, 148, 160, 162, 167, 192
Delhi, 24, 27, 34, 143, 163

Dobbs, Col Richard S., 124, 127, 132, 146-9, 160, 182, 184, 190
Douglas (IoM), 8, 12-15, 18, 52, 53, 73, 103, 181, 182, 184, 194
East India Company (London/ England/ United), 2, 3, 22, 26, 30, 32, 35-7, 58, 92-3, 104, 110, 112, 144
Fencible Corps, Manx (1779), 21
Fort St George – see Madras
Fraser, Col James S., 118-21, 125, 128, 130, 133, 144, 190
Harris, Gen George (Baron 1799), 63, 64, 66, 82, 108, 117, 191
Harvey, Henry, 97, 99-103, 105-6, 110, 111, 158
Hastings, Warren, 1, 4, 36, 40, 44, 151
Hildesley, Bishop Mark, 18-20
Hyder Ali, 5, 26, 27, 34, 37, 40, 64, 65, 113, 119, 121, 130, 157, 158, 189, 192, 195
Hyderabad, 15, 23, 27, 28, 39, 40, 48, 61-5, 71, 78, 96, 100, 107, 109, 114, 128, 133, 148, 163, 166, 187, 190, 191, 192, 195, 196
   Nizam of, 27-8, 40, 49, 62-4, 163, 166
India Act (1794), 36, 46, 194
Isle of Man
   Church, 11-12, 17, 18
   General, 7, 12-15, 22
   Government, 7-11
Kirby (IoM, Mark Wilks's estate), 54, 72, 97, 98
Kirk Michael (IoM), 17, 18, 97
Kirkpatrick,
   Lt Col James, 65, 148, 191
   Lt Col William, 64, 191
Kurnool, 65, 92, 137, 195
Lewis, Mrs, 89, 91, 134, 148
Macaulay, Lord (T. B.), 1, 2, 4, 120-1, 122-4, 150-1, 165
Mackenzie
   Capt Colin (Mysore Surveyor), 66, 71, 191
   Lt Colin, 109, 125, 191

Mackintosh, Sir James, 96, 123, 191
Madras, 2-4, 14, 15, 22, 23, 30, 33, 34, 37, 39-51, 56, 58, 60-1, 67-72, 76, 80, 85-6, 88, 91-7, 99-107, 109, 111, 113, 114, 116-18, 121, 122, 124, 128, 129, 132, 133, 135, 139, 141, 143-5, 150, 153, 15-61, 163-5, 166, 168-9, 171-80, 185, 187, 189, 190-96, 199, 200
Malcolm, Gen Sir John, 4, 5, 62, 64, 75, 76, 82, 83, 90, 107, 108, 113, 189, 192
Maratha Confederation
   General, 23, 28-9, 40, 61, 81-2, 106, 198
Martin, Major George M., 84, 140, 146, 179, 185, 192
Marx, Karl, 97
Maughold (IoM), 13, 14, 20, 52-4, 58, 71, 102, 106, 181, 194
McHutchin, Capt. Thomas M., 3, 132, 136, 148-91
Meuron, Charles-Daniel de, 59, 60, 193
Meuron, Régiment, 59, 60, 64
Minto, Baron, 99, 101, 104, 107
Moore, Sir George, 13, 20, 22, 42, 54, 73, 182, 190, 193
Morison, Col. William, 102, 104-6, 109, 111, 116-18, 124, 149, 153, 193
Mornington, Earl of (Marquess Wellesley), 61, 62, 64, 67, 71, 81, 83, 84, 134, 135, 170, 191, 192
Mysore
   City, 4, 5, 14, 15, 23, 25-7, 39, 40, 41, 44, 46, 49, 50, 61, 62, 64-7, 69, 71, 75-7, 82-4, 86, 87-9, 93, 94, 100, 109, 113, 114, 116-39, 144, 146, 148, 151-60, 162, 163, 166, 16878, 180, 182, 184-99, 204
   Commission, 4, 129, 131-2, 138, 168, 174, 185, 190, 191
   State, 1, 4, 27, 66, 93, 113, 129, 153, 166, 196

Napoleon I, Emperor, 83, 93, 98, 104
Nilgiris, 23, 109, 122, 129, 138, 145, 146, 164, 195
Nizam-al-Mulk - see Hyderabad, Nizam of, - see Hyderbad
Nundidroog, 48, 89, 93, 95, 130, 136, 146-8, 155, 168, 175, 178, 190, 192
Poorniah/ Purniya, Diwan, 44, 64, 86, 101, 113-14
Rama Sawmy, 77, 109, 193
Ramsay, Lady Susan, 135, 138-40, 142, 147-8, 182
Ramsey (IoM), 12-15, 18, 52-6, 70, 72, 182-4, 192
Régiment Meuron – see Meuron, Régiment, 59, 60, 64
Regulating Act (India, 1774), 35
Seringapatam, 15, 26, 27, 40, 41, 47, 48, 63-6, 68, 76, 77, 80, 82, 88, 90, 96, 100, 108, 117, 126, 139, 189, 191-6
Sivaji, 28, 29, 195, 198
St. Helena, 2, 97-8
Stuart
    Col/ Gen James, 46
    Gen James, 51, 59, 63, 75, 119
Taubman
    Major John, 21, 22, 72, 97, 98
Tipu Sultan, 39, 41, 44, 46, 62, 64, 91, 121
Trevelyan, Charles E., 3, 12, 151, 163-8, 172-6
Tweeddale, Marquis George Hay, 128-9, 135, 140, 142
Vellore, 46, 63, 65, 72, 90, 91, 94, 99, 189, 193
Vereenigde Oostindische Compagnie (VOC), 30-2, 59, 100
Vira Raja (of Coorg), 119, 123, 194

Wadiyar
    Family, 5, 26, 27, 64-6, 113, 115, 121, 186, 187, 191
    Maharajah Krishnaraja Wadiyar III, 5, 66, 71, 113-14, 118, 122, 125-7, 132-3, 136-7, 151, 153, 167, 169-71, 174-6, 181, 185-6
Wellesley
    Arthur (later Duke of Wellington), 5, 61, 63, 64, 66, 72, 75, 82, 83, 98, 106, 107, 113, 116, 192
    Henry (later Baron Cowley), 61-4
    Richard –see Mornington, Earl of,
Wilks
  family, 16-17, 98
  (John) Barry, 54, 56, 86, 98, 101
  Anne – see Collet, Mrs Anne,
  Col Mark, 54-6, 67, 70-3, 76, 93, 96
    early life, 19-211
    journal, 38-9, 42-3
    Resident at Mysore, 4, 75-86, 93-7, 113
  James, 16-18, 19, 20, 54, 70, 72-3, 193
  Laura – see Buchan, Lady Laura,
  Mrs Margaret (née Wood), 17, 18, 195
  Mrs. Elizabeth (née Christian), 19, 54
  Mrs. Harriot (née Macleane), 47, 48, 50, 51, 54, 56-9, 72-3, 79, 81, 85, 90
  Rev James, 17-19, 20
Wilson
  Bishop Thomas, 11, 17, 18
  James, 166, 172, 173, 175-6
  Mrs 'Eliza', 175
Wood, Sir Charles (later Viscount Halifax), 141, 144, 160, 166-8, 171, 173, 176, 186